South Park
FAQ

South Park FAQ

All That's Left to Know About the Who, What, Where, When, and #%$* of America's Favorite Mountain Town

Dave Thompson

APPLAUSE
THEATRE & CINEMA BOOKS

An Imprint of Hal Leonard Corporation

Published in 2014 by Applause Theatre and Cinema Books
An Imprint of Hal Leonard Corporation
7777 West Bluemound Road
Milwaukee, WI 53213
Trade Book Division Editorial Offices
33 Plymouth St., Montclair, NJ 07042

The FAQ series was conceived by Robert Rodriguez and developed with Stuart Shea.

Printed in the United States of America

All photos are courtesy of Photofest.

Book design by Snow Creative Services

Library of Congress Cataloging-in-Publication Data

Thompson, Dave, 1960 January 3–
    South Park FAQ : all that's left to know about the who, what, where, when, and #%$* of America's favorite mountain town / Dave Thompson.
      pages cm
    Includes bibliographical references and index.
    ISBN 978-1-4803-5064-9 (pbk.)
    1. South Park (Television program) I. Title.
    PN1992.77.S665T54 2013
    791.45'72—dc23
                                                                2014012027

www.applausebooks.com

To my mother, Sheila Ann Thompson, who I sincerely hope would never have allowed me to watch this show when I was little.

Contents

Acknowledgments

Thank you to everyone who lent a hand, offered an opinion, or threw in an utterly unreasonable demand (expletives delighted) as I wrote this book, but especially to Amy Hanson, for her uncanny recognition of the pop cultural references that I completely missed; and to John Cerullo, Marybeth Keating, Wes Seeley, and Gary Morris for bringing the project to life.

And finally, to all the other people who threw something strange into the casebook, even if it was just sympathetic glances in the direction of a teetering pile of DVDs. Karen and Todd; Linda and Larry; Betsy, Steve, and family; Jo-Ann Greene, Jen, Dave and Sue, Gaye and Tim, everyone at Captain Blue Hen in Newark, Oliver, Trevor, Toby, Barb East, Bateerz and family, the Gremlins who live in the heat pump, and to John the Superstar, the demon of the dry well.

Introduction
Respect My Authority

"When we started out, we didn't know anything about political correctness. We were just two guys from Colorado, and it was because we didn't know any better that we did the kind of humor we did. We like being rebellious, and we like flying in the face of what people think we should say."

—Trey Parker

It's the same with just about any TV show you can mention, and probably a few that you'd be better off keeping quiet about. If there is one topic that is guaranteed to really annoy a fellow viewer, even more than asking how they could even like that show in the first place, it's the prickly poser of "what's your favorite episode?"

I lost count of the number of times I was asked that when I mentioned to friends that I was writing a book about *South Park*. And I lost count, too, of the number of times they replied, "Phooey! [fill in your own choice] was much better than that." Or words to that effect.

So, to get it out of the way right away, I'm going to list my personal five top of the *South Park* pops. And if you don't agree, you are welcome to cross them out in violent crayon and add your own in their place.

- "Spookyfish"—for giving us a true taste of Halloween, mangled up with a taste of *Halloween* too.
- "Sarcastaball"—for delivering a beautifully well-timed slice of social commentary, splashed across a scenario that could easily happen tomorrow. If it hasn't already.
- "Scott Tenorman Must Die"—for reminding us of the true depths of depravity to which a third or fourth grader's imagination can sink.
- "The Return of the Fellowship of the Ring to the Two Towers"—for demonstrating just how unprepared most parents are for the day when they must discuss the undiscussable.

- And just about anything involving Terrance and Philip, because if you don't think fart jokes are the funniest thing on Earth, then why are you watching the show to begin with?

Actually, that's unfair. Poop jokes are just as funny. So are jokes against gingers, Jews, gays, straights, racial minorities, religious stereotypes, Goth kids, vampire kids, the disabled, the tall, the short, the pompous, the pathetic, the British, the Canadians, the famous, the feeble, the young, the old, the blank-space-to-fill-in-some-suggestions-of-your-own . . . in fact, in the world of *South Park*, more or less everything and everyone is funny. And the more we are told not to laugh at it, the funnier it is.

An eight-year-old gluing somebody else's pubic hair to his face and claiming to be Kris Kristofferson. That's funny.

An eighteen-year-old determining that a more or less monosyllabic kid in a wheelchair would make the perfect lead singer for his metal band. That's funny.

Australian wildlife expert Steve Irwin turning up at a Halloween party with a stingray barb in his chest, just weeks after the real Steve Irwin was killed by a stingray barb in the chest. That's . . . funny?

No, it isn't.

Well, maybe it is a little.

In fact, maybe it is a lot.

Yeah, that's funny. Not because Irwin's death, or the nature of it, was any cause for mirth. But because (and yes, it's a cliché but that doesn't mean it's not true), sometimes laughter is the only worthwhile response to any kind of tragedy. The best medicine, as they say. A panacea for your pain.

It isn't a matter of belittling something that for all intents and purposes is extraordinarily sad. It isn't a matter of making light of something that we should all be in darkest mourning about. It isn't even a matter of watching a disaster unfold on live television and thinking, "That'd make a great Halloween costume." It's a matter of putting tragedy behind us and getting on with life in a better frame of mind.

During World War II, as the Nazis rained bombs down on Britain, a song went around the shelters and hospitals that might not have changed the fact that the city was burning, that the bombed had lost everything, that people were dying. But it made the survivors smile regardless.

Hitler has only got one ball
The other is in the Albert Hall

His mother
The dirty bugger
Cut off the other when he was small.

Did Hitler really only have one ball? Did his mother even contemplate removing one of her infant son's testicles? And did she then deposit it deep within one of the most prestigious concert venues in the world? Probably not. But a lot of people sang the song then, and they were still singing it twenty, thirty years later. Today, they'd most likely be arrested for mocking the sacrifices of that terrible conflict and glorifying one of modern culture's manifold He Who Shall Not Be Nameds. Ho hum. Modern culture's loss.

Another war, another song. Oddly, but grimly, apt in the light of sundry recent concerns. This one dates from World War I, when the Germans routinely deployed mustard gas against their entrenched English foe.

I got gassed last night, I got gassed the night before
Going to get gassed tonight if we never get gassed no more
When we get gassed, we're sick as we can be
Cos phosgene and mustard gas is much too much for me.

Could you imagine someone singing that song today?

No. But could you imagine somebody thinking about singing it and then censoring themselves before someone else does?

Cough.

Increasingly, we live in a world where opinion is pinioned by the need not to offend, nor even risk offense, by saying—even lightheartedly— something that someone might feel belittled by. Including people who aren't actually present when the remark is made.

The soccer manager who told his charges the old joke about a monkey and an astronaut, and was promptly accused of racism by somebody else entirely.

The teen playing a video game who made an off-the-cuff remark about shooting up a school and eating his victims' hearts. A fellow player overheard the exchange, and the kid was arrested and threatened with eight years in jail.

The . . . and so on and so forth. All it takes is one person who doesn't understand, appreciate, or maybe even acknowledge the existence of humor (however humorless the humor might be), and it doesn't matter if he is the only person in the world who doesn't sneak a smirk at the gesture. One complaint is worth a thousand chuckles, and the only positive that comes out of the experience is the possibility that maybe one day, the rest of the world will tire of these petty-minded dictators and start complaining about them instead.

Which is why we love *South Park* so much.

For there, exaggerated political correctness and microscopically focused nitpickery are already like a red rag to a bull in the eyes of creators Trey Parker and Matt Stone.

Like Cheesy Poofs to a big-boned eighth grader.

Totalitarianism is totalitarianism, no matter how loudly you condemn the people who actually point that out, which is one of the reasons why *South Park* has never rested in its campaign to highlight humbuggery wherever it may dwell.

True political correctness means respecting other peoples' right to say whatever they like, no matter how much it might offend you, because that is the only thing that guarantees your right to say whatever you want to. Chip away at other people's right, no matter how worthy your intentions may be, simply opens the door for other, perhaps less worthy people to take the process to its logical conclusion and outlaw free speech altogether.

Trey Parker and Matt Stone. Without whom, none of this would be necessary.

Or, as Gerald Broflovski patiently explained to his son Kyle, "We live in a liberal-democratic society, and democrats make . . . laws [that] tell us what we can and can't say in the workplace, and what we can and can't do in the workplace."

"Isn't that fascism?" asked Kyle.

"No," replied his father. "Because we don't call it fascism."

None of this is news, of course. From the outset, *South Park* set out to puncture ego, slaughter the sacred, and generally poke holes in the manifold (and ever-growing) absurdities, conceits, and hypocrisies that comprise a large part of modern life. And generally, it has succeeded. As Parker told *Esquire* in 2011, the key to *South Park* is the fact that its protagonists, four everyday middle school Colorado-born boys, are generally smack in the middle of everything, pointing out that both sides are as bad as one another. "Any side who thinks they're totally right is fucked up. That's the heart of every show."

There will always be the occasional episode in which the barbs fall short or the target twists away; just as there will always be the occasional one that even confirmed *South Park* addicts might admit went too far to make a point that wasn't really worth making to begin with.

Contrarily, however, there are a great many episodes that continue to astonish, sometimes years after their original broadcast and years, too, after whatever the original butt of the joke might have been is forgotten. We are, after all, assailed with so much rancorous junk masquerading as news and current affairs these days that our brains should no longer be described as computers. They're more like shredding machines, dismissing and destroying far more "headlines" a day than they ever actually pay attention to.

Oh, and that thing news readers do before the commercial break, the "when we come back, we'll tell you why you may not want to wear any underpants tomorrow" teaser? Seriously, guys, if it was that important, you'd tell me now. Channel change.

Matt Stone outlined *South Park*'s approach.

"On one hand, it's really fun when you flip off the principal and the principal yells at you. But in general, we do the show because we want people to like it. We are entertainers. We're trying to entertain people. At the same time, we've been doing it long enough to realize we're still not a mainstream show . . . we're still on cable, we still consider ourselves an alternative show." Far more people, he acknowledged, dislike *South Park* than enjoy it, but unlike most television shows, that was fine. "Twenty percent of people got this joke, and they love us for it, and we'll piss off the other 80 percent just for them."

The very best of *South Park* teases, as well. But it's a knowing tease, a worthy tease, taunting the viewer with just enough information that you think you know where the story is going . . . but you cannot believe anybody has the balls to take it there. Again, a lot of the targets are as ephemeral as the headlines they are drawn from, but that is not an issue. The fact that . . . to draw a cultural irrelevance at random from the stockpile . . . Honey Boo Boo is even sufficiently well known to be considered a worthy target for the South Park sniper is itself sufficient condemnation of the culture that the show so gleefully ridicules, and of course she is not alone.

To concentrate on *South Park*'s status as the devourer of worthless worlds, however, is to overlook its other primary purpose, to act as a mirror to what we might call everyday society. South Park itself is Anytown USA, as accurate a reflection of small-town life as any live-action television series has ever mustered, and a lot more honest as well.

The characters that inhabit the town may seem at times like exaggerated stereotypes, but that is because we are watching them and expecting them to be so. At the same time, however, we recognize every one of them, from our own circle of friends, acquaintances, work colleagues, neighbors, and within each of them we espy aspirations that are equally familiar from that same circle. The Marsh and Broflovski families are exquisitely true to life in their overall normalcy, but so are Mr. Mackey and Ms. Crabtree in their absurd eccentricity.

Indeed, excise the more fantastical elements of South Park life (the town's propensity for regular destruction, its magnetic attraction to extraterrestrial aliens and religious deities, and its love of a certain talking poo), and little that occurs in South Park would feel out of place in any American-or-elsewhere community.

South Park shows us our own lives with all the filters switched off, and the fact that its heroes are a bunch of fourth graders does not detract from that intention in the slightest. No matter, for example, how many real-life politicians have been skewered by the show, Eric Cartman has "parodied" many more simply by saying and doing the exact same things as them; and it's only the fact that he is a fourth grader that prevents us from making the connection every time.

"What we're sick of," the show's creators told *In Focus*, "and it's getting even worse, is you either like Michael Moore or you wanna fuckin' go overseas and shoot Iraqis . . . . We find just as many things to rip on the left as we do on the right. People on the far left and the far right are the same exact person to us."

They usually get away with it, too. True, *blogs.Villagevoice.com* was among those sources that reported, in 2011, on growing evidence that the Church of Scientology "investigated" Parker and Stone back in 2006, in the apparent hope of finding something incriminating against them. True, too, that a DreamWorks spokesman reportedly told *DeadlineHollywoodDaily.com* that Steven Spielberg's portrayal in "The China Probrem" (in which the movie mogul is shown repeatedly raping Harrison Ford) was "tasteless," before asking "How can that be shown on basic cable?"

But condemning *South Park* as "tasteless" is a little like condemning trees for being wooden, or blankets for being warm. As Trey Parker remarked in a 2006 interview: "You can only say 'You can't do that' so many times to Matt and me before we're gonna do it." Their secret, then, lies in their ability to come up with scenarios that nobody told them "not to do," because nobody else could have thought of them in the first place.

Thou shalt not portray Barbra Streisand as a robotic Godzilla-type monster that destroys the town before being vanquished, in turn, by the Cure's Robert Smith. But if you do, you still shouldn't be surprised if she turns up at your Broadway play fifteen years later. An incredulous Stone told *Esquire*, "The cast told me she was there, and I was like, 'No fucking way.'"

Thou shalt not portray Radiohead as a bunch of heartless Brits, laughing at a boy who has just lost (and then inadvertently eaten) his own parents.

Thou shalt not pretend to disguise the prophet Muhammad as a bear, before revealing it to have been Santa all along.

Thou shalt not portray Oprah Winfrey as the owner of a talking vagina that pulls a gun and takes a hostage, before killing itself following the death of her anus.

Thou shalt not . . . and so forth. The men the *Denver Post* once described as "unlikely kings of pop-culture subversion . . . two snickering goofballs who bonded more over breaking wind than breaking barriers in a 1992 University of Colorado film class" succeed not only because they break boundaries, but because they take the time to think up fresh boundaries to break. Including those that they themselves could be said to have set.

The season fifteen episode "You're Getting Old," for example, riffed around the complaints (that, in all honesty, have been circulating since season two) that the show wasn't as funny as it used to be. That it had "turned to shit"—which is what absolutely everything in the episode then proceeded to do.

Horrified bloggers sharpened their keyboards, outraged not at the fact that the episode wasn't the funniest *South Park* ever, but that Parker and Stone were apparently acknowledging their decline without suggesting any kind of remedy to the "problem." In other words, satirizing fandom's own expectations and feelings about the show by turning the fans themselves into the butt of the joke. A joke, judging from those aforementioned blogs, that very few of them got.

"We [were] making fun of Kevin James and Adam Sandler," Parker explained. "But we have to include ourselves in there, too,"

If celebrities have proven reluctant to complain about their treatment at the hands of *South Park*, however, *South Park* has been considerably more willing to avenge itself for its treatment at the hands of celebrities.

When the real Phil Collins pipped the *South Park* song "Blame Canada" to a Grammy award, an imaginary one promptly became one of the show's favorite victims. When the living filmmaker Michael Moore appeared to suggest that a short piece of animation in *Bowling for Columbine* was the work of Parker and Stone, they created a marionette of him, then had it blow itself up in the (non-*South Park*) movie *Team America: World Police.*

When Isaac Hayes abandoned his series-long role as Chef, following an episode that ridiculed his Scientology beliefs, he was rewarded with one of the bloodiest and messiest deaths ever depicted on television. And when a hitherto-anonymous ginger kid posted an anti-*South Park* rant on YouTube, he ensured that gingers everywhere would be next in the cartoon's firing line.

Precisely as the rest of us expected.

The most crucial element in all of this, however, is that *South Park* is, first and foremost, a comedy show, and no matter how outrageously it might stretch the limits of what actually is and isn't funny, the program lives and dies by laughter. Which, as it hurtles toward its twentieth consecutive season, is a remarkable achievement.

One of the hardest things about writing comedy, especially when that comedy has a life span that goes beyond a couple of seasons of a sitcom, or a couple of years on the stand-up circuit, is that you do eventually reach a point (as we saw earlier) where it becomes an accepted belief, even among your own fans, that you used to be a lot funnier.

It's not a phenomenon that is unique to comedy, although it does feel more rife there. Bands that outlive their first few albums will eventually encounter the dewy-eyed nostalgics who think the music was better when its makers were starving. Authors are often asked to look back at their first few books and try and recapture the old questioning hunger.

But they are also, and often by the same people, shown the respect that graceful aging demands. A Beatles fan might think their first LP was their most enjoyable, but few disagree that *Sgt. Pepper*, five years and as many seismic changes later, was their most important. Charles Dickens made a bang with *The Pickwick Papers*. But *Great Expectations* kicks its ass in every department. And so on.

Comedy is rarely given that same grace, because comedy is targeted at a different part of the witness's brain. A song that makes you dance will always make you dance. A book that makes you feel warm and fuzzy will always do that. But a thing that makes you laugh . . . no. Or not for the same reasons.

Good comedy is a combination of a lot of things, but paramount among them are disbelief, absurdity, juxtaposition, and timing. Take the Fishsticks joke that so outraged a drawing of Kanye West, for example:

"Do you like fishsticks?"
"Yes."
"Do you like putting fishsticks in your mouth?"
"Yes."
"What are you, a gay fish?"

Remove any of those attributes and you chip away one of the key platforms of the moment. Even the medium can distort the intent.

Two nuns are sitting in the bath. One says "where's the soap," and the other says "yes it does, doesn't it?"

Repetition is the death of a joke. It's why nobody over the age of twenty-one laughs when a gaggle of students start reciting old Russell Brand routines at one another for the umpteenth time; and why no one over the age of forty should believe it necessary to dead parrot entire *Monty Python* sketches in crowded rooms. After a while, even the stiffest Norwegian blue will lose its bloom.

The people who devise such routines, however, the comedians themselves, are not so fortunate. If they reiterate the old favorites, they are justifying the argument that they're not as funny as they used to be and are forced to rely on the "old favorites" in order to justify the ticket price.

But if they don't perform them, and just bring out new material, then they're cheating people who came to see them hoping to mingle with old friends again. Even if those same people will then complain that all they heard was the old stuff.

Kenny died at the end of almost every *South Park* episode for five full seasons, by which time even his cartoon friends were tired of the joke. But the moment he stopped dying, people reacted as though they had lost a family member. And if the jokes that replaced those many deaths are regarded by those same people as something less uproarious than the original premise (which they will be, because familiarity is very hard to replace with its opposite), then it's true, *South Park* is not as funny as it used to be.

Those people are not mourning something that made them laugh every time they heard it, however. They are mourning the novelty that made them laugh in the first place. Of all the spoken and theatrical arts, comedy is unflinchingly cuniculate, and it is all too easy for a comedy writer to find him- or herself backed against the far wall without any place else to go. But it is also cunctipotent, meaning there is always a way out if you look hard enough, and aren't afraid to double back and twist new meaning from old words.

It is the difference between Robin Williams telling a joke, then pulling a face at the end of it, to remind us he's the funniest man alive; and Billy Connolly breaking down in the midst of an otherwise unfunny sentence, because his body language alone delivers the punch line. If something is so funny that even he is unable to say it aloud, then you know it's going to be good.

What is Mr. Hankey, after all, but an ambulatory reincarnation of the wee jobbies with which Connolly once peppered his repertoire, and more straight faces have probably been cracked by reference to those two characters alone than any other single bodily function in television history.

All of which allows us to draw just two conclusions.

The first is that *South Park* has only gotten funnier as it aged, and its creators shed the shackles of what even they considered was suitable material for a television program. And the second is that jobbies themselves are very funny. Particularly when, as Billy Connolly also pointed out, they happen to be beige.

So, clean yourself up, sit yourself down, and let us step together into the world of *South Park*. Apparently, you have some questions you'd like to ask?

What's So Special About Christmas?

South Park's Festive Beginnings

"When you grow up in Colorado, you don't think, 'I'll write a Broadway musical!' Or, 'I'll go to Hollywood and make a TV show!' That just doesn't happen. But in the 1990s, that was the heyday of independent films, so we thought, 'OK, we can make independent films and still live in Colorado.'"

—Matt Stone

The story begins . . . .

In film school at the University of Colorado in 1992, where students Trey Parker and Matt Stone are hard at work cutting figures out from construction paper and creating an animated short entitled *The Spirit of Christmas*.

They were, Stone later remarked, something of an odd couple in the class, the only two people who preferred comedy to art; who refracted their vision through movies that were more notable for what they weren't than for what they were. They weren't "Black-and-white lesbian . . . sexual exploration pieces." The only two, he said with a laugh, who didn't want to be Martin Scorsese.

They were rejecting a world that they would, in later years, parody with ruthless effectiveness when they brought the Sundance Independent Film Festival to an episode of *South Park*. "Independent films are those black and white hippie movies," sniffs Cartman. "They're always about gay cowboys eating pudding." And sure enough, one of the movies on display was titled precisely that.

There were no gay cowboys in Stone and Parker's first *South Park* setting. The opening credits referred to it as "An Avenging Conscience film," and the first thing you heard, the first thing you saw, was four kids, more or less recognizable to us all today but, at the time, quite unlike any third grader you had ever drawn.

Other students in their class may have wanted to be Martin Scorsese. Parker and Stone wanted to be Terry Gilliam, the artistic iconoclast whose bizarre visions and sanity-taunting imagery were among the manifold threads that made up *Monty Python's Flying Circus*, a British half-hour comedy show that was quite unlike anything that television had ever disgorged in the past.

"As we've said in every interview," Parker once repeated in another, "I remember that was the show—it was like Thursdays at 10:00 at night, being in third and fourth grade and watching that show, and not even getting a lot of it, but just knowing it was really funny. I think that's why Matt and I hit it off so well . . . because we had this very big *Python* background."

"Still to this day," Stone agreed, "when our heads are getting a little big, if we go and put on an old Flying Circus . . . you just watch that and you're like—'what the hell are we doing?' We do that every once in a while to check ourselves."

The Pythonic influence howls loudly across *The Spirit of Christmas*, and it howls across its four juvenile leads, as well. A group of third graders, blessed with all the charm and style that comes so naturally to that age group, clad in the clothing that was nothing different from anything you might see a "real" third grader wearing, but that defined each of the kids regardless. You knew, before they'd even done anything, that these kids were trouble. Or, as Parker told the *National Post* in 1998, "Third grade is really the time when you are at your peak of bastard-dom. That's where the gold mine is."

The characters.

One was . . . let's be polite and say he was big-boned, with a moonlike face only partially eclipsed by a pale blue hat. One was blond and didn't do much. One wore a red hat, blue clothes, and was supremely sensible. And the fourth was lost within the voluminously hooded confines of an orange anorak. In another life, he could have been Ally Sheedy's character throughout the first half of *The Breakfast Club*, lost in the folds and communicating solely through grunts and squeaks. Except he will never metamorphose into a swan. He will remain a duckling for the remainder of his life.

However long (or short) it might be.

None of which is especially relevant to the boys' conversation, which revolved around the rights and wrongs of putting yet another hat, a magic one this time, on the snowman they had apparently just finished building.

It was not a good idea. Sensible Boy, who managed to last the entire four minutes of film without claiming a name, cautioned against it. A snowman in a magic hat, he declared, is a sure-fire killer. But Blondie didn't care. "Let's do it anyway," he insisted, preluding his dare-devilry with a well-defined F-bomb; and so the fun began, as the kids struck up a Christmas carol and placed the hat on their snowman's head . . .

At which it immediately turned into a monster. Who promptly killed Kenny . . . who, in this case, was the big-boned kid, but the effect was the same. While Kenny lay bleeding copiously into the snow, blondie and sensible threw themselves into a gloriously profanity-strewn argument over whether that "fucking hat" should ever have been placed on Frosty's "fucking head" in the first place.

And then, the inevitable question. "What do we do now?"

We turn to Santa for help, of course. There he stood, red and round, hohoho-ing away like the seasonal behemoth that he was, except he wasn't, because Santa was suddenly transformed into the snowman, and another boy bit the dust. There was just blondie and sensible left to go now, and there was no one around to help them.

"Oh Christ," said one, despairingly.

"Jesus," said both, nervously, and away to the nearest manger they hurried, where a few words of devout prayer aroused the Baby Jesus from his straw-bound slumbers to destroy the evil Frosty with just two well-aimed tosses of his death-dealing halo. And so the boys learned a valuable lesson.

Christmas isn't about Frosty and Santa. It's not even about Jesus. It's about presents.

Of course.

Parker explained, "Part of what we loved about [Monty] Python was when they were saying stuff that, if you said in school, you got smacked in the mouth. What was so funny about it is like, 'oh, you're not supposed to make fun of that, are you?' And so, immediately you make—just Jesus made out of construction paper is funny. You know, it's like we didn't even have to have him say anything. And I remember when we were doing *Spirit of Christmas*, and I cut him out and I'm laughing the whole time. I showed it to Matt and we're just like, 'Huh-huh-huh!' It's just inherently funny.

"When we started talking about this show," he continued to a crowded Aspen Film Festival audience in 1998, "even when we were doing the shorts . . . it was like there was always a leader kid. Matt and I didn't grow up together, but we both were talking about—we had this one fat kid. 'Oh, everyone had the fat kid,' or 'at one time, I was the fat kid' . . . and you

In search of Alfred G. Packer, voracious man-eatin' sonofabitch and the hero of Parker and Stone's first Sundance sensation.

always had the poor kid . . . who died every week. It started off a very cliché group of boy friends that just sit around and cuss at each other. The most fun for me about *South Park* has been Cartman, because to see him grow . . . in *Spirit of Christmas*, he's just a big fat fuck that just bitches a lot. And to go from that to him having a tea party with his stuffed animals and doing their voices and stuff, has been great."

In 1992, when *The Spirit of Christmas* (aka Jesus vs. Frosty) was created, that was all still to come. But it drew a little closer three years later. That was when, at the behest (and a $1,200 commission) of Brian Graden, a friend who was also a Fox network executive, Parker and Stone revisited the idea for a second short, intended this time as a video Christmas card.

They had not been idle in the interim, of course. Indeed, in an alternate universe, the world might still be celebrating the creation and success of the duo's next project, *Cannibal: The Musical.*

It is the story, in words and music, of Colorado pioneer Alfred Packer, a Civil War veteran who was charged and convicted with the murder and cannibalism of five fellow prospectors; and subsequently (1968) immortalized by the Alfred G. Packer Memorial Grill at the University of Colorado at Boulder.

According to one admittedly sensationalist source, the presiding judge, M. B. Gerry, showed Packer no mercy whatsoever. "Stand up yah voracious man-eatin' sonofabitch and receive yir sintince. When yah came to Hinsdale County, there was siven Dimmycrats. But you, yah et five of 'em, goddam yah. I sintince yah t' be hanged by th' neck ontil yer dead, dead, dead, as a warnin' ag'in reducin' th' Dimmycratic populayshun of this county. Packer, you Republican cannibal, I would sintince ya ta hell but the statutes forbid it."

Merciless cannibalism, appalling diction, and party politics! Who could possibly resist?

Cannibal: The Musical was written and directed by its star, Parker; Stone was producer, and the pair figured they could probably get $1 million for its video rights—a nice profit on a movie that probably cost no more than $100,000 to make. Instead, a few guerrilla screenings at the Sundance Film Festival marked the musical's high point, but its possibilities did convince them to move to Los Angeles.

The revisited *Spirit of Christmas* (aka Jesus vs Santa) was a little over a minute longer than its predecessor, but this edition of the epic also allowed the team to abandon their original cutouts in favor of the computer animation that, successive technological advances notwithstanding, has remained largely the same ever since. (With the exception of what would become the actual series debut episode, "Cartman Gets an Anal Probe." Produced independently as a pilot for an as-yet unsolicited show, this one returned the duo to a dark room for many days, laboriously drawing every second of action.)

First, the original cardboard cutouts were scanned and redrawn using a popular vector graphics editor called CorelDRAW. The results were then imported into PowerAnimator, the same highly integrated 3D modeling, animation, and visual effects suite that was employed for the movie *Terminator 2: Judgment Day*. (This was later upgraded to the newly launched Maya system shortly before work began on *South Park*'s fifth season.)

PowerAnimator was a wise choice, in that it allowed the show to retain its early "amateur" style, at the same time as establishing that style as something unique. Few people first watching *South Park* considered the animation to be of any quality whatsoever, complaints that would eventually spur Stone and Parker into creating Terrance and Phillip, in an (admittedly successful) attempt to show those naysayers what bad animation really looked like.

In fact, what detractors still to this day describe as cheap-looking cutout animation is one of the elements that has rendered *South Park* so successful. Revolving around children, the show almost looks as though it was drawn by children, and one only needs to imagine *South Park* reanimated to the standards of *Ice Age* or *The Little Mermaid* to realize that "better" art does not necessarily make for better viewing. A point that was reinforced by the opening credits to season seventeen, all 3D graphics and sweeping vistas.

What *South Park* understood, and this is another lesson that Parker and Stone drew from *Monty Python*, is that great animation is as much about setting a scene and maintaining a mood as it is anything else, and neither would be well served by a 3D Towelie nodding out in front of us.

With its four juvenile heroes all clearly recognizable as the creatures they would become, *The Spirit of Christmas* now named them as well: the rotund Cartman; the well-concealed Kenny; Kyle, who celebrates Christmas despite being Jewish; and Stan, who constantly demands a sensible explanation for everything.

Cue a compensatory chorus of "Dreidel Dreidel Dreidel"; cue what we now know is a characteristically coarse response from Cartman; and suddenly, down came Jesus.

"What are you doing in South Park?" asked Cartman, calmly.

"I come seeking retribution," answered Jesus, gently.

"He's come to kill you cos you're Jewish, Kyle," responded Stan, fearfully.

"Oh fuck," replied Kyle, understandably.

But no. It seemed that the following day would be Jesus's birthday ("your birthday's on Christmas? That sucks") and he had some unfinished business to attend to. A final showdown with Santa.

"You have blemished Christmas for the last time, Kringle," he declared to his festive archenemy. "I'm here to put an end to your blasphemy."

The titans clashed. Kenny was killed. But Santa and Jesus were too evenly matched for their battle to have a decisive victor. They needed help, and both called on the surviving boys for aid.

But whose aid should they go to? Santa reminded Stan of the choo-choo he received when he was three. Jesus pointed out that he died for their sins.

It truly was an intractable dilemma, one whose resolution lay with just one man, an Olympic figure skater and latter-day television chef who was the only person on Earth who could answer the eternal question.

"What would Brian Boitano do?"

He would remind the combatants that without Jesus, there would be no Christmas Day. And without Santa, the spirit of Christmas might have been forgotten long ago. Then, as he skated off into the distance, and the reconciled Christ and Kringle headed off for an orange smoothie, the boys were left to contemplate what they had learned from the events of the day. That, at Christmas, it doesn't matter what you believe or what religion you are. Christmas is about . . .

"Ham," said Cartman.

"Presents," said the others.

And lunch, responded the rats, who devoured Kenny's headless corpse in less time than it took to sing "Dreidel Dreidel Dreidel" again.

Now there's a Christmas card to remember.

The Internet was still in its infancy back then. According to figures supplied by the International Data Corporation (IDC), by the end of 1996, the net was the plaything of just thirty-six million people worldwide. Up from sixteen million a year before, but still a mere 0.9 percent of the planet's entire population. By comparison, today there are around three billion users.

Such innocent times. Newspapers (remember them?) and television still took their stories from actual events, as opposed to scouring "social media" to find out what was "trending." Journalists left the house in pursuit of information, rather than getting fat at the laptop; Apple was a fruit, YouTube was an (admittedly obscure) insult, and Microsoft described a penis after a very cold bath. So, when you read today that Parker and Stone's Christmas video went "viral," remember that not only did the term not exist back then, its reach would scarcely even be worth commenting on today.

Still the germ of a notion found room in which to blossom, and, by early 1997, Parker and Stone were actively developing a potential television program, an animated half hour called *South Park*, headlined by perhaps the unlikeliest set of heroes since . . . well, MTV's runaway hit *Beavis and Butt-Head* may possibly have raised their heads here, in that a couple of foul-mouthed teenagers were only a few years removed from a quartet of foul-mouthed third graders. But despite some superficial similarities, there were also many more vast differences, as *Slate* magazine's Dana Stevens observed.

"*Beavis and Butt-Head* appealed to a cult audience of jaded, pop-culture-savvy young men, and for this reason, they're often compared to the kids on *South Park* (which is clearly indebted to the earlier show, right down to the touchy-feely teacher who likes to say, "Mmm-kay?").

America's *other* favorite juvenile delinquents, Mike Judge's Beavis and Butt-Head.

"But the elementary-school heroes of *South Park* are smart-ass social critics, taking down liberal and conservative pieties with an equal-opportunity cynicism that reflects the libertarian beliefs of their co-creator Trey Parker. The high-school burnouts Beavis and Butt-Head have no such ambition; they are sublimely passive losers, both products and harbingers of the end-of-history anomie of the mid-'90s."

Looking at the show's longevity compared to its high school counterparts, too, *South Park* posed problems to anybody making comparisons. "It's impossible to imagine a post-9/11 *Beavis and Butt-Head*. Not because the show was devoid of political content, but because the world it so ruthlessly satirized, a suburban cocoon of mindless consumption and complacent self-regard, abruptly ceased to exist at the beginning of this millennium."

Still, the genesis of *South Park* was very much the sum of its creators' influences. "When we started *South Park*, we didn't know how to write at all," Parker admitted to *AV Club* in 2008. "And we've sort of become writers as the show went on, and learned structure, and learned—if you look at the first few seasons, they're just a mess. And thank God we got by on them, because they were so shocking and new and crappy, and that was funny."

They were also autobiographical, at least after a fashion.

The pair met at university. Trey Parker (Randolph Severn Parker III) was born on October 19, 1969, and grew up in a largely Mormon area in Conifer, Jefferson County, Colorado. South Park County lay next door, and he did in fact enjoy a year of schooling there, at South Park High in Fairplay.

Parker's early ambitions were musical. Aged fifteen, he and a friend named David Goodman recorded and sold a cassette tape's worth of songs titled *Immature: A Collection of Love Ballads for the '80's Man* (whose contents very much adhered to the album's title), and, for one semester, he studied at the Berklee College of Music in Boston before transferring to the University of Colorado at Boulder (UCB) to study film and classical music, double-majoring in music and Japanese. In later years, several of his earliest cinematic efforts would find their way onto eBay and thence into his "official filmography," much to Parker's own astonishment.

"We had to do foreign press recently, and this Swedish guy says, 'Tell me about your first film, *Giant Beavers of Southern Sri Lanka*.' And I was like, 'Dude, I was twenty, and it's a three-minute fucking thing. That's not my first film.'"

Another college short, *American History*, is remembered not only for winning its creator a Student Academy Award, but also for debuting the animation style that would be reborn for *South Park*.

Matt Stone (Matthew Richard Stone), meanwhile, was born in Houston, Texas, on May 26, 1971, but grew up in Littleton, Colorado, where he attended Heritage High School, before moving on to university, graduating with degrees in film and math.

Precisely the kind of backgrounds, therefore, that one would expect to combine as the creators of a walking, talking fece named Mr. Hankey. Who, according to legend, was single-handedly responsible for the Fox television network declining the opportunity to produce a *South Park* television series.

In the years since the network was launched as America's fourth broad-cast television channel, Fox had pushed a lot of boundaries; comedic (*Married with Children*, the first sitcom to take the English slang for a male masturbator, Wanker, and reposition it as a county in Wisconsin), cultural (*21 Jump Street*, the show that made a star of Johnny Depp), and beyond. But even they drew a line at what Stone and Parker had in mind.

MTV was less squeamish. *Beavis and Butt-Head* had proven there was a market for cartoons that came with a bit of a bite, and another animated smash would certainly allow them to lose yet another half an hour's worth of the tiresome music videos that people still seemed to expect Music Television to broadcast.

Parker and Stone, however, were less enamored. MTV might make the show a hit. But they might also, and just as easily, market it as a children's show, and expect it then to be designed in that same direction. Which, despite the animated medium, really wasn't the idea.

Parker explained to *Rolling Stone*, "There's this whole thing out there about how kids are so innocent and pure. That's bullshit, man. Kids are malicious little fuckers. They totally jump on any bandwagon and rip on the weak guy at any chance. They say whatever bad word they can think of. They are total fucking bastards, but for some reason everyone has kids and forgets about what they were like when they were kids."

Uncut magazine's David Bennun reiterated those observations. "Kids are mad little buggers. Anyone who works with children will tell you so, although they may phrase it differently. Not all kids are vicious, bloodthirsty, wee bastards. Just most of them. You probably were. Maybe you don't remember it, because you can't imagine a time before you had a conscience, any more than you can recall a time before you could read.

"Kids aren't evil, just astoundingly callous. They have next to no empathy. And whatever empathy they do have is more likely to be reserved for pets or television than for fellow humans. It's no wonder they grow up to be adults. What is a wonder is that no one thought of *South Park* sooner. An animated series about children who actually behave like children."

South Park would fill that void with vibrant passion. It just needed to find the right mind to make that happen.

Enter Doug Herzog, an executive at Comedy Central, the channel formed in 1991 from the merging of two upstart comedy networks, the Comedy Channel and Ha! A series of six episodes of *South Park* was commissioned, and a premiere airdate was set. In 1998, Debbie Liebling, Vice President, West Coast Development & Production and Comedy Central Executive Producer recalled the early phase of the ensuing relationship for an audience at the Aspen Film Festival.

"I had just closed a deal with two very unassuming guys for a pilot based on a very insane short entitled *The Spirit of Christmas*. At the time, Trey Parker and Matt Stone could barely afford parking to get out of our office building. All of us at Comedy Central were pretty confident that this show would be hilarious, and we were hopeful it might draw a little bit of attention to the channel. But none of us had any idea it would become the pop cultural phenomenon that it has, and that Trey and Matt would be the subject of a panel here two years later, sharing the bill with fifty ... other cultural icons. But clearly, through their hard work and vision, they've earned it . . . .

"They work around the clock," she continued, "paying attention to every detail on the show, both on-air and off-air. They're prolific writers. They believe in their choices and they stand by them. And the honesty and integrity that you see in their work is there because that's the honesty and integrity in their characters."

She outlined the events that shaped the eight months since *South Park* premiered on Comedy Central: planning a full-length *South Park* feature film and a television soundtrack album. Their cartoon had placed them on the cover of *Rolling Stone* magazine. They had appeared as guests on *The Tonight Show with Jay Leno*, won a CableACE Award for Best Animated Series, and a NOVA from the Producers Guild of America, recognizing them as the most promising producers in television. And that, Liebling concluded, was "just their first year of show business."

A year that began on August 13, 1997, when America discovered what happened the day that Cartman got an anal probe.

South Park has not looked back since then. Or, if it has, it does so with bemusement. "There's tons of interviews, right after [the show's] first year, when people asked us, 'How long do you think you can do this?,'" Parker reflected in 2010. "And there were so many times that we would answer back, 'Well, it's not like we're going to be doing this when we're 40.' I turned 40 in October."

2

South Park

It's Just a Typical, Normal, American Town, Right?

It was the magnificently named Zebulon Pike who discovered South Park. Or at least made it sound like the kind of place where people might want to live. Exploring the Colorado Rocky Mountain range in the first decade of the nineteenth century, it was Pike who heard and then publicized the rumor that there was gold to be found in the South Park basin. Four years earlier, it was said, a Kentucky trapper named James Pursley had found gold . . . and then gone on his way. Apparently he didn't like mining.

It took time for anybody to act on Pike's tip. In spring 1839, settlers bound for Oregon passed through the region but didn't really hang around for too long, and it was another twenty years before South Park truly found its place on the map, as the Pike's Peak Gold Rush (named for the mountain that was named after Zeb) sent hopeful prospectors scattering through the mountain range in search of fresh strikes.

They found them in South Park, along the west side of the park and in the Mosquito Range, in Tarryall Creek and over by Fairplay, and within a year, Park County boasted some 10,000 residents, fully one-third of the entire population of Colorado Territory. Merchants followed the miners, families followed the merchants.

Silver was discovered. Uranium. Coal. Semiprecious stones. The population boomed. The first camps became communities, the communities grew into towns. Fairplay and Alma, Jefferson and Como, Hartsell and . . . South Park?

Actually, South Park doesn't exist. But if it did . . . .

If it did, it would have boomed and busted, grown and then be ground down, reacting to the highs and lows that visited the rest of the local community, the decline of the mining, the growth of other nearby cities, the coming of the railroad, the construction of the highways.

Either way, the town of South Park remembers its heritage in exactly the same fashion as any other community of its nature might. Just outside town, the visitor can find the aptly named Pioneer Village, a lovingly fashioned facsimile of South Park as it once appeared, flawlessly recreating life in 1864 and offering a startling counterpoint to the hustle and bustle of the South Park of today.

For what was once a small mining outpost populated by grisly old gray-bearded miners named Jeb, waving pickaxes in the air, singing "My Darling Clementine," and avoiding the attentions of any local cannibals, has mushroomed into a bustling town of some 4,388 people, most of whom seem to have grown happily accustomed to the two factors of local life that best distinguish their community.

One, that there are friendly faces everywhere.

And two, that bad things happen to good people.

Nowhere is this better illustrated than by the town's annual Civil War enactment, held under the aegis of one of its most distinguished elderly residents, the centenarian Marvin Marsh.

Little-remembered by Civil War scholars in the outside world, but locally highly decisive, the Battle of Tamarack Hill was a resounding victory for the Union forces. Most of the time, anyway. But once, in 1999, history was rewritten with a vengeance.

Three boys were at the root of all that occurred. Two of them, Stan Marsh and Kyle Broflovski, were on the victorious Union side; the third, Eric Cartman, was aligned with the defeated Southern force. This particular year, however, Eric—a notorious sore loser—intended to rewrite history.

Dressed as General Robert E Lee, Cartman convinced his troops to forgo the usual light refreshment encouraged by the event's sponsors, Jagerman's S'mores-flavored schnapps, in favor of getting absolutely drunk out of their minds. He then persuaded them to beat the Union for real and, having done so, to bring the rest of the country under Confederate rule.

Though they were equipped only with blank ammunition, the drunken horde marched across the country, fueled by further copious amounts of alcohol, and having taken control of Washington, D.C., Cartman was ready for his final triumph. Pull this off and, according to the terms of a bet he laid back in South Park at the outset of the adventure, Kyle and Stan would have to act as his slaves for an entire month.

A document of surrender was drawn up, and a drawing of President Bill Clinton was poised to sign it. One hundred and thirty-four years after

The gang's all here. With assorted grown-ups, too.

the official end of the Civil War, the final result is about to be reversed. The South had risen again.

Or had it? In their own disguises of President Lincoln and Jefferson Davis, Stan and Kyle arranged a reenactment of their own, recreating the original Southern surrender. The Confederate forces melted away, and now it was the victors' turn to reap their rewards. Cartman was to act as their slave for a month.

Or was he?

Sadly, if the North truly had won the war, then slavery had been abolished. Cartman remained a free man.

Such events as this firmly establish South Park as a seething microcosm of modern American life, a place where the ebbs and flows of both current and historical events not only impact on the day-to-day existence of the community, but can do so in often outrageously shocking ways.

And throughout all the vicissitudes of fate and circumstance, the stoic people of South Park simply do what everyone else in the world does. They go with the flow, knowing that once the crisis has passed, life will return to normal. Injuries will heal. Damage will be repaired. The town will be rebuilt. No matter what cataclysms with which a capricious fate might visit South Park, at the end of the day South Park will still be standing, ten thousand feet above sea level, just off Route 285, on the banks of the South Platte River, nestled within one of the most breathtakingly picturesque landscapes in America.

It is a vacationer's paradise.

Denver, Aspen, Boulder, Conifer, Eagle, and Greeley are all within easy reach. Winter sports are a year-round attraction (probably because the local climate dictates that it is almost always winter there). South Park's own Stark's Pond boasts some of the most spectacular aquatic life-forms in the country, while the bracing Rocky Mountain air still resonates with the restorative magic that once inspired American medicine to litter the region with TB clinics and sanatoriums.

So restorative that it can defy death itself. Anyplace else in the world, people would laugh to hear of a local resident who claimed to have been killed close to one hundred times and still be around to tell his tale. In South Park, the locals just nod knowledgeably and say "you must be talking about the McCormick kid."

South Park is a center of religious pilgrimage. Figureheads from most of the world's greatest religions (and some of the sillier ones too) have made regular appearances around the town, oft-times transforming it into some kind of multifaith amalgam of Mecca, Jerusalem, the Ganges, and Lourdes, all at the same time.

It is a focal point for UFOlogists, a nexus for students of the paranormal, a celebrity getaway, and a hotbed of musical talent. Like Woodstock in New York and Altamont in California, South Park is fabled and famed as a festival site, with the legendary Chef Aid concert living on in the memory even of people who have never heard of it.

South Park hosts the heartbeat of modern technology, with both the Sperm Bank of South Park and the South Park Genetic Engineering Ranch positioned at the forefront of their respective fields. South Park's world-renowned rhinoplasty surgery has attracted some of the biggest names (and noses) in the world, and the town is one of the few communities in the entire world that can claim to have produced two Nobel Prize nominees in the same year.

South Park is a happening place!

Around the Town—Things to Do and See in South Park

For the modern tourist or visitor, South Park is best approached by air, and better still via the town's own carrier. Owned by the proprietor of the town's locally renowned Chinese restaurant, City Wok, City Airlines are known statewide for the distinctive yellow livery of their fleet of one Cessna aircraft.

Touching down after a breathtaking flight over the mountains, first-time visitors are directed to the Airport Hilton, a venue that—aside from offering the visitor all of the luxury and comfort that one normally associates with the Hilton hotel chain—also hosts a variety of conventions in its beautifully appointed Sunset Room. These have included the first Ginger Pride rally, a subsequent meeting of the Ginger Separatist Movement and the Coonicon 2009 convention. All were wild successes. After a fashion.

Of course, a major Colorado hotel would not be complete without a touch of tragedy, and while the Hilton probably cannot rival the world-famous Overlook in shining terms of blood-soaked walls, spectral twins, and mysterious anagrams appearing in mirrors, still ghost hunters await the day when a frightened guest reports the first-ever sighting of Ms. Stevenson, the former South Park kindergarten teacher who plummeted to a grisly death from the hotel roof following her much-publicized elopement with her pupil, Ike Broflovski. A salutary lesson that prompted the following statement from an outraged bystander. "If you don't go with Christ, you could end up like that splattered bitch on the pavement."

Back in the realm of the more or less living, history buffs will enjoy such architectural delights as City Hall and the courthouse, while the arts are catered to by regular movie showings at the Bijou Cinema and a thriving community theater. The town's religious needs are well served by a range of churches, while the local school—rebuilt to almost identical specifications following a disastrous fire—has been featured regularly on national television.

South Park is a shopper's paradise. Among the longest-established businesses on the town's picturesque main street, the aforementioned Tom's Rhinoplasty offers the latest in nasal reconstruction techniques, with Barbra Streisand purportedly numbered among its many satisfied clientele. (Streisand was once also rumored to own a $4 million condo on the slopes above the town, although this might be confused with the one she also owned in Aspen.)

EV Games, forever on the cutting edge of modern gaming technology; a well-appointed FedEx Office; the local branch of Unplanned Parenthood; Lolly's Confectionary Factory; Jimbo's Guns; Lamont's Dance Studio; and the Photo Dojo are all familiar sites on and around South Park's picturesque Main Street, while animal lovers will certainly want to pay a visit to the Indian Burial Ground Pet Store, home to a wide variety of very unusual furry, feathered, and scaly companions, and the repository, too, for another of the quaint local legends with which South Park abounds.

A very colorful local myth insists that much of the pet store's distinctive stock was actually drawn through a swirling portal from an evil alternate dimension, created when the store's owner accidentally dug up an ancient Native American cemetery, urinated on the remains, reburied them upside down, and then erected his pet store on top of them.

"Why?," he was once asked.

"I don't know," he replied. "I was drunk."

Like that of the Hilton, tales such as this go a long way toward explaining why South Park has been described as one of the most haunted towns in America. It's a reputation that not only earned it a visit from television's intrepid Ghost Hunters team, it also resulted in the isolation of a whole new form of supernatural evidence.

According to crudely rendered representations of Jason Haws and Grant Wilson, plumbers by day, fearless psychic investigators by night, and founders of The Atlantic Paranormal Society (TAPS), the liquid warmth that formed, independently, around their groins, traced down one leg, and then produced a mysterious pool at their feet was "definitely [the product of] some paranormal activity." It was during an investigation in South Park that this phenomenon was first captured on camera.

Other long-standing South Park businesses include South Park Pianos, the South Park Pharmacy, the betting club Sports Book, and Jim's Drugs RX. Sadly, however, the town recently lost its sole video rental store, with both the local Blockbuster and a replacement operation owned by local businessman and geologist Randy Marsh having fallen victim to changing times and technologies.

Finally, South Park Mall features every major retailer you could possibly hope or expect to find, often selling precisely the same items as you could have purchased at home, in an environment that looks precisely the same as the one you left behind. Mallards, Toy Safari, Body World, the Red Robin where Tom Hanks and Beyoncé did not get married one blood-soaked Black Friday, the works. A little slice of home from home, then, and make sure you don't miss visiting the local branch of "Paris Hilton"'s Stupid Spoiled Whore franchise.

Nightlife is very important to South Park. Though rarely frequented, the Comedy Club and the nightclub Les Bos are both paramount among the attractions, while Viggos cappuccino and coffee house has offered performance debuts to a wide variety of local talent, including beat poet Randy Marsh, following his unfortunate appearance on television's *Wheel of Fortune* in 2007.

For visitors wishing to sample rural community at its most primal, meanwhile, the ever-popular Skeeter's Bar and Cocktails has been described as the only bar in town. Which is unlikely, but it does possess a working jukebox, whereas its only true competition, the bar at Mick's Bowling, offers only bowling. And Guitar Hero. But it was also the birthplace of the music legend Steamy Ray Vaughan, one of a surprising number of top musical performers to have been born and bred in town.

Elsewhere, the town's reputation for fine dining is catered to by a veritable smorgasbord of eateries. These range from such nationally known chains as Bennigan's, IHOP, and Denny's, to a wealth of private enterprises that cater to every palette.

Under the guidance of airline tycoon Tuong Lu Kim and his singing superstar wife Wing, the City Wok offers the finest in Chinese cuisine; next door, City Sushi reflects the growing trend for consuming raw fish and seaweed. The internationally famed Harbucks coffee chain, with its distinctively non-phallic Camel logo, is a welcoming oasis for anyone who does not want to drink locally manufactured coffee that tastes of rancid sewage; the locally owned Tweek Bros. Coffeehouse is there for anybody who does.

For family dining, the local branch of the evergreen Raisins franchise, staffed by its trademark cast of over-cosmeticized and underdressed pre-teen girls, is always a popular choice; and has prompted at least one juvenile customer to remark, "If I were a little older, no doubt I would be aroused."

For seniors, however, the Country Kitchen Buffet not only offers a wide menu of comfort foods, it is also of local historic interest. The buffet was the center of military operations during that short period of time during which the AARP invaded and occupied South Park to protest recently passed town ordnances legislating against the number of road accidents caused by local senior citizens.

Only the fast thinking of a small band of townspeople ended the conflict; recalling how the closure of the Country Kitchen Buffet in nearby Steamboat Springs led to the mass extinction of that town's senior population, they barricaded the establishment's doors and caused the hostile forces to surrender. The Country Kitchen Buffet was ultimately destroyed during the Mecha-Streisand crisis, but will doubtless reopen again at some point. Old people do need to eat sometimes.

Finally, for fans of continental dining, Whistlin' Willy's is South Park's award-winning pizzeria, and was formerly known as Crust E. Krotch's.

South Park and its environs are also home to a wide variety of cultural and entertainment attractions, including the Museum of Tolerance and Cartmanland, a massive amusement park built over the site of the former North Park Funland by a local fourth grader using funds bequeathed to him by his late grandmother. Visitors are warned, however, that opening hours have been known to vary, and a strict admissions policy is enforced.

The water park Pi Pi's Splashtown is also a major attraction, home to such thrilling features as Pi Pi's New York Splash, featuring FDNY ships equipped with powerful water cannons; the wave pool Pi Pi's Swashbuckler; the pyramid-shaped Lost River in King Tut; the Journey to the Center of the World; the volcanic Pele's Revenge (a hilarious re-creation of the destruction of Martinique in 1902); the relaxation-themed Lazy River and the Zipline water slide.

It should be added that the future of the entire park was, several years ago, endangered after health officials discovered that the urine-to-water quotient of the pool exceeded national safety limits of eighty-three parts pee to seventeen parts water, with a peak ratio of 98-2 actually creating a vastly destructive tidal wave. However, recent reports suggest that these levels have been reduced considerably.

Another amusement park, Super Phun Thyme, is located just two blocks from the renowned Pioneer Village, but adult visitors are certainly not overlooked in the rough and tumble rush for juvenile pocket money.

Just a few miles outside of town, the Three Feathers Indian Casino is a gambler's paradise, its popularity and renown so pronounced that plans were once laid to demolish South Park in its entirety, to make way for a superhighway that drove straight into the heart of Denver. Thankfully this scheme has never been acted on, and town and tribespeople continue to live harmoniously together.

Of course, no vacation can ever be considered complete without a visit to the local emergency room, and visitors to South Park can count themselves fortunate that the town is equipped with one of the most experienced (if not especially accessible) hospitals in America.

Hell's Pass Hospital has been at the center of innumerable medical emergencies over the years, each of which has added immeasurably to the facility's expertise, although hospital administrators will be the first to acknowledge that with such great responsibilities, there have come occasional trials.

However, the once-revolutionary employment of a nurse with no arms, and the hospital's outside-the-box practice of not separating donor blood from infected test specimens have both subsequently proven their worth; while among the hospital's most remarkable accomplishments can be numbered its handling of an outbreak of chicken pox, the repair of a barbed-wire infected hemorrhoid, and several falls from roofs. (Although not Ms. Stevenson's Hilton plunge.)

Hell's Pass also leads the field in the Death or Vegetable debate, while the nearby Colorado Medical Center is at the forefront of crack baby care and research.

And finally, if your visit to South Park should prove so enthralling that you wish to end your days there, both the Shady Acres retirement home and Looming Sunset Assisted Living await.

Welcome, then, to South Park.

"Ample parking day or night, people spouting: 'Howdy, neighbor!'"

3

And Now for Something Completely Vaguely Similar

What Is This Python of Which They Speak?

"Right as South Park came out we were at the Aspen Comedy Festival and we sat down with some of the Monty Python guys—before our Gods. They said, 'So South Park seems to be pretty successful.' And we said, 'Yeah and we got this and we're going to do that' and Terry Gilliam said, 'Don't over-extend yourselves.' And he was so right, and we've been over-extending ourselves for the past decade."

—Trey Parker

Exploding penguins, menacing hedgehogs, and bisected bees are not what one would describe as natural targets for humor; abattoirs, funeral parlors, and Australian table wines likewise, and it will be with considerable bafflement that future generations, midway through some modern course on light entertainment of the early 1970s, first broach the topic. What, they will ask, is amusing about a naked man playing the organ? A xylophonist replacing the keys of his instrument with live mice? Goldfish with whooping cough, and the Spanish Inquisition?

And why should John Philip Sousa's "Liberty Bell" still conjure up images of a swiftly descending, very large foot?

Well, as Terry Jones reliably suggested midway through an advertising film the creators of *Monty Python's Flying Circus* made for the Birds Eye frozen food company in 1971, maybe they should "ask some housewives."

It is now forty-five years since *Monty Python's Flying Circus* first appeared on British television screens; forty since it first arrived in America. A comparable timescale would be to ponder the state of humor almost half a century before the advent of the Pythons; what were people laughing at in 1924? And was it still as funny in 1969 as *Monty Python's Flying Circus* remains today?

What, too, of the *Pythons'* original audience? It has indeed grown up to become squawking housewives and recalcitrant pet shop proprietors; smarmy chat show hosts and irate military men. And television comedy has grown up with it.

Who, watching prime-time reruns in the mid-1960s, for example, could ever have foreseen a day when the suave sophistication of *South Park*, the dry intellectualism of *Beavis and Butt-Head*, and the mannered satire of *Married with Children* could even find a place in American television listings, let alone a respectable Nielsen rating? About as many people, in today's age of political correctness, as could imagine a time when phrases like "a dagger up the clitoris," characters named "Mr. Smokestoomuch," and the concept of cheese shops that don't sell cheese were staples of evening viewing.

Yet *Monty Python* retains its hypnotic hold on our imagination, a hold that only seems to tighten every time one or other of the surviving former members opens his mouth to make us laugh—or, in some cases, doesn't open his mouth at all, but manages to make people smirk through inference alone.

In 2013, as this book was being written and the US was girding its loins for confrontation with Syria, the Internet buzzed with news of an antiwar message put out by John Cleese, which truly seemed to be couched in such typical Python humor that . . . well, that it surprised a lot of people when it turned out to be a hoax. And surprised considerably less when it turned out there were some people who didn't believe it was a hoax to begin with.

That's the problem with the Pythons, you see. It doesn't matter how much you know about them, you never really know them at all. And if that can be considered a measure of their success, then it is a success that defies even those admirers who describe them as a phenomenon. The Pythons are a way of life, and there are annoying little people on college campuses across America for whom the ability to quote verbatim slabs of Pythonesque dialogue remains a power to be proud of.

"I just spent four hours burying a cat."

"Four hours to bury a cat?"

Monty Python demonstrate the "Upper Class Twit of the Year".

"Yes. It wouldn't keep still."

Monty Python's conquest commenced immediately after the show began running on PBS in 1974, when the first three British series became one of that august organization's most successful imports ever. There was even talk of a Marvel comic based on the series, and by 1976 *Python's* American distributors, Time-Life, were fielding offers from the networks for the fourth series.

Although the Python team themselves had expressly forbidden their work to be sold to commercial television, a deal was struck with ABC, and the two-year-old fourth season premiered on prime-time television with a ninety-minute special, compiling the first three shows of the six-show series. It was a disaster, or so Python mainstay Michael Palin complained, and perhaps the astute TV historian can draw parallels between the fate of the Pythons and that awaiting *South Park* so many years later.

"[ABC] had made numerous cuts in accordance with some Federal— official but arbitrary—code of censorship; we felt that what they'd done was de-gut the programs totally, to such an extent that they just were not Python."

Entire sketches were excised, links were lost; odd words were removed from the text, victims not only of network squeamishness, but also the need to cram in as many commercials as any single show could bear. The end result, as Python biographer Roger Wilmut put it, "looked as if the Python team had produced seventy minutes of boring, pointless material."

The Pythons headed hurriedly for the courts, to obtain an injunction against ABC's projected second show; Judge Lasker found in their favor, but taking into consideration the amount of money ABC had at stake, ruled that the projected second compilation could be broadcast, provided it was preceded with a disclaimer, pointing out the Pythons' objections to the show.

ABC appealed and had the disclaimer dropped (the show was broadcast with a simple "edited for television" caption); Python then returned to the offensive, and this time, they not only won damages (and control over the manner in which their work could subsequently be presented), they also found themselves enshrined in American legal history for establishing what remains, from an artist's point of view, one of the most important points of law in the book, the artist's right to exercise control over his work.

What was most remarkable about all this, at least so far as most discerning Python fans were concerned, was that Roger Wilmut actually got it right. The fourth series was, for the most part, boring and pointless, and did in fact need to be edited down.

Aired in Britain between October 31 and December 5, 1974, the fourth season of *Monty Python's Flying Circus* had been touch and go from the start. John Cleese, the cast member who, to many viewers, was Mr. Python, had quit at the end of the previous series, leaving many people to speculate that the show was doomed by definition. The BBC certainly felt that way and seriously considered canceling the show before a summer 1973 Python tour proved there was still life (and, onstage at least, Cleese) in the old dog. There were not, however, many good sketches. *Monty Python* would never return to the small screen.

The *Monty Python* story begins, as does most modern British comedy, with *The Goons*, the anarchic 1950s broadcasts that made cultural heroes of Harry Secombe, Spike Milligan, Peter Sellers, and Michael Bentine. For the first time in broadcast history, unbridled silliness was allowed to masquerade as humor for the delectation of a nation, and in the wake of *The Goons'* success, both on radio and, later, television, similar lunacy erupted from the very quarters where *The Goons* had proven most popular, Britain's halls of higher learning, the Universities of Oxford and Cambridge.

The convoluted skein of interrelated television and stage shows that grew out of these unsuspecting hotbeds of humor, fondly loved revues such as *Beyond the Fringe*; satirical current affairs shows like *That Was the Week That Was* (hosted by the late David Frost); and lunatic children's hour blockbusters like *Do Not Adjust Your Set*, were the testing ground on which the future Pythons fired their first shots.

John Cleese first emerged as one of the writers behind the 1961 Cambridge Revue *I Thought I Saw It Move*; Graham Chapman debuted (alongside Cleese) in the following year's *Double Take*. Over at Oxford, Terry Jones appeared in 1963's bizarrely titled **'****'**; and was then joined by Michael Palin for 1964's *Hang Down Your Head and Die*. And by 1965, all four were writing for David Frost's biting *The Frost Report*, where they were joined by a younger Cambridge veteran, Eric Idle.

Individually and collectively, the five-some continued to work together through the remainder of the 1960s, both as writers and performers, fermenting the weird chemistry that would, with the addition of Carol Cleveland and vicious American cartoonist (and *Do Not Adjust Your Set* veteran) Terry Gilliam, launch the Flying Circus.

Highly creative though the team was, all they really knew was that they wanted to create a comedy show within which short sketches, cartoons, and jokes were linked (or not) depending on the mood of the players.

There would be no punch lines; rather, visual puns and stream-of-consciousness association would simply lead one sketch to the next, with Terry Gilliam's cutout cartoons the glue that held the others' sketches together. He recalled, "I was given a starting point and an ending point, from where the last sketch ended to where the next one began, and I just let my mind wander in between."

Such creations as the man-eating push chair, the killer cats, and a wide-ranging arsenal of disembodied body parts followed, themselves held together by an unrelenting savagery. They would also become a key element in the development of *South Park*, both from an artistic point of view (the early drawn characters were very Gilliam-esque) and in terms of the most impossible creations morphing into the semblance of reality that was the town of South Park itself.

Another major influence on the gestating *Python*, and one whose reflection can also be seen in *South Park*, was ex-Goon Spike Milligan's recently launched *Q5*. Terry Jones recollected, "He just totally ripped up all form and shape. Milligan started a sketch and then it turned into a different sketch, then it turned into something else." As the team outlined their ideas to BBC producer Barry Took, Milligan's genius was at the forefront of their minds.

Took, whom they all knew from *The Frost Report* (and beyond), was sufficiently enthusiastic to win the team a thirteen-show commission from the BBC; others within that establishment, however, were less overwhelmed by the anarchic promise of the self-styled Baron Von Took's wacky protégés. One even dubbed the whole affair "a flying circus," a derogatory name that the sextet—who had hitherto been playing with such titles as "Owl Stretching Time" and "Bunn, Wackett, Buzzard, Stubble and Boot"—nevertheless leaped on with gleeful abandon.

But whose Flying Circus was it to be? For a time, it was almost Gwen Dibley's, a name Palin spotted in a Women's Institute magazine and found pointlessly amusing. But somewhere else along the line, Idle thought of "Monty," Cleese contributed "Python," and after a few days of reasoned consideration, that was the name that was delivered to the BBC. *Monty Python's Flying Circus* it was.

Producer Ian McNaughton, assigned to the fledglings after Took's initial delivery, was delighted. "We chose the title for three carefully considered reasons," he later explained. "Because as far as we knew, there was no one called Monty Python. Because it had nothing to do with flying. Because it was not a circus."

The first series of this new show was broadcast on October 5, 1970, at 11:00 p.m. "Whither Canada?," as the episode was (again, revealingly!) titled, featured seven basic sketches, including two parodies of contemporary television ("It's Wolfgang Amadeus Mozart" and "It's the Arts"), plus "Famous Deaths," "Italian Lesson," "Whizzo Butter," "Picasso/Cycling Race," and "The Funniest Joke in the World." Which might even have been a forerunner of "Fishsticks," except nobody ever survived hearing it.

The *Daily Telegraph* newspaper responded to what the BBC described as a "nutty, zany, comedy show" the following morning. "The comedy was sophisticated and had much of the delightful absurdity which has not been seen on television since the Marty [Feldman] show," enthused reviewer Norman Hare. "It took toll of interviewers and other features of television that need the sending up process."

Cleese, for one, appreciated Hare's words. "One of the loveliest things that people used to say to us," he remarked, "was that once the show came off the air, and the next thing came on, which was a regional magazine program, it was impossible to watch it without finding it terribly funny."

Hare's reference to the bug-eyed Feldman, meanwhile, was not entirely gratuitous; Palin and Jones had both written for the two broadcast series of Marty, and at least one Python sketch, the current affairs type exposé of young men who get their kicks from dressing up as mice, had originally been written (but rejected) for the Feldman show a year or so previous.

Neither was Hare far off the mark when he commended the team on its treatment of television stereotypes; indeed, if *Monty Python's Flying Circus* did have any one specific target, it was the increasing pomposity (and the exponentially broadening trivialization) of television—another area that *South Park* has truly excelled in.

"We were acutely . . . aware that the best parodies of television are done on television," Cleese acknowledged as, with ever more glee and guile, Python took on everything from soap operas to TV movies, from documentaries to chat shows, and on to the viewers themselves.

Game shows such as Blackmail, in which unsuspecting contestants are invited to pledge increasing amounts of money to prevent their greatest indiscretions being revealed; Upper Class Twit of the Year, an Olympian contest between archetypal English aristocrats; and the self-evident Most Awful Family in Britain became a staple of the show. The oft-favored footage of a theater full of old ladies happily applauding some unseen performer was based on the then-typical BBC-invited audience—according to Palin, in fact, it looked exactly like the crowd that awaited the first-ever Python recording.

This process of mocking its public culminated with the introduction of The Colonel, a veritable voice of reason whose admonitions to "stop this, it's silly" parroted the vocal minority whose outraged complaints swamped the BBC switchboard every time the corporation broadcast anything out of the normal. *Monty Python's Flying Circus*, of course, was simply begging for their attention.

The Colonel (whose expression was to become as popular a catch-phrase as Cleese's "and now for something completely different") would prove a valuable aid in the scripting of sketches. As the first series went along, so the team grew more and more adept at setting up a situation, and then allowing it to develop ever more surreal layers before finding a way of winding it down. The Colonel, striding on-screen amidships, demanding an end to the silliness, proved to be the perfect culmination.

Although he first appeared in episode one's "Joke Warfare" sketch, the Colonel (played by Chapman) really came into his own in the eighth episode of the first series, interrupting army recruit Eric Idle's discourse on why he doesn't fancy the idea of getting killed. "That's a very silly line. Awfully bad." Other victims of the Colonel's sense of moral value included a sketch in which a pair of swarthy foreign protection racketeers try putting the squeeze on the British Army ("things get broken, Colonel"); and a mini-documentary on the menacing evil of Hell's Grannies.

The BBC were very slow in appreciating the success of *Python*. Although the administration was initially keen on the idea, shortly after work on the first series was completed, the upper echelons of the corporation underwent a sizable change as the open minded Director General Hugh Greene quit, to be replaced by a considerably less tolerant regime.

Python suffered immediately. The show's late-night slot was one of those openings in the schedule during which the various BBC regions were free to pre-empty the head office's programming with whatever else they wanted, generally local interest specials and news digests. And so, while the London-based media went Python crazy, many parts of the country remained practically Python free until the show went into repeats the following year.

"I think if the authorities had been aware of what we wanted to do right from the beginning, we would never have been allowed to do the program," Graham Chapman once mused. "I don't think the BBC really wanted us around the building very much, in fact we seemed to get worse and worse offices as we went along, and for the last series, we were in a shed near the gate."

Indeed, without the support of the media, it seems unlikely that the BBC would have even considered commissioning a second series. With *Monty Python*'s cult status assured, however, the BBC's record division set to work culling the best (or at least, the most appropriate) moments from the first series for a soundtrack LP, the first in a series of *Python* albums that themselves did as much as the television series to popularize sketches and expressions. Indeed, in the years before VHS and DVD came along, those LP records were the only way anyone could relive favorite *Python* moments again and again. And they did.

It was a well-designed set, including such highlights from the first season as Eric Idle's "nudge nudge wink wink" assault on a well-mannered businessman; a succession of sexually explicit children's stories; a self-defense class featuring murderous, fruit-bearing assassins; and the appearance of sundry Nazi leaders at a small west country bed-and-breakfast. There was also an airing for a sketch that has since become synonymous with *Monty Python*, featuring Michael Palin, John Cleese (portraying a long-running but seldom-named character called Mr. Praline), and a disputably deceased parrot.

Strangely, in view of its subsequent ubiquity, "The Pet Shop" was not an especially successful sketch. In its original format, in fact, the actual debate over the parrot's animation was swiftly subverted by the action's rapid progress through a brief argument over whether or not the town name "Ipswich" is a palindrome of "Bolton," before the Colonel turns up to condemn the whole thing as "silly."

On record, too, the parrot sketch comes in a decidedly poor second to its culmination, where the by now thoroughly beleaguered Cleese approaches a railroad complaints office, only to be confronted by an especially overwrought clerk. Ignoring his customer entirely, the clerk bemoans his lot before expressing his true ambition—to be a transvestite lumberjack. And if there was any single "hit" from the first series, that was it: "The Lumberjack Song." But the parrot lives on, and was even paid tribute by *South Park* in the short "Dead Friend Sketch"—with Kenny, inevitably, standing in for the parrot and Cartman likewise perishing when the giant Monty Python foot lands on him.

A second series was commissioned and recorded. Once again, however, the show's late-night slot left it subject to the programming whims of sundry provincial TV chiefs, and once again, those chiefs were often able to find something to substitute it with.

In London, too, the BBC found itself increasingly perplexed by the show. Originally broadcast between September 15 and December 22, 1970, the second series again has its share of classics—in April 1971, a *Python* compilation even won the prestigious Silver Rose at the Montreaux Festival, a mighty accolade indeed for a show that completely baffled its own bosses. But still the censors' scissors were never far away, and often with very good reason.

"What you discover is that stuff with an element of shock does have the ability to make an audience laugh much more than stuff without it," Cleese acknowledged, a point that was hammered home by the "we're so fucking sorry" apology that appears on the 1974 *Drury Lane* live album, and the entirely gratuitous reference to "four cunts, one clitoris, and a foreskin" that opens the *Holy Grail* movie soundtrack album.

Still, Cleese denies accusations that Python deliberately intended upsetting people by remarking, "the more you are in this business, the more you tend to abandon taboos you may have held when you were fifteen, twenty or even twenty-five. So some of the things we do, which are no longer shocking to us, may be quite shocking to a Presbyterian minister's daughter, brought up in Ayr."

Or to a BBC watchdog, raised on *Dixon of Dock Green* and *University Challenge*. A sketch revolving around a cannibalistic funeral home was permitted onto the screens only if the Pythons arranged for the audience to show its distaste at the concept. A piece that combines wine tasting with urine, "The Wee-Wee Sketch," was banned outright, while one of Gilliam's cartoons of a prince who foolishly ignores a malevolent black spot that is growing on his body was redubbed for future broadcasts, in case it upset cancer sufferers. Instead, in some misguided attempt at alleviating the inherent tastelessness of the original concept, it targeted victims of gangrene.

Other moments, however, remain pristine, even in the eyes of the establishment. The Spanish Inquisition (which no one expects) swiftly made the transition from televisual entertainment to cultural mainstay, as highlights of the sketch entered every viewer's vocabulary, and comfortable chairs became a byword for hideous torture. John Cleese's silly walks took on an even greater life of their own, bedeviling their creator to this very day. And then there were the Piranha Brothers.

Doug and Dinsdale Piranha, as every British viewer would have instantly known, parodied the recently jailed Kray Twins, London gangsters whose criminal empire held London society enthralled, even as their activities grew increasingly more brazen. Finally imprisoned, the Krays' influence remained pervasive; the arrival of one of Doug Piranha's "associates" at the end of the sketch, to suggest politely that it should be brought to an end, was an echo of the Krays' own continued ability to squash unwanted publicity with a few well-chosen words in the appropriate ear.

In 1971, the team established their own Python Productions company, to oversee the marketing of their career. Removing themselves from BBC Records, a recording deal was negotiated with Charisma, a label hitherto best known for such progressive fringe rock acts as Genesis and Van Der Graaf Generator. A book deal was concluded; a colorful sprawl full of stupidity, smut, and occasionally, inspired genius, 1971's *Monty Python's Big Red Book* (which of course was blue) became an instant best seller (two years later, the hardback *Brand New Monty Python Bok*, followed by the softbound *Brand New Monty Python Papperbok*, repeated the feat).

And the team's first feature film, *And Now for Something Completely Different*, was released in October 1971. Essentially a compendium of favorite sketches from series one and two, the movie was originally intended to introduce the Pythons to the American market, with its British impact a barely considered possibility. Instead, with almost Pythonesque contrariness, the movie crashed and burned in America, while becoming a massive hit at home.

All this activity took time, of course. Filming of series three did not begin until December 1971 and was to drag on for almost six months. It was October 1972, therefore, before it could begin transmission, and all concerned admit that the slow gestation of the material caused the overall strength of the series to suffer. John Cleese, in particular, was losing interest, announcing his intention to quit the cast at the end of the series (he would, however, remain on board for stage shows, movies, and vinyl).

Although the television series remained a primary source of material, the team's third album also featured a great deal of new material, a testament to the sheer creativity of the Pythons. John Cleese and wife Connie Booth's "A Fairy Tale," the highwayman Dennis Moore, and Sam Peckinpah's "Salad Days," the latter a brilliantly realized collision between

In the land of Python, nothing was sacred, nothing was out of bounds.

The Wild Bunch and a BBC costume drama, all rate amongst the comedy highlights of 1972.

So does Eric Idle's "Eric the Half a Bee" (originally conceived, but excised from, the "Fish License" sketch), an album cut that was also released as a November 1972 single. Indeed, so successful, and (as it transpired) universal, was the Pythons' humor that even today, much of their material remains relevant, impervious to the deprecations of either time or fashion. Evidently, the concept of innocent soccer players being turned into Scotsmen by the blancmanges remains cogent however far into time and space one travels.

The Pythons' pataphysical ability to grasp slivers of contemporary society and bend them out of shape remains one of the series' strongest points, and one of its most powerful influences—as Matt Stone and Trey Parker have frequently admitted.

Contemporary satire, of course, was nothing new in British entertainment, and the thinly veiled appearance of sundry (predominantly right-wing) social and political icons had long been a staple of comedy. Where Python stepped beyond the norm was in the depth to which those figures were veiled, a process that has actually allowed the characters to take on a life of their own, long after the people they were modeled on have faded to obscurity.

Some of the show's best-loved denizens were simply exaggerated stereotypes: the bellowing Gumbys, the squawking Pepperpots, and of course, the Colonel. But elsewhere, neither dignity nor propriety prevented such real-life political figures as Enoch Powell and Reginald Maudlin becoming so absorbed within comic culture that today, it is difficult to believe that anybody ever labored under such instinctively humorous handles.

Cleese's departure from the series, coupled with the BBC's continued insouciance, ensured that there would be another long wait for a new television series, although there would be no letup in the team's activity.

Back in 1970, the Pythons staged a live show at the Belgrade Theater in London. Now, in 1973, the Pythons—with Cleese and former Bonzo Dog/ *Do Not Adjust Your Set* songwriter Neil Innes both on board—set out on the Anglo-Canadian (!) outing that they called the First Farewell Tour, an evening of "jokes which will be appearing for the last time before retiring."

It was a grueling routine, a series of one-night stands that left Palin, hoarse from the nightly exertions of Gumbyhood, suffering from laryngitis on top of the natural exhaustion that afflicted everybody else. Despite this, the Pythons obviously enjoyed live performance, and in February 1974, they launched a season of shows at the Drury Lane Theatre in London, armed with a well-honed repertoire that included both a selection of old favorites ("Albatross," "Nudge Nudge," "Pet Shop," "Lumberjack Song") and a liberal serving of newer material.

The Australian philosophers whose homophobic pledge of "No Pooftahs" was amongst the most quoted catchphrases of the age were similarly one of the highlights of the stage show; so were the Four Yorkshiremen—an exercise that took colloquial stereotyping to its ultimate, but strangely still lifelike, extreme. Travel to the northern wastes of England, to "the Third World" of Python's *The Meaning of Life* movie, and wizened old men named Obediah really do sit around waxing nostalgically about a youth spent "down mill" and the social deprivations surrounding it.

"I had t'get oop in t'morning at ten o'clock at night, half an hour before I went t'bed, drink a cup of sulphuric acid, work 29 hours a day down mill and pay mill owner for permission t'come t'work, and when we got home, our dad and our mother would kill us and dance about on our graves singing hallelujah."

Also included was the greatest Python game show yet, an exercise in unmitigated brutality called "Spot the Braincell," in which Mrs. Scum competes for such star prizes as a blow on the head or a knee in the temple; and best of all, a lengthy Election Special, designed to coincide with the real-life political contest being waged in Britain at that time.

Perfectly parodying the BBC's traditional coverage of such an event, and introducing such immortals to the hustings as Kevin Phillips Bong and Jethro Q. Walrustitty, "Election Special" is a succession of quick-fire puns, well-mannered digs, and quite ferocious insults, many of which were targeted ruthlessly at real-life political candidates.

Enoch Powell, whose old constituency of Wolverhampton Southwest was taken by the unequivocally named Rastas O'Dingah O'Dingah, was a renowned racial scaremonger; Tarquin Fintinlinbinwimbimlinbin-Bus Stop-F'tang-F'tang- Ole-Biscuit-Barrel was patently modeled on any one of several double-(or more)-barreled Conservative bastions; and the little pink pussycat who beat the Liberal Party in Barrow was, in fact, simply a veiled reference to the Liberals themselves, as they reeled from tabloid revelations about their party leader's sexuality. All of which, when laid bare, is utterly meaningless forty years on, but remains cloaked in a veneer of humor when regarded in its own right. Another tribute, then, to the Pythons' skills.

The rampant success of the live shows, with an audience simply baying its approval as the cast relived some increasingly hoary sketches, remains astonishing. Several members of the cast compared their reception to rock concerts, a parallel that was only exaggerated by the audience's own behavior: fans knew the sketches, knew the words, and chanted along with the performers.

Like the Rolling Stones unearthing "Satisfaction" for one more trip round the stadium circuit, or Roger Daltrey reminding us of the days when he hoped to die before he got old, a bus he has now well and truly missed, it matters not that years of repetition had stripped any genuine sense of meaning from the words; had reduced the sketches, in fact, to anthemic status. Like a good (non-Australian) wine, Python jokes really did seem to improve with age. "I don't know what it is," Michael Palin once remarked. "Like the Spanish Inquisition sketch, it improves on the telling. When you actually see it, it's not done all that well in a way, it creaks a bit. But . . . it matures in the mind."

The fourth, and final, television series finally aired in Britain between October 31 and December 5, 1974. It ran into immediate criticism. The jokes just weren't very funny any longer.

Cleese's departure had done more than break up a winning team; it also shattered a winning chemistry. The magic of *Monty Python*, as Michael Palin once explained, was drawn from the six principles "pulling in different directions." Without Cleese, whom many observers credit with providing a certain restraint to the wilder flights indulged in by his colleagues (it is widely believed that it was he who alerted BBC censors to the aforementioned "Wee Wee Sketch"), Python lost its sense of gravity, in every meaning of the word. The result was a formless foaming of misplaced frenzy.

Watching (and rewatching) series four, it was easy to assume that the team was losing its edge, and maybe—without Cleese—it was. With him, however, there was no sense of surrender, a fact that was hammered home by the spring 1975 release of Monty Python's second feature film, the epic *Monty Python and the Holy Grail*, a twisted parody of the Arthurian legend that would eventually spawn the mega-successful Spamalot stage show.

Python took to the road again in the wake of the *Holy Grail*, visiting the US for a two-week season at the City Center in New York; then, without ever acknowledging a split, the Pythons would spend the remainder of the 1970s spinning off on their own projects: Cleese's *Fawlty Towers*, Idle and

Innes's *Rutland Weekend Television*, Palin and Jones's *Ripping Yarns*, Gilliam's *Jabberwocky* movie, and so forth.

"Working in a group is great fun, but you need your own individual identity as well," Graham Chapman explained. "If you're stuck together for almost a year doing a television series, it becomes very difficult to have a separate existence other than within the group. You virtually have to ring up to ask if it's all right to have a bath."

Of course, the Pythons themselves were not yet finished; indeed, for many fans, their next move was their best yet, 1979's feature film *Monty Python's Life of Brian*. Originally conceived (as *Jesus Christ—Lust for Glory*) in the fevered aftermath of *Holy Grail*, *Life of Brian* was not, as many critics supposed, actually based on the Bible. The tale of Brian Cohen, an innocent man who finds himself mistaken for some sort of messiah, was however freely adapted from it, and of course, there were problems from the beginning.

The film's original backers, EMI, withdrew from the project very early on—Beatle George Harrison eventually financed it, claiming that it was the only way he'd ever get to see it. The movie (but not, strangely, the soundtrack album) was banned in Ireland, while two American states, bending to the will of outraged Christian and Jewish organizations, also forbade the movie from playing within their jurisdiction.

Equally mortified by the movie's content was the crowd of extras gathered outside a house for one morning's shooting. *Life of Brian* was filmed in Tunisia; consequently, many of the extras, male and female, were Muslim—a religion that forbids its female followers to witness male nudity. One can, then, only imagine the squeals of very real horror that greeted the sight of a full-frontal Graham Chapman, throwing back the shutters to greet the new day.

Controversy, meanwhile, followed controversy; having been reviled by the Catholic Church over *The Life of Brian*, the Pythons were next on the receiving end of John Denver's wrath. Their next album, 1980's wryly if accurately titled *Monty Python's Contractual Obligation Album*, included a saucily defaced cover of "Annie's Song," although one wonders which planet Denver's advisors were living on when they sued Python for defamation of character. When the satirical comedians applied for permission to cover the song, it was stated, they had not made it apparent that their intention was ridicule.

Monty Python's second summer of activity lasted three more years, a period bookended on the one hand by a series of shows at the Hollywood

Bowl (September 26–29, 1980), which would subsequently spawn a movie-length documentary; and on the other by one final movie, the chaotic but delightfully visual *The Meaning of Life*. The scene in which Mr. Creosote eats until he explodes remains a classic in the annals of bad taste, while Idle's ode to conception, "Every Sperm Is Sacred," has rightfully taken its place in the songwriting hall of fame (not to mention on the accompanying, remix-packed soundtrack album).

But the end was nigh. Any hopes that a third reunion was in the cards were ended first by John Cleese's virtual adoption by Hollywood, in the wake of the smash hit movie *A Fish Called Wanda*, and then by the passing of Graham Chapman, on October 4, 1989 ... it was, of course, a masterpiece of ironic timing that he should die the day before the next Python album release, a compilation of songs suitably titled *Monty Python Sings*.

Monty Python's Flying Circus occupies a unique place in the annals of world comedy. While much of what was considered daring about them has now become so integral a part of the comic landscape that it is all but meaningless today, still great swathes of the show's dialogue has become one with the language, in Britain and abroad. America, of course, remains ferociously loyal to a brand of humor that, many people remain convinced, is still only barely understood here, while European and Japanese markets, too, have taken the team to their hearts.

Video rentals and sales have remained constant since the shows and movies first appeared (in an escalating variety of formats) in that medium; regular reissues of the albums, again in a bewildering number of permutations, have kept Python snaking out of the record stores. A 2014 reunion of the surviving cast members proved one of the year's most eagerly awaited, and rabidly received, comedy events; it was also one that Terry Jones acknowledged was inspired by *South Park*.

He told *Big Issue*, "It was Matt Stone and Trey Parker ... who got the ball rolling. They suggested doing something with us and we thought, that's a good idea. But then we thought that we should change it and do something together ourselves, so that was the spark that lead to us all getting back together."

And you always know when the shows are back in syndication when you ask what's on the television and discover that whatever it is, it looks like a penguin.

A penguin that promptly explodes.

4

You Can't Do That in Front of the Children . . .

Can You?

"The big lie of our whole career is that right-wing fundamentalists are always trying to shut us down. It has literally never happened. The Mormons haven't, the Christians haven't—OK, the Scientologists did, but they don't count. But when we make fun of liberal people, they're like, 'What?!' I think religious conservatives are more used to taking a beating."

—Matt Stone

hat is the difference between an episode of *South Park* and the nightly network news? Apart from the fact that *South Park* is usually a lot more balanced?

Less than you might think.

Both rely on a group of familiar faces to bring you "team coverage" of whichever event is under the spotlight.

Both are almost obsessively conscious of the stories that matter most to the average American (at the same time as having absolutely zero significance in either political or historical terms).

And both are often still being scripted right up until the moment when they are broadcast. Even those episodes that appear more interested in breaking wind than breaking news.

To gather, and list, every occasion on which *South Park* has investigated, or reflected, on a story that the news channels insist is of national or international import would not, of itself, be important. For the same reason that nobody has ever published an episode guide to CNN *Headline News*, so *South Park* has become such an integral element of modern cultural commentary that, very often, it is the show's response to an event, or a personality, that lingers in the mind long after the event itself has been forgotten.

This is not a unique phenomenon. Fellow Comedy Central stalwart Jon Stewart and HBO's *The Newsroom* (successor to creator Aaron Sorkin's *West Wing*) likewise visit the latest headlines in order to offer an alternate and thought-provoking take on current affairs; while the satirical puppet show *Spitting Image* spent much of the 1980s teetering on the brink of sundry deadlines as fresh new stories broke in the hours before transmission.

The difference was, *Spitting Image* comprised a series of generally unrelated, short sketches, any one of which could be pulled at the last minute to make way for something more topical.

South Park, with its continuous narrative spread over an unbending twenty-two minutes (commercials bump it to its scheduled thirty), does not have that luxury. But it succeeds in its intentions regardless, to offer up—for the length of each season—an unflinching cultural history of the times in which we live and the sheer absurdity of the depths to which so-called news programs will stoop in their death race for increased viewing figures.

Preparation for each week's edition of *South Park* generally begins on the Thursday before transmission the following Wednesday, Parker and Stone heading a brainstorming team that, over the years, has included such staff writers and consultants Pam Brady (scriptwriter for the movies *Hamlet 2* and *Hot Rod*), Nancy Pimental (*The Sweetest Thing*), *Saturday Night Live* stalwart Bill Hader, and Norman Lear (veteran producer of *The Jeffersons*, *Sanford and Son*, and *All in the Family*).

From these sessions, a script is produced and then delivered up for production, a process that can take anywhere up to four or five days, but that has pushed into a sixth on occasion, as the writers respond to what we might call "late-breaking news." On more than one occasion, an episode has been completed and delivered to Comedy Central just hours before the show's scheduled airtime at 10:00 p.m. (EST).

The episode celebrating Barack Obama's 2008 Presidential election, "About Last Night," for example, aired less than twenty-four hours after his victory was confirmed and included elements of Obama's own victory speech; 2003's "Christmas in Canada," in which we hear of deposed Iraqi leader Sadaam Hussein's discovery in a "spider hole," treated a story that had only made the networks three days earlier.

When great swathes of American society became inexplicably obsessed by the doings of reality television's Honey Boo Boo, *South Park* struck out with its own interpretation of the phenomenon, prompting a frankly furious response from the real thing's mother. And in 2010, the show's two hundredth edition, aptly titled "200," was widely excoriated for mocking Islam's prohibition on the depiction of Muhammad (by pointedly not depicting him), a follow-up to the all-too-real furor that followed a Danish newspaper's inclusion of such a depiction in a recent cartoon.

Someone, somewhere, once said that trying to choose the most controversial episodes of *South Park* is like ... well, just add in your own Herculean task. What was the worst David Bowie album of the 1980s? Which is the most annoying Tom Hanks movie? Who is the least believable mainstream politician? Everybody has their own opinion, and there's way too many to choose from, regardless.

You could point to almost any episode of *South Park* and isolate at least one fairly large segment of the population that will be alienated in some way, a broad and ever-moving target that ranges from Canadians, Mormons, and Scientologists to rednecks, rockers, and people who don't like talking poo.

The good folk at Apple have felt the sting of the *South Park* tongue, as have the pioneering comics at Fox and even the show's compadres at Comedy Central. So have the NFL and the NRA, the AARP, and the brains behind *Family Guy*. In fact, it sometimes feels that if something moves, it's worthy of a shot—and the cheaper the shot, say the show's proponents, the more valid the assault will be. Or the more absurd. Your choice.

In 2009, Judge Lynn Cook-Stanhope, presiding over a court room in Calgary, Canada, condemned *South Park* for inspiring two local teens to take part in a "Kick a Ginger" day. Which was dedicated, as you might expect from such a name, to kicking ginger people. *South Park*, the judge declared, is a "vulgar, socially irreverent program that contributes nothing to society." Furthermore, it was unfortunate that the show's creators, Trey Parker and Matt Stone, would never be called to account for encouraging such action in the first place.

Stone and Parker, on the other hand, would argue that they can never be accused of taking sides against any minority, no matter how any viewer cares to interpret their stories. And why? Because they treat them all with equal disdain. As was proven in the offending ginger kids story. Half of it is devoted to Cartman hating redheads and preparing for their annihilation; half to him leading the carrot-topped oppressed out of bondage and planning to annihilate everybody else. The only message the episode offered was that both were ultimately as stupid as one other.

Naturally, it is all too easy for any enemy of the show to miss such underlying messages of tolerance and understanding, for that is very often the point. The fact that there are two sides to every story isn't simply a fundamental component of human makeup, it is the underlying principle of both democracy and free speech. A world, or even a nation, in which everybody spoke and thought with a single mind wouldn't simply be colossally boring, it would also put Stone and Parker out of a job, together with almost every other comedian, writer, musician, commentator, journalist, and politician.

Of course, the authors of the American Constitution probably never foresaw a day when an entire nation (as it sometimes seems) could be divided over the rights or wrongs of a simple cartoon. But there again, on the other hand, perhaps they did. Political cartoons, ferociously lampooning the statesmen and events of the day, were as much a part of everyday life in the 1770s as they are today, and perhaps even more so.

In a world without radio, television, movies, or the Internet, the printed page was as keen a weapon as the sharpest modern documentary, and the cartoon was the keenest of them all, because even the illiterate could understand it. The spread of, and support for, the Protestant Reformation of the sixteenth century was at least partially fired by artists such as Hans Holbein the Younger and Lucas Cranach the Elder; while the madness of King George III and the cast of politicos who danced around him was a common feature in the work of James Gillray. Indeed, no less an authority than Wes Bel and Tim Najmolhoda, authors of the University of Michigan's webpage on "Comic Art in Eighteenth Century England," have this to say about Gillray's work: "[It was] characterized by obscenity and monstrous distortion. Much of his art was offensive in the extreme. He did not try to achieve either beauty or realism in his works. Instead, the characters of his cartoons were twisted and unshapely. They were often nightmarish and ugly. He sought to bring out the worst in his victims."

Does anything here sound familiar?

There is more. According to author Vic Gatrell, an expert on the cartoon art of the era, "In the 1790s, Isaac Cruikshank could ridicule a great aristocrat's Jacobin sympathies by having him defecate into his coronet and urinate on a bishop's mitre while gazing at the portrait of George III with which he intends to wipe his bottom. In William Dent's 'Public Credit' (1791), the Treasury Secretary's vast backside farts defiance at his political opponents. James Gillray's 'Evacuation of Malta,' during the 1803 peace negotiations, has the bare-arsed and terrified Prime Minister

Addington defecating territorial concessions to Napoleon into a French officer's cocked hat."

Far from being a modern perversion that reflects only the grotesque depths to which society has now sunk, *South Park* is in fact merely the latest beneficiary of a cultural legacy that dates back almost to the age of Christopher Columbus. Who himself was nowhere near as pleasant a man as history sometimes likes to paint him.

Indeed, that perhaps is the most vibrant of all definitions of satire and, by extension, *South Park*. It reminds us that things are not always what they seem, and the more insistent history, government, or a lobby group becomes, the closer we should be inspecting their claims.

And so it is that states as far apart (geographically and culturally) as Connecticut and Georgia have enacted bans on *South Park* merchandise being taken to school, while a group calling itself Action for Children's Television denounced the show as "dangerous to the democracy"—presumably missing out not only on everything we've already said in this chapter, but also the fact that *South Park* is not, and has never been, marketed as a children's program.

Yes, it's a cartoon. But so were the Tijuana Bibles of 1930s' shock and renown, a series of rudely produced booklets that depicted political and showbiz figureheads of the day indulging in the wildest and most crudely drawn sexual acts imaginable.

The fact that, back in 1999, a survey of British eight- to ten-year-olds saw Eric Cartman elected their favorite television character is hardly a reflection on either the show or its makers. It is the parents who allow kids that age to watch a program that routinely features death, dismemberment, abuse, and bad language who should be questioning themselves.

After all, it does have a "mature" rating, together with an opening disclaimer that leaves nobody in any doubt as to its content. And if a parent should continue unable to trust his or her own judgment, then listen to the wise words of the Parents Television Council.

South Park, they decreed, is a "curdled, malodorous black hole of Comedy Central vomit."

Got that? A curdled, malodorous black hole of Comedy Central vomit. That's a pretty unequivocal condemnation, no matter how modern one's parenting skills might aspire to be.

But wait! There's more. No less august a body than the Christian Family Network published an educational guide devoted to "protect[ing] our youth from vile trash like *South Park*," arguing that the show physically undermined their own attempts to "restore morality, and protect life for the individual, family, and community."

What about the day when readers of the British Daily Telegraph newspaper were informed by writer James Delingpole that the satire aspired to by *South Park* "is the most gratuitously offensive in the history of television"? That the show is "ugly to look at, unpleasant on the ear, badly drawn, execrably voiced, puerile, cynical, expletive-ridden, vulgar, trashy and almost entirely free of likable or, indeed, psychologically plausible, characters"?

Did nobody take that as a warning not to let little Fifi and Jeremy watch it before bedtime?

Okay, so Delingpole also revealed himself to be a fan of the program, continuing on, "It also happens to be possibly the funniest programme on television and certainly the boldest, bravest and most socio-politically acute."

But boldness, bravery, and acuteness are not necessarily qualities that people look for in a television program. Why think about the message when it's far easier, quicker, and garners more headlines if you simply slaughter the messenger?

Again, *South Park* is not, and will not be, the first animated television show to draw down such censure. Throughout its history in the early-mid 1990s, Mike Judge's *Beavis and Butt-Head* was regularly the subject of complaint and concern, and that despite running with its own series of disclaimers:

> "Beavis and Butt-Head are not real. They are stupid cartoon people completely made up by this Texas guy whom we hardly even know. Beavis and Butt-Head are dumb, crude, thoughtless, ugly, sexist, self destructive fools. But for some reason, the little wiener-heads make us laugh."

This was subsequently changed to the even more cautionary:

> "Beavis and Butt-Head are not role models. They're not even human. They're cartoons. Some of the things they do could cause a person to get hurt, expelled, arrested, possibly deported. To put it another way: Don't try this at home."

"Don't try this at home." That's a warning that dated back to the days when no less wholesome a superman than Superman himself apparently started encouraging his fans to wrap themselves in a bedsheet cloak, and then leap out of windows in the belief that they could fly. With, apparently, tragically messy results.

Of course, if disclaimers of this nature actually worked, it is doubtful whether they would be required in the first place. After all, anybody smart enough to read, absorb, and accept those dire warnings would already be smart enough to know what was and wasn't acceptable, or even feasible, behavior to indulge in themselves. And so *Beavis and Butt-Head* offered the authorities and watchdogs of the early 1990s precisely the same kind of target as *South Park* would, later in the decade (and beyond).

A target whose misdemeanors may or may not have been fantastical, but that certainly came in for its share of—if true—genuinely condemnable complaints. The firework death of a cat in Santa Cruz, just months after *Beavis and Butt-Head*'s MTV debut in March 1993, was seen as a copycat response to a similar killing in the show.

That same October, a mobile home fire in Moraine, Ohio, that killed a little girl was blamed by the grieving mother on her little boys' exposure to Beavis's penchant for fire raising. Indeed, so serious was this event that Beavis was banned from ever again shouting "fire, fire!" So he started shouting things that sounded like it, instead, but the boys weren't out of the woods yet.

In 1994, the watchdog group Morality in Media blamed *Beavis and Butt-Head*'s influence for the death of an infant, struck by a bowling ball hurled off a Jersey City overpass by a teenaged boy—an episode of the show has recently shown the pair loading a bowling ball with explosives and dropping it off a building.

What was interesting about both this case and the earlier Ohio incident is that it later became apparent that neither of the perpetrators had actually seen the episodes on which their actions were blamed; did not, in fact, even subscribe to cable television. Observations, according to other forces within the media, that suggested the often precipitous rush to blame controversial television programs for sundry societal ills might not always be rooted in reality and fact.

Stone told *Hollywood Interrupted*, "early on in *South Park*, we would have Cartman say, 'Shut up Kyle, you're a dirty Jew.' Cartman is a little racist, and he just heard that someplace. Kyle always tells him to fuck off. In the beginning we were told you can't do that because there would be a lot of people out there that would repeat it without irony. That somehow they'll think it's okay to say, 'You're a dirty Jew.' And we'd say, no they're smart in the middle of the country, they get it.

"In Hollywood, there's a whole feeling that they have to protect Middle America from itself. We can all laugh at Jew jokes and gay jokes, and I can make a black joke because I'm enlightened here in Hollywood, but don't put that on TV because when people in Nebraska hear it, they're going to yell the 'N word' at the next black person. Political correctness started from there, with the idea that the middle of the country can't handle sophisticated jokes. And that's why *South Park* was a big hit up front, because it doesn't treat the viewer like a fucking retard."

Indeed, *South Park* has offered its own regular commentary on these claims, most recently via the season seventeen episode "Informative Murder Porn."

Shocked and outraged by the amount of time their parents devoted to watching so-called true-life documentaries about murderous spouses, and fearful that the shows could only lead to tragic copycat behavior, the boys campaigned to have such shows banned altogether. Of course they were rebuffed, so instead they programmed the family TVs' parental lock with a question that no parent on Earth could answer. Or so they thought . . . .

Which proved not only that the war against unsuitable television programming cuts both ways, but also that the most cunning lock in the world will never be truly fail-safe. Just as *South Park* had already proved, thirteen years earlier, that the most fail-safe electoral system in the world is no match for a good dose of cunning. And, in so doing, brought bitterness ringing down around the heads of Parker and Stone from the Republicans who gathered around George Bush as he battled for victory in the aftermath of what most people considered a reasonably decisive defeat in the 2000 presidential election.

Most people, but not them. And doubtless they flinched angrily as Mr. Garrison attempted to resolve a similar impasse following an attempt to elect a kindergarten class president in a contemporary episode of *South Park*.

"Recount," demanded Filmore Anderson's supporters.

"You lost, Filmore!," responded Mr. Garrison. "Don't be such a baby!"

Which, we all agree, was no way to speak, even obliquely, to the newly declared President of the United States. But while James Gillray must surely be pirouetting in his grave by now, it is joy and not despair that animates him so. For "speaking that way to the president" is precisely the point of the show. And precisely what its critics hate the most.

Beavis and Butt-Head was held accountable for the action of its titular characters, and ultimately proved that people are quite capable of being stupid on their own without even needing to glance at the television set. So *South Park* was set upon for a modus operandi that *Beavis and Butt-Head* could never truly be accused of.

For being too clever for its own good.

For not simply picking at what we might call the scab du jour, but fully excavating it as well. And the more recent and painful that scab might be, the better. Only Jon Stewart's *The Daily Show*, also aired by Comedy Central, is better placed to harpoon the absurdity of modern society, primarily because great swathes of the political right wing seem to treat it as a valid and vital part of the mainstream news media.

But *South Park* goes even further, following up the harpoon by driving a stake into their victim's writhing corpse as well.

"We get to express our frustration through a little fat kid screaming at the top of his lungs," Stone explained to *The AV Club*. "So it can be taken semi-seriously. We get to enjoy that same distance that the Jon Stewarts of the world get to too. They demand that they be taken seriously, and as soon as someone takes them seriously, they crack a joke.

"I love the fact that Trey and I have gotten awards for being topical and satirical, but at the end of the day, we are just making jokes. If you ask me how to really solve the health-care crisis, I have fuckin' no idea, and I don't want to be a part of it. But I can make a little fat kid yell some emotional truth about it. That's what we've figured out over the years. If you're gonna make it a TV show, you would never do the actual politics of something, but you would do the emotions behind the politics. Who cares if it's a right-or-wrong policy—here's how it makes me feel. You're not gonna get into a policy discussion with Cartman and Mr. Hankey and Jesus and shit."

More than once, an episode passes by without great swathes of the audience truly understanding what is being skewered, simply because they had managed to live their lives to date without ever encountering . . . for example . . . Honey Boo Boo, World of Warcraft, or Jared Fogle.

Perhaps you have forgotten author James Frey, who wrote a best-selling self-help book about his recovery from a life of hardship and pain, only for it to be subsequently revealed that he had not been exactly truthful in his storytelling.

Cue mass condemnation, cue a public furor, cue what came so close to a public witch hunt that, when a towel named Towelie was discovered telling lies of his own on the *Oprah Winfrey Show*, Oprah did indeed rouse an army of outraged readers bent on lynching the dissembling little cheat. But you don't need to have read *A Million Little Pieces* in order to appreciate the *South Park* episode "A Million Little Fibers," just as you don't need to believe that Oprah had a gun-toting, talking vagina in order to appreciate Towelie's plight.

Another one.

If you weren't aware that actor Mel Gibson once made a more-or-less interminable movie about how painful a death crucifixion is, then you might devote the entire span of *South Park*'s "The Passion of the Jew" to wondering why a Hitler-clad Cartman has suddenly become fixated on the star of *Mad Max* as the figurehead of a new and terrifying brand of anti-Semitism.

You might even confuse it with the anti-Semitic rants the real-life Gibson allegedly gave vent to when arrested for drunkenness two years later, in 2006. Indeed, even for people who do consider themselves "informed," there are moments while watching old episodes of *South Park* when you feel a little like some future archaeologist, trying to make sense of the twentieth century with just the tiniest scraps of context-deprived papyrus to guide you.

And you might never guess that Parker and Stone were completely taken by surprise when that particular episode turned out to be one of the best-loved of all *South Park* episodes. "We thought it was crap," Parker said. "We came to work two days later, and people loved it, and we're like, 'Whaaaa? People love that piece of shit?'"

The brilliance of *South Park* is that (a) it still makes sense without that foreknowledge, and (b) once you do seek out the source material, it's impossible to view it through any prism beyond the cold, clear logic with which it has just been dissected. For that is another of *South Park's* talents. It doesn't simply lampoon its victims. It asks questions about them as well, and usually answers them in a manner that is very hard to argue with.

So, with all that in mind, what are the most controversial/offensive/ whatever other word you might choose to use episodes?

The episodes that created the most horrified, astonished, or simply disbelief-packed response not necessarily from their victims but from the outside world?

The episodes that, were you to watch one while texting, would demand you wear out the O, M, and G keys on the touch screen. What is peculiar, however, is how seldom the targets themselves rise to the bait. For example . . . .

Followers of the Mormon faith might have had occasion to look away from the screen as the episode "All About Mormons" offered up what the Church of Jesus Christ of Latter-day Saints declared to be its "gross portrayal of Church history." But its scope was narrow and exquisitely tightly focused, and the Church itself acknowledged that no harm was done. "Individual Church members no doubt felt uncomfortable. But . . . it inflicted no perceptible or lasting damage to a church that is growing by at least a quarter of a million new members every year."

"Uncomfortable." Hardly a resounding triumph for the forces of animated evil that other, non-Mormon, elements of the media would have had us believe; and probably no more than Stone and Parker intended. "We knew a lot about Mormonism," Parker explained.

"We grew up around a lot of them. They were kind of lost in time. They are a very Disney religion." Indeed, it was that aspect of the faith, he acknowledged, that inspired him and Stone to create *The Book of Mormon*, the Broadway sensation that took them into the second decade of the twenty-first century.

"Just looking at Mormons you think: Wow, watching a bunch of them on stage singing a song would really be nice! They really have that kind of charisma. I think if it was about crappy people and people who were just kind of really fundamentalist and serious and angry then it wouldn't be a very fun musical to go and see."

Where *South Park* truly succeeds, then, is on those occasions when it upsets people beyond its immediate target. Such as the time a powerful Russian Pentecostal group tried to persuade their nation's government not merely to ban *South Park* from ever befouling the country's airwaves again, but to close down the channel that had the nerve to be broadcasting it in the first place. And all because they didn't like Mr. Hankey, the Christmas Poo.

A drawing of Harrison Ford could have been excused for feeling a little sore after being raped, several times, by drawings of Steven Spielberg and George Lucas in "The China Probrem," an episode designed to question the movie industry's insistence on beating a successful "franchise" to death. In this instance, the Indiana Jones cycle. But it was not Ford, Spielberg, or Lucas who raised their voices most loudly in protest. It was the Parents Television Council, who accused the episode of "exploiting the sensitive topic of rape for a trivial movie satire."

Likewise, when Comedy Central itself put its foot down over the contents of an episode, it was not because the boys had convinced themselves that Jared Fogle, the advertising front man for Subway sandwiches, had AIDS (he actually had aides ... a personal trainer, a dietitian, and so forth). It was because the suggestion that Butters's mom and dad routinely hounded their son might be seen as somehow approving of parental abuse.

"HEAVEN ON BROADWAY. 'THE BOOK OF MORMON' ACHIEVES SOMETHING LIKE A MIRACLE. A CELEBRATION OF THE PRIVILEGE OF LIVING INSIDE THAT IMPROBABLE PARADISE CALLED A MUSICAL COMEDY."
NEW YORK TIMES BEN BRANTLEY

All singing, all dancing, all Mormon. Parker and Stone take Broadway.

And still Parker has insisted, "People have the misconception that we start our projects by sitting down and saying, 'All right, who can we rip on?' and we don't ever come at it that way, it's always, 'Oh, here's a good story, here's something interesting, here's something fun and happy and silly.'"

Language has also landed *South Park* in trouble. In the episode "With Apologies to Jesse Jackson," the uncensored and unapologetic use of the "N-word" (how odd that it can be said on television but not in any reporting of the show itself) may have been intended to make a very valid point ... that is, demonstrating for an audience who "just don't get it" how the term is offensive to the people it's used against.

But it raised hackles regardless, and sent them soaring so high that people quite lost sight of the one question the show really had to ask. Which was, how can society ever be expected to understand the lessons it should be learning if political correctness has rendered the topic itself out-of-bounds?

Equally bafflingly, one can sit through any number of prime-time television dramas and hear sufficient cussing and obscenity to color the average inner-city turf war. And the following day, the critics will speak in awestruck tones of the edgy artfulness of the show's reflection of real life as it is lived.

Transpose that same language to a mid-evening cartoon, on the other hand, and maybe exaggerate the cussing to a point where no less than 162 "shit"s were dropped in just twenty-two minutes (that's one every eight seconds, fact fans), and again, jaws smack floors in horror and outrage, and trembling hands reach out to change the channel and watch something less gratuitous instead. Like *Deadwood* or *Chicago Hope*. Over five thousand people were so incensed by the episode "It Hits the Fan" that they were moved to e-mail their dismay to Comedy Central.

Good thing they didn't watch *Bigger, Longer & Uncut*. After all, if it's good enough for the Guinness Book of Records . . . .

South Park's assaults on popular culture are not always successful. "World War Zimmerman" looked askance at the 2013 trial of Florida neighborhood watchman George Zimmerman, for the murder of a young black, Trayvon Martin, and the fears, voiced by many media observers, that his eventual acquittal might lead to widespread racial rioting. As targets go, so far, so good.

But three months separated that verdict (in July) from the episode (in October), months during which the immediacy of the early outrage had very much died down—compare that with the mere six weeks that divided the still-fresh scars of 9/11 from *South Park's* first commentary on the subject.

Likewise, the world had already moved on from the Brad Pitt movie *World War Z*, which the episode also spoofed, thus giving the entire story a spookily "are you sure this isn't a repeat"-like feel before its first airing was even over. The fact that it was also very clumsy didn't help. There was social commentary aplenty in the story line itself, but the targets (the hypocrisy of justice, the absurdity of certain laws) were scarcely the sacred cows for which *South Park* was once religiously accused of slaughtering.

However, the multitude of complaints and problems that dogged the computer launch of the Affordable Healthcare Act in October 2013 made a gloriously effective theme for the season seventeen highlight "Taming Strange." Regardless of whether or not one agrees with the Canadian Healthcare minister who admitted, "Anyone who thinks streamlining health care into an integrated health care system would go smoothly deserves a giant queef in their face."

But talking of religion . . .

Religion is an obvious target for any comedy show, and *South Park* made its own position very clear from the outset, the first time that Cartman ever deployed the Broflovski family's Jewish faith as a weapon against their son Kyle.

Parker told the *Denver Post*, "I grew up with the religion of *Star Wars*, frankly. That's when I realized there is something bigger out there . . . and it's called The Force. [But] people have a lot of different beliefs, and at the end of the day, we all have deeply held beliefs that probably don't make sense to anyone else. We just try to keep it in the context of how we can treat each other right and laugh about it without being too offended about it."

We have already mentioned (or will be doing soon) the show's assaults on Scientology and Mormonism. Several other episodes, however, have also routinely been highlighted as maybe going a step too far.

When the issue of child abuse in the Catholic Church hit the headlines early in the millennium, *South Park* dispatched Priest Maxi to the Vatican City to combat what the entire rest of the church appeared to believe was an irrevocable fundament of the religion itself. One that packed plenty of historical precedent, too. As far back as the 1720s, the French writer and philosopher Voltaire was overheard (or rather, loudly proclaimed) that the vast majority of his health issues could be traced back to boyhood, "when those damned Jesuits . . . buggered me to such a degree that I shall never get over it as long as I live."

That he made this pronouncement at a high-class dinner party, shortly after he learned to speak English (but, presumably, before he learned to speak politely as well) is immaterial. So is the fact that he was promptly asked to leave the gathering. Three hundred years later, the same words were being spoken by hundreds of similar victims. Small wonder that Father Maxi was willing to risk his life to remedy the situation, because who could deny that it needed remedying?

Season nine revisited Catholicism, by electing the night before the Feast of the Immaculate Conception as the most suitable occasion on which to investigate the long-standing Catholic fascination with bleeding statues of the Virgin Mary.

Normally, however, they bled from their eyes or the palms of their hands. "Bloody Mary"'s blood came gushing from her rectum.

Weeping, bleeding, and otherwise leaking statues of the Virgin Mary have been around for centuries, with the last century or so positively teeming with them. The Church's own position on the subject is tentative, with far more being pooh-poohed (or, more politely, disproven) than have ever been even halfway acknowledged. And only two, one in Syracuse, Sicily, in 1953 and another in Akita, Japan, in 1988, have ever been given official recognition.

Of course, the Church's reluctance to give credence to every putatively fluid-oozing Mary has made little impression on the millions who do believe in miracles, and who flood in their hundreds (or more) to visit any halfway believable phenomenon they hear of. As recently as 2012, believers in the Philippines witnessed a Marian statue that excreted palm oil and bled from the face. In 2004 in the Lebanon, a statue blinked its eyes and oozed scented oil; and in 1989, again in the Philippines, Mary is recorded as weeping tears of pig's blood.

For viewers of "Bloody Mary," then, a statue leaking blood from its rectum, at St Peter's Church in nearby Bailey, would inevitably become a major attraction for Colorado's pilgrims. Much to the discomfort of the visiting (cartoon) Pope and much to the fury of the (real-life) Catholic League for Religious and Civil Rights. At their behest, Joseph A. Califano Jr., a member of Viacom's board of directors, released a statement calling the episode an "appalling and disgusting portrayal of the Virgin Mary" and pledged to have it reviewed.

Further afield, New Zealand's Catholic Bishops' Conference attempted, albeit unsuccessfully, to have the episode banned in that country. But such storms were little more than teacup-sized when compared to what happened when *South Park* appeared to go up against the Muslim faith's prohibition on depictions of the prophet Muhammad.

Because now, to paraphrase the season five opener, the shit really hit the fan.

The plot was simple. In the aftermath of the worldwide furor that engulfed the Danish newspaper cartoonist who depicted Muhammad in one of his cartoons, Parker and Stone devised a plot in which the Fox network cartoon *Family Guy* announced that an uncensored depiction of Muhammad would appear in the next episode of the show.

Family Guy is not, it is safe to say, one of Stone and Parker's favorite shows. Indeed, Parker informed the *New York Times*, "We kept running into people that are just like, 'Oh, you guys do *South Park*—I love that show, and *Family Guy*. That's the best. You must love *Family Guy*.' And we were like, "No, we [really] hate *Family Guy*.'"

Fox's *Family Guy*. Not one of South Park's favorite shows.

What better target could there be, then?

Fearing a repeat, or worse, of the Danish controversy, the people of *South Park* panicked, and "Cartoon Wars I" ended with a cliffhanger . . . would *Family Guy* forge forward with its plan?

Yes! Kyle convinced a Fox executive to go ahead with it, no matter how many threats might be issued by militant opponents. But as if to disprove the old artistic insistence that you can do anything with a cartoon, the actual broadcast of *South Park* featured a blacked-out image and the words "Comedy Central has refused to broadcast an image of Mohammed on their network." Which seemed a little strange, being as he had already appeared in the episode "Super Best Friends" back in season five, without anybody paying much attention whatsoever.

It was a rare moment of discord between show and broadcaster, as Matt Stone told the *AV Club*. "We don't get a single note like, 'Eh, we don't like that scene . . . Can we put the boys in the middle more?' We haven't for, like, ten years. But we do have Standards & Practices look at the script, and Legal does too. But we probably get more leeway than most shows. And if we want to do something special—like, we . . . did this Tourette's show, and we said 'In order to do this show, we need to say "shit" a bunch, or else it doesn't make any sense.' So we made a case for it, and they let us say 'shit' a bunch. And they let us say 'cock,' too. But it was within the realm of Tourette's, so it was okay, I guess. So there's always a negotiation process, and if we can give a reason for it that's defendable to them, and to our advertisers, then they let us do it."

Muhammad, apparently, was not defendable. So they tried again in "200." And again, Muhammad was either censored or unseen throughout. But this time, voices were angrily raised—not for depicting (or not) the prophet, but for mocking the religious restrictions that surrounded that depiction. The New York–based radical Muslim organization Revolution Muslim even took to Twitter, with username Abu Talhah Al-Amrikee praying for Allah to kill Stone and Parker and let them "burn them in Hell for all eternity."

Elsewhere, he invoked the 2004 assassination of Dutch filmmaker Theo Van Gogh by a Muslim extremist, captioned "Have Matt Stone and Trey Parker Forgotten This?," and continued, "We have to warn Matt and Trey that what they are doing is stupid and they will probably wind up like Theo Van Gogh if they do air this show."

Apologies were demanded from as far afield as Malaysia, where the conservative Islamic PAS party insisted Parker and Stone repent for showing Muhammad dressed as a bear (even though it turned out to have actually been Santa in disguise), although PAS vice-president Mahfuz Omar did make a very valid point when he said, "The show itself spells of bad intention, and the depiction of the Prophet is provocative. It creates religious tension."

More was to follow. The second part of the story, "201," saw Comedy Central censor the word "Muhammad" throughout the episode before its broadcast. In the UK, British Comedy Central screened a repeat of "The Tale of Scrotie McBoogerballs" in lieu of the episode and canceled a scheduled repeat showing of "200."

Even South Park Studios' own website, repository for all things *South Park*, has been rejoined from including these two episodes in its collection of streams (a fate that has also devoured "Super Best Friends").

And the month after the "200"/"201" controversy, the *Daily Telegraph* reported that police investigating an attempted bombing in New York's Times Square, close to the Viacom offices, had themselves considered the possibility that it targeted "the makers of *South Park*."

In the event the aborted attack proved to have other motives entirely. But the fact that a link had even been considered was a harsh reminder that the world has changed immeasurably since the days when the TV critic was a program maker's worst enemy.

After all that, then, should there be any question of whether it's a suitable kids' program?

Yes there is, as Trey Parker discovered in 2011.

"My girlfriend who I've been living with for two years has a ten-year-old. So I actually have a kid who really wants to see *South Park* and wants to see this show. And I catch him watching *South Park* and I'm like, 'Hey! Jesus. This is what I do.'

"But it's fine. There are some times when I sit and watch an episode with him and I'm like, 'Oh my God. It's all about the Holocaust and it's not what I believe.' With him, it's like, let him pick up the burning stick. He'll figure out it's on fire and try not to do it again.

"You just gotta let them do what they're going to do and watch what they're going to watch, and hopefully they have a relationship with you where they'll ask you if they don't understand something. Hopefully you see that Cartman is not the good guy here. You're not supposed to be like him."

And you are especially not supposed to *like* him.

5

One Hundred Celebrities

Poorly Impersonated, of Course

This isn't always easy to believe, but very few of the show's highest-profile victims actually respond to the taunting to which they have been subjected. What goes through their mind in the privacy of their own home may never be known, but it's nice to think that they are all big enough to take a cartoon blow on the chin with the same resolve as they accept the plaudits they are most accustomed to receiving.

Take Tina Yothers, for example, the *Family Ties* actress whom *South Park* once depicted in an extraordinarily unflattering light. Matt Stone was out "with the guys" once, and "I [met] this girl ... and they're like 'here's Tina.' And I say hi and start talking to her and everybody starts laughing. Turns out it was Tina Yothers and they're like 'this is Tina Yothers, you made fun of her.' She thought it was great though. She's fronting a band [Jaded], [and] she uses the soundbite to kick off her shows. She wasn't picking costumes, that's why I didn't recognize her."

Another victim, Brian Boitano, employed the song "What Would Brian Boitano Do?" (from *South Park: Bigger, Longer & Uncut*) in one of his shows, and even had members of his cast dress like the *South Park* boys. He also penned the introduction for Stone and Parker's *The South Park Guide to Life* book in 2008.

Paris Hilton even reportedly claimed to be flattered by her appearance in the show. Which, retorted Stone, "shows just how fucked up she is. That's terrible that she's flattered by it."

Parker told *Playboy*, "We're almost at the point where we know what will happen. We'll rip on someone, and the next day we'll get a call from their publicist saying, 'So-and-so saw the show last night and just loved it, and really loves *South Park* and you guys. Thank you.'"

The thanks do not always seem 100 percent sincere, of course. Often, Parker continued, "they're trying to put out a fire .... Because they know

Brian Boitano. What would he do?

they can call and say, 'Fuck you,' and then we'll rip on them more. Or they can say they love the show, thinking we'll be like, OK, that's cool, let's leave 'em alone. And it usually works. Because, except for Barbra Streisand, there's really no one we rip on because we hate them. We really are just deconstructing stardom. That's why it's just any random celebrity—we don't go for the Backstreet Boys, because that's too easy."

Or Tom Cruise. But did Tom Cruise go moaning to the media following the admittedly merciless impaling of both himself and his Scientology faith in the episode "Trapped in the Closet"?

No he didn't. He may, as was reported, have threatened to abstain from promoting his latest movie, *Mission Impossible III*, because Comedy Central was ultimately owned by the same company, Viacom, as also owned Paramount Pictures. But that was only a rumor, no more or less substantial than the follow-up gossip that claimed he recanted when a scheduled repeat of the episode was canned by the network; or that which insisted Isaac Hayes resigned from his series-long role as Chef in a similar state of dudgeon.

In fact, the only piece of concrete evidence for the entire "controversy" was a statement released by Parker and Stone, responding to it.

"So, Scientology, you may have won this battle, but the million-year war for Earth has just begun! Temporarily anozinizing [sic] our episode will not stop us from keeping Thetans forever trapped in your pitiful man-bodies. Curses and drat! You have obstructed us for now, but your feeble bid to save humanity will fail! Hail Xenu!!!"

In the event, the episode was rebroadcast two months later and was subsequently nominated for an Emmy; Hayes went on record stating that his departure from the show had nothing to do with its depictions of Scientology, while Cruise insisted that he would even not "dignify" the rumors by saying whether or not they were true.

Which is probably the best approach to take.

"Having celebrities on the show was all about the deconstruction of celebrities," explained Stone. "People wonder why we rip on celebrities, when all around there are pages of shit glorifying celebrities like Winona Ryder. And celebrities view themselves as the fucking Mozarts of their time. Even fucking Ray Romano thinks he is an enlightened individual. These people all think they are enlightened artists and therefore speak for the country. Half the people in this country can do what they do, but for some reason they think their opinion matters."

When Kanye West was depicted as a humorless egotist who assumed that a harmless joke was a personal insult, he promptly responded with an all-caps blog posting that not only acknowledged the episode as "pretty funny" (or, more accurately, PRETTY FUNNY), he also agreed "I GOT A LONG ROAD AHEAD OF ME TO MAKE PEOPLE BELIEVE I'M NOT ACTUALLY A HUGE DOUCHE BUT I'M UP FOR THE CHALLENGE. I'M SURE THE WRITERS AT SOUTH PARK ARE REALLY NICE PEOPLE IN REAL LIFE."

Yes. Of course they are.

1. Ben Affleck—revealed as the missing son of a couple suffering from TPS, a medical condition that makes people's faces look like butts.
2. Christina Aguilera—of all the myriad side effects of Ritalin, the once-so-fashionable drug designed to prevent children from behaving like children, hallucinating an Aguilera-faced monster is surely one of the most terrifying.
3. Ayman Al-Zawahiri—the Al-Qaeda leader issued a jihad against *Family Guy*, complaining it "isn't even that funny of a show."
4. Stephen Baldwin—ruthlessly massacred with his brothers by the Canadian Air Force.
5. Glenn Beck—the self-styled controversial commentator was clearly a role model for Cartman as he delivers the ultimate conspiracy theory. Student-body president Wendy wants to kill Smurfs.
6. Pope Benedict XVI—the highest authority (the Queen Spider must have been busy) available to determine whether a statue of the Virgin Mary is really bleeding out of its ass.
7. Justin Bieber—popular singer crushed like a bug by Cthulhu.

8. David Blaine—escapologist, magician, and the sinister head of the Blaineology cult.
9. Wolf Blitzer—CNN newsman who reports with characteristic verve and panache on the slow collapse of Obama's deal with the Chinese.
10. Bono—the singularly named pop star and the longtime record holder of the world's biggest jobbie. In fact, he turns out to be the world's biggest jobbie, a turd born and raised as a future pop singer—thus explaining, it is said, how he could accomplish so much that is good yet still seem like "such a piece of shit."
11. Tom Brady—footballer who becomes a keen advocate of the bleachy sports drink Butters's Creamy Goo, and who is later erroneously prescribed Ike's laxatives instead of hormones—with truly garish on-field consequences.
12. Gordon Brown—short-lived and swiftly forgotten British Prime Minister who, abetted by a covert gang of fellow world leaders, joins Randy Marsh in laundering space cash discovered aboard an alien craft that crashed in South Park.
13. Kobe Bryant—one of several celebrities attending a sex addicts meeting.
14. Jimmy Buffett—a last-minute replacement for Sir Elton John at an AIDS-Aid party raising funds for the HIV-stricken Cartman.
15. Ted Bundy—together with fellow serial killers John Wayne Gacy and Jeffrey Dahmer, Bundy is in charge of supplying the cake for Satan's party.
16. Tim Burton—hapless director who apparently hasn't had a good movie idea since *Beetlejuice*, so he keeps remaking the same movie (with the same music) with Johnny Depp.
17. George W. Bush—conspiracy-prone American president.
18. Felipe Calderón—the Mexican president who announces a public holiday when Butters immigrates to Mexico.
19. James Cameron—*Avatar* filmmaker who successfully raises the bar that society has spent the past decade lowering.
20. Drew Carey—serial "shit" sayer, subsequently executed by a Knight of Standards and Practices.
21. Fidel Castro—Cuban leader who renounces Communism after receiving a letter from Kyle.
22. Dick Cheney—having already shot one of his own friends while on a hunting trip, you'd have thought the former vice president would have had no trouble taking out Kyle and Stan. But he does.

23. Michael Chertoff—former Homeland Security head who is also secretly a guinea pig bent on conquering the world.

24. Bill Clinton—one of Liane Cartman's many lovers, and another former President of the United States.

25. Hilary Clinton—the wife of the above, and the unwitting centerpiece of a British plot to finally win the Revolutionary War.

26. Johnny Cochran—the lawyer who got O. J. off succeeds in securing a guilty conviction for Chef, via the cunning deployment of the infamous Chewbacca defense.

27. Phil Collins—singing drummer who wins the love of South Park juniors following the mass prescription of Ritalin.

28. Gary Condit—former US Congressman who attends a support group for people who have lost a close relative but had nothing to do with their death. O. J. Simpson and John and Patsy Ramsey are also members.

29. Bill Cosby—one of several wealthy blacks who relocates to South Park in the belief (fostered by Token) that it is the new Aspen. Kobe Bryant, Diddy, Will and Jada Pinkett Smith, Snoop Dogg, and Oprah Winfrey also fall for the scam.

30. Katie Couric—namesake for the scientific measurements by which human excrement is calculated. One Couric equals two and a half pounds.

31. Russell Crowe—host of the show *Russell Crowe: Fightin' Round the World*. In which he travels round the world fightin'.

32. Tom Cruise—actor and Scientologist.

33. Ann Curry—the morning television hostess who, alongside cohorts Matt Lauer, Meredith Vieira, and Al Roker, is reduced to violent vomiting after Butters appears on their show to discuss his best seller *The Tale of Scrotie McBoogerballs*.

34. Richard Dawkins—evolutionary biologist who enjoys a short-lived sexual relationship with Mrs. Garrison.

35. Paula Deen—one of a host of celebrity chefs who visit South Park to film *Hell's Kitchen Nightmares I*. Alton Brown, Bobby Flay, Jamie Oliver, Mario Batali, Giada De Laurentiis, and Guy Fieri are her cohosts.

36. Neil Diamond—impersonated by Krishna during the battle with Mecha-Streisand.

37. Princess Diana—attends Satan's Halloween party dressed as Lara Croft.

38. Leonardo DiCaprio—one of the prostitute Ming Li's customers.

39. Diddy—the erstwhile Puff visits South Park to lecture Stan on the need to vote.

40. Ronnie James Dio—a performer at the South Park Elementary Bay of Pigs Memorial Dance.

41. Celine Dion—ex-wife of fellow Canadian and controversial comic Terrance. Their daughter Sally was once kidnapped by Saddam Hussein.

42. Duane "Dog" Chapman—the television bounty hunter and his crew are hired to track down a teacher suspected of an improper relationship with Ike.

43. Bill Donohue—the head of the Catholic League declares himself Pope and jails Jesus. Who is then killed by Kyle, thus springing him from his cell via his talent for miraculous resurrection and enabling him to kill Donohue.

44. Michael Douglas—actor who attends a meeting for sex addicts along with Eliot Spitzer, Charlie Sheen, Michael Jordan, Ben Roethlisberger, Bill Clinton, David Duchovny, David Letterman, and Billy Bob Thornton.

45. Queen Elizabeth II—seen committing suicide following the unravelling of her plot to reestablish British sovereignty over the United States.

46. John Elway—Cartman briefly believes the former quarterback to be his father.

47. Brett Favre—Thousand Island dressing, a sauna, and the then-Packer star in one of Mr. Garrison's favorite sexual fantasies.

48. Jared Fogle—Subway sandwich spokesman who launches a campaign to give everyone aides. Meaning nutritionists and personal trainers. Not AIDS. Meaning a disease.

49. Steve Forbes—one of the tech heads invited to take a sneak peak at Mr. Garrison's revolutionary breakthrough in the world of personal transportation, "IT." Steve Jobs, Bill Gates, Donald Trump, and Yasmine Bleeth also attend.

50. Morgan Freeman—seen reading an excerpt from Butters's second book, *The Poop That Took a Pee*.

51. Jo Frost—TV Supernanny challenged to introduce the concept of discipline and good behavior to Cartman. She is reduced to tears and eating her own excrement.

52. Kenny G—molests Mr. Garrison.

53. Mel Gibson—maniacal Australian who refuses to recompense disappointed viewers of his movie *The Passion*. He will, however, pursue them halfway across the country, half naked.

54. Kathie Lee Gifford—prize giver and merciless haunter of Mr. Garrison's dreams.

55. Newt Gingrich—politician much prone to debating.

56. Philip Glass—renowned experimental composer, and a controversial choice for scoring *South Park's* first nondenominational Christmas pageant.

57. Whoopi Goldberg—hostess of the 42nd Annual Nobel Prize Awards.

58. Selena Gomez—hostage to Cartman's promise not to be a bully.

59. Al Gore—former vice president devoted to warning the world about the dangers of ManBearPig.

60. Tom Green—offers Howard Stern a $20,000 blowjob.

61. Kathy Griffin—namesake of an award at South Park Elementary's first annual comedy awards show.

62. Gene Hackman—Hollywood hero who succeeds in ending the peril of the fetus-devouring Christopher Reeve.

63. Tom Hanks—discerning actor best remembered for his role in *Bosom Buddies*. Oh, and that movie written by a fat third grader that also stars a monkey.

64. Tom Hayward—BP CEO forced to apologize for the Gulf oil spill. And also for drilling on the moon, thus releasing Cthulhu.

65. Jennifer Love Hewitt—an employee and sideshow at the Cow Days Festival.

66. Paris Hilton—multitalented heiress who visits South Park to open a store called Stupid Spoiled Whore. She then disappears into Mr. Slave's anus.

67. Faith Hill—singer for whom the "bunching-up-your-shirt-so-it-looks-like-boobs" craze of "Faith Hilling" is named.

68. Adolf Hitler—a guest at Satan's Halloween party, where he came dressed as the Verizon Guy.

69. Honey Boo Boo—compulsive consumer of "sketti and butter," provided by her mama, Mama Fat and Nasty.

70. Saddam Hussein—Iraqi dictator whose conquest of Canada is only narrowly averted by farts. Also, a former lover of Satan.

71. Enrique Iglesias—the unwitting inspiration behind Mr. Garrison's "IT" transportation system.

72. Steve Irwin—having already been enlisted by the FBI in its search for the Ice Man, the late Crocodile Hunter then appears at Satan's Halloween party without a costume.

73. Alan Jackson—creator of a truly inspirational album full of 9/11 songs.

74. Jesse Jackson—having already commented on the disenfranchisement of the black students in Mr. Garrison's kindergarten class, the Reverend again encounters South Park's finest when Randy Marsh visits to apologize for using the "N" word on national TV.

75. Michael Jackson—facially deconstructive man-child who moves to South Park to live under the name Michael Jefferson.

76. Steve Jobs—Apple head and inventor of the HUMANCENTiPAD.

77. Sir Elton John—one of the guests at Chef Aid.

78. Magic Johnson—one of the team who discover a cure for AIDS. A "$180,000 shot directly into the bloodstream" will do it.

79. Angelina Jolie—apparently her pubic hair is where lice go to live in bliss.

80. The Jonas Brothers—Mickey Mouse–backed trio packaged to unsuspecting teenaged girls as the epitome of purity and innocence.

81. The Kardashians—slaughtered by a crazed fan after reading *The Poop That Took a Pee*, although Kim at least survives to date Kanye West and, during an elementary school discussion of the evils of photoshopping, be compared to a hobbit.

82. Nicole Kidman—Australian actress who tries desperately to persuade her then-husband Tom Cruise to exit the closet.

83. Lil' Kim—organizes a competition, the winner of which will appear in her next video. Her breasts are the same size as her head.

84. Don King—boxing promoter who represents Satan in his forthcoming bout with Jesus.

85. Larry King—CNN interviewer who discusses stem cell research with Christopher Reeve.

86. Ted Koppel—veteran newsman who interviews the boys about their attempts to protect classic films from their own directors.

87. Korn 00000—Nu-metal heroes whose visit to South Park sees them tangle with ghost pirates.

88. Osama bin Laden—apparently had a tiny penis. And farty pants.

89. Mills Lane—referee for the great Satan vs. Jesus fight.

90. Geddy Lee—his version of "Candle in the Wind" is about farts. Much like the rest of his repertoire, then.

91. Jim Lehrer—stalwart newsman who interviews two prospective candidates for the new school mascot, Giant Douche and Turd Sandwich.

92. Jay Leno—*The Tonight Show* host with a killer chin and a penchant for booking "washed-up actress from a sitcom" onto his show.

93. Shari Lewis and Lamb Chop—unsuspecting objects of one of Mr. Garrison's darker fantasies.

94. Jennifer Lopez—famed singer who loses her fame after her record company signs up a new J.Lo. Cartman's hand with lips drawn on it.

95. George Lucas—directorial icon who teams with Steven Spielberg to rape Harrison Ford.

96. Charles Manson—escaping from prison with Cartman's uncle, the former murderous (and, at the time of writing, newly married) cult leader meets Mr. Hankey at the mall, and is utterly overcome with the Christmas spirit.

97. George R. R. Martin—the author of *Game of Thrones* is inadvertently (but very willingly) drawn into the boys' preparations for the impending Black Friday apocalypse, before being slaughtered by impatient shoppers. There will be winter. There will be dragons. And there will be lots and lots of floppy wieners.

98. Billy Mayes—enraged-mammoth-voiced TV infomercial host whose death did not preclude his continued afterlife in commercial land. Haunting little Ike, he is later revealed to be among the dead celebrities awaiting Michael Jackson's arrival aboard the Purgatorial Plane. Walter Cronkite, David Carradine, Bea Arthur, Dom DeLuise, Ricardo Montalban, Patrick Swayze, Natasha Richardson, Ed McMahon, Farrah Fawcett, Oscar Mayer, and Ted Kennedy are also aboard.

99. John McCain—leader of a jewel heist team comprising renowned cat burglar Sarah Palin, Barack Obama, and his computer hacker wife Michelle.

100. Sarah McLachlan—once-famous singer who takes up the cause of crack babies.

6

Humble Folks
Without Temptation

"People do [come up and do] the Cartman voice or something from South Park, which is cool, but it's like 'Why would we want to hear that?' I don't know why people do that. It's really the last thing in the world we want to hear. People come up and do one line from an episode or they do a voice and I'm like, 'I remember, I kinda work on the show.' I dunno if they think I'm gonna go, 'hey you're awesome?'"

—Matt Stone

Like every other community in the world, South Park is made up of many different people, from a multitude of backgrounds. Families and friends. Movers and shakers. Hunters and gatherers. Crips and Bloods. All combining within the vast, glorious melting pot that we call "community."

Some of them might even be people we would like to befriend in our own lives. But probably not.

Big Gay Al

Forever at the forefront of gay rights activism, longtime South Park resident (and former Boy Scouts troop leader) Big Gay Al is best known in town as the proprietor of Big Gay Al's Big Gay Animal Sanctuary, where wild animals of all sexual persuasions live in considerably more harmony than human beings ever succeed in doing.

He is also a vocal supporter of a grassroots campaign to realign the word "faggot," applying it not to gays but to Harley bike riders. Sadly, the movement did not become a nationwide phenomenon, but it retains its efficacy regardless. Harley bike riders get even more upset than gays when the word is used to describe them.

Big Gay Al is married to his same-sex partner Mr. Slave, although they have yet to fulfill Matt Stone's prophesy that "Slave and Al will adopt a Chinese boy and name him Jerome, and a little black boy and name him Cato."

Allison

Allison was Mr. Garrison's lesbian lover during his brief sojourn as Mrs. Garrison.

Bradley Biggle

An alien from the planet Ko-Tojn, fourth-grade student Bradley Biggle was born under the name of Gokzarah and arrived on earth charged with employing his unique super powers to save the planet. Unfortunately, these powers seem to have been confined to Mint and Berries with a tasty, satisfying crunch, hence the boy's superhero alias of Mintberry Crunch.

Bradley's sister Henrietta is one of the Goth kids whose dark and gloomy presence occasionally unenlivens the lives of their South Park school friends, and whose existential angst is apparently embroiled in perpetual warfare against vampires, Emos, poseurs, and conformity. In fact, the Goth kids' loathing of artificial uniformity in all its guises is so all-encompassing that they have rejected all clothing bar their own unique and extraordinarily well-thought-out outfits.

The children's mother, Mrs. Biggle, by the way, is also known as Demon Jizz. That is not her superhero identity, however, it's just what Henrietta calls her.

The Black Family

When the Blacks arrived in South Park, they were first Afro-American family in town to not be related to the school Chef, and the first super-rich family, too. Mr. Black, a lawyer, and Mrs. Black, a respected chemist for a major pharmaceutical company, have one child, a boy named Token, a gifted singer and bass guitarist who takes no crap from anybody, and whose secret superhero identity is TupperWare.

Despite the family's obvious and ostentatious wealth, incidentally, it should be noted that when *Lord of the Rings* fever swept South Park's youth, the best costume Token could muster was a colander on his head.

Blockbuster Employee's Ghost

His name is unknown, his fate is unrecorded. But the spectral figure of a fully uniformed sales clerk from the long-deceased video rental chain is said to haunt the former site of South Park's one branch of Blockbuster.

Trent Boyett

Preschooler Boyett was sentenced to five years in juvie for setting the fire that hideously disfigured teacher Mrs. Claridge. Bent on exacting revenge, he was released several years ago.

The Broflovski family

Prior to the advent of the legalistically inclined Black family, Gerald Broflovski was South Park's go-to lawyer. A member of the City Council, on which he serves as city attorney, he is a respected and tenacious battler who has represented almost everybody in town at one point or another, but is probably best remembered for his defense of Chef during the infamous "Stinky Britches" court battle. And also for his tendency to allow his lust for money and power to override his instincts as a servant of the law, such as the time when he devised and instigated a Ponzi scheme to convince the staff and students of South Park Elementary to sue one another for sexual harassment.

He also passed a local law outlawing cats.

The Jewish Broflovski's personal life tends to be calm; he lives well but not ostentatiously with his overbearing wife Sheila and two sons Kyle and Ike. However, he is also on record as Colorado's first Jewfin, after he underwent radical dolphinoplasty surgery. The operation was subsequently reversed.

Of the two boys, Kyle, the eldest, is generally regarded as a calming influence among his peers, a voice of compassionate reason when things go awry (as they so often do), an attribute reflected by his criminal record (see chapter eight). He enjoys a typical fourth-grade relationship with his parents, but he is devoted to his brother, despite Ike being an adopted Canadian who is shaped like a football. Which is probably why Kyle enjoys kicking him so much. Kyle's secret superhero identity is the Human Kite.

Ike himself is as precocious as his brother is conscientious, and despite his tender years has already proven himself to be sexual Lothario, an intellectual genius, a gifted psychic, and a potential criminal genius, as his prominent role in the notorious Obama/McCain diamond heist reveals.

Jack Brolin

Brolin is one of those really annoying people who always seems to turn up when you've done something wrong, to lecture you on how you could have avoided disaster. His secret superhero identity, therefore, is Captain Hindsight, and he apparently has three sidekicks, named Shoulda, Woulda, and Coulda.

Timmy Burch

Wheelchair-bound fourth grader Timmy is both mentally and physically handicapped. His vocabulary is restricted to just a handful of words and phrases ("Timmy," "Jimmy," "Gobbles," and "Livin' a lie"), although in his guise as lead singer with the rock band Timmy and the Lords of the Underworld, such limitations do not appear to be at all a disadvantage. Timmy's superhero alter ego is Iron Maiden.

The Cartman family

A single mother struggling to raise her only son alone, Liane Cartman is Eric Cartman's superindulgent but often overly forgiving parent, an alleged hermaphrodite whose premotherhood career in pornography and modeling saw her feature on the cover of *Crack Whore* magazine and star in several German *scheisse* movies.

In addition, her rampant promiscuity has allegedly encouraged her to have sex with most of the people in the country—including the Denver Broncos, Diane Crabtree, Mayor McDaniels, Sheila Broflovski, a cyborg named (but not resembling) Bill Cosby, and Jack Tenorman, a married man (and father of Eric's kindergarten classmate Scott), who after many years was revealed as Eric's own dad. Unfortunately, any reunion was postponed by the fact that Eric had previously arranged for the man to be murdered and eaten, as a means of avenging himself on Scott.

Certainly Eric is a trial for Liane, no matter how hard she tries to overlook his misbehavior. His weight problems are dismissed as mere big-bonedness and have nothing to do with his abject gluttony and obsession with fried chicken. (It does not help that she is also an excellent cook, a talent that even Satan has acknowledged. Among her more outlandish specialties is chocolate chicken pot pie with icing on top.)

Liane encourages the boy's childishness in the apparent belief that it makes him more charming, yet she seems also to have inculcated a wide range of her own personal prejudices into his makeup. Eric's hatred of Jews, hippies, gingers, gays, African Americans, and many more minority groups appears to be the sole legacy of Liane's own beliefs, but he remains unblinkingly devoted to his mother (so long as she lets him have his own way), establishing her as probably the only person on Earth against whom he does not nurse an intractable grudge of some form. His secret super-hero identity is the Coon.

Liane's niece Alexandra is an occasional visitor to the household, while her father has visited (or been visited) at least once, on which occasion he treated his grandson to an obscenity-strewn, and intricately, intimately detailed retelling of the Aristocrat Joke. Retold by Cartman during a movie devoted entirely to the joke, Penn Jillette and Paul Provenza's 2005 *The Aristocrats*.

Dating back, it is said, to the music hall era, when it was deployed as a weapon against the hypocrisy of the ruling classes, the Aristocrat Joke goes something like this:

A family walks into a talent agency, a mother, father, their son and daughter, and a baby. "Our family," announces the father, "has a magnificent act. If you permit us to perform it, you will sign us immediately."

The talent agent is unconvinced. His experience tells him that family acts are seldom less than facile and cloying. But the mother convinces him to give them two minutes . . . and those two minutes turn into the most depraved, disgusting and disturbing moments of the agent's entire life. There is no perversion that the quintet does not perform on one another, no bodily function or orifice that is left unexplored, no taboo that is not examined in microscopic detail. Until finally the two minutes is up, at which point the agent its silent for a moment before finally spluttering, "Jesus, that's a hell of an act. What do you call it?"

To which the father replies, "the Aristocrats!"
"I don't get it," says Kyle.
"Neither do I," replies Cartman.

Diane Choksondik

The late Mrs. Choksondik (or Mrs. Makes-Me-Sick and Mrs. Chokes-On-Rocks, as her pupils mockingly rechristened her) was a deeply unpopular fourth-grade teacher at South Park Elementary.

Known for her steadfast refusal to wear a bra, a fashion statement that allowed both gravity and stray kittens to wreak havoc on her large sagging breasts, and for her controversial antimale approach to sex education, Mrs. Choksondik was also embroiled in a passionate, and deeply secret love affair with school counselor Mr. Mackey.

Following her death, a quantity of her lover's semen was discovered in her stomach, but rumors that her name proved somehow self-fulfilling have never been proven.

Jesus Christ

Although he is not a full-time resident of South Park, the Son of God is widely believed to have a holiday home in the area, and He frequently intervenes in local affairs. His cable access show Jesus and Pals is a long-running feature of local programming. He is also allied to the superhero group the Super Best Friends.

Billy Circlovich

A sickly child, Billy's moment of stardom came when he was featured on the local news, awaiting a bone marrow transplant and needing just $600 more to be able to afford it. Apparently he believed the Tooth Fairy would make that final donation.

Mrs. Claridge

A former South Park preschool teacher, Mrs. Claridge was forced to retire following a fire that left her disfigured, wheelchair bound, and capable only of speaking in electronic beeps—one for yes, two for no. One of her pupils, Trent Boyett, was subsequently sentenced to five years in juvie for setting the blaze.

Mr. Conners

The somewhat inept coach of South Park Elementary's Junior Wrestling Club.

The Cotswolds

Two homeschooled kids named Mark and Rebecca. Mark would like to go to public school and is occasionally seen hanging round town. Rebecca wouldn't and isn't.

Veronica Crabtree

"Muffin," as she was known to sundry truckers, was for many years the driver of South Park's one school bus. Best remembered for her bird's-nest-like hair and for her personal catchphrase "Sit down and shut up," it came as something of a surprise when Ms. Crabtree discovered a shining new talent as a stand-up comedienne, whose rise up the echelon of entertainment ultimately saw her appear on *The Tonight Show*. Sadly, her talent was snuffed out when she was murdered by the notorious Left Hand Killer.

Cthulhu

The dark lord of Lovecraftian lore first appeared in the pages of *Weird Tales* in 1928, before becoming a semistaple of HP's other horror writing and, in the hands of other writers, the focus of an even wider folkloric mythos.

For obvious reasons, he is not a South Park resident per se. But when an oil company succeeds in drilling on the moon and releasing Cthulhu from the alternate dimension in which he traditionally resides, there is only one power on Earth that can halt his violent rampage: the superheroes known as Coon and Friends.

Damien

The son of Satan, Damien first arrived in South Park expressly to challenge Jesus to fight his father. Enrolled into South Park Elementary, Damien was initially unpopular with his school colleagues, earning the nickname "Fartboy." However, his talent for mocking another of the boys, the English transplant Pip, soon saw him win over many of his erstwhile tormentors.

The Donovan Family

Fierce atheists, the Donovans own a shoe store at the South Park Mall, a fact that is generally regarded as the explanation for their only son's otherwise inexplicable popularity with girls. Fourth-grader Clyde is the second fattest kid in South Park, has packed a colostomy bag since the age of five, and, according to rumor, is missing a testicle.

His superhero alias is Mosquito; his super power is the creation of stunning lemon bar recipes.

Ms. Ellen

A substitute fourth-grade school teacher whom Wendy Testaburger arranged to have fired into the sun.

Flo, Aunt

Stan's Aunt Flo was once a regular visitor to the Marsh household, dropping by for five days every month and reducing the family to fractious chaos as Randy was forced to sleep on the couch and Sharon became subject to unpredictable mood swings. Yet when Aunt Flo passed away, horribly murdered by the goldfish she bought for her nephew, Sharon irrationally discovered that she missed her.

As did Cartman, who mistook the old lady's Parkinson's disease tremors for a fun-fair attraction.

Herbert Garrison

Arkansas-born Herbert Garrison was raised in an age when child molestation was seen not as a crime but as a form of affection—leading to intense feelings of rejection when he realized that his own father had no interest in his body.

Graduating college with a degree in mechanical engineering, Garrison instead moved to South Park to take up the post of third-grade teacher, despite having no teaching qualifications or, indeed, any knowledge of the subjects he was expected to teach. Following the death of Ms. Choksondik, he also assumed responsibility for the fourth grade.

Mr. Garrison's confused sexuality has never been far from the surface, although its most frequent manifestations were transferred to Mr. Hat, a puppet that accompanied its owner everywhere. Class discipline, too, was often left to Mr. Hat and, following the latter's disappearance, Mr. Twig.

Mr. Garrison was well into midlife before finally accepting his homosexuality and embarking on a spree of experimental lifestyle choices, often with the aid of his leather-clad teaching assistant Mr. Slave. Subsequently, Mr. Garrison would undergo a sex change operation and become a lesbian (see Janet Garrison), before having the operation reversed.

He was also imprisoned for the attempted sexual molestation of Eric Cartman, leading him to lose his job and spend some time living as a hermit in the nearby mountains.

Janet Garrison

Janet Garrison was the identity that Herbert Garrison assumed following his sex change operation, but her tenure at South Park Elementary was cut short following her refusal to incorporate evolution into her classes. She was replaced on the faculty by Professor Richard Dawkins, and the pair began a relationship that ended only after Eric Cartman revealed that Janet was once a man.

It was on the rebound from this shattered relationship that Janet discovered her latent lesbianism, and for a short time she became a passionate supporter of lesbian rights. However, an episode of *Oprah* featuring a woman-to-man transsexual who became pregnant led Janet to reconsider her sexuality. Her penis was regrown using her own DNA, and Ms. Garrison was once again Mr. Garrison.

Ned Gerblanksi

South Park's greatest war hero, Vietnam veteran Ned served in the same platoon as Jimbo Kern, and together the pair allegedly destroyed the entire Viet Cong army. However, Ned was permanently disabled when a hand grenade exploded prematurely and blew off his arm. A former chain-smoker, he then contracted throat cancer, resulting in the loss of his voice box. He speaks now with the aid of an electro-larynx.

Nut Gobbler

Ms. Gobbler is a kind-hearted prostitute, cursed by a long-term urinary tract infection.

Bridon Gueermo

Bridon is a highly talented song, dance, and basketball prodigy, the son of a theater-obsessed madman and a mother who suffered her husband's abuse unstintingly until the day Bridon snapped and smacked the old man. At which point, she punched the old bully on the nose as well.

Baahir Hassan Abdul Hakeem

South Park Elementary's first Middle Eastern pupil, which naturally established him as a suspected (if utterly unproven) radical terrorist.

Jimbo Kern

Stan Marsh's maternal uncle (he and Randy are half brothers), Jimbo is another Vietnam veteran, having served alongside Ned Gerblanksi in the operation that led to the destruction of the entire Viet Cong army.

A lifelong supporter of the NRA, Jimbo hosts the cable access show *Huntin' and Killin'*, and his ambition is to appear on the cover of *Guns & Ammo* magazine. Among Jimbo's other leisure pursuits can be numbered drinking, hanging out with his buddies drinking, and taking the children on hunting expeditions while drinking.

Kevin

Kevin may or may not be one of South Park scientist Dr. Alphonse Mephesto's more successful projects, a strange monkey-like humanoid who has proven the doctor's most valued and loyal assistant over many years of bizarre and sinister experimentation.

Tuong Lu Kim

Otherwise known as City Wok guy, Tuong Lu Kim is proprietor of both the City Wok Chinese restaurant and the smaller City Airlines. He was responsible for building a Great Wall around South Park to ward off Mongol invaders, and also suffers an unfortunate speech impediment that makes it impossible for him to pronounce a "sssss" sound (as in the word "city," for example) as anything other than "shhhh" (as in the word "shitty," for example.)

His wife, named for and vaguely resembling the popular Chinese singer Wing, is herself a Chinese popular singer, brought to the US by the Chinese mafia.

Mr. Mackey

School counselor and occasional teacher Mr. Mackey is widely regarded as one of the most level-headed members of the South Park Elementary faculty, rarely flustered, seldom enraged, and prone to reinforce his every point with a casual, friendly exclamation of "mkay?"

However, he is also prey to occasional misunderstandings and miscalculations, such as the time a sample of marijuana he was utilizing in a drug education class was stolen. He was subsequently fired, and, having also lost his apartment, he briefly became a drug user himself. During this period he married a fellow addict; the pair then honeymooned in India, before Mackey alone was rescued by the A Team. Disturbingly, although the marriage was consummated, Mackey was so high at the time he had no memory of the event.

He is easily led by technology, such as the time he installed a new computer system into the school, then hired an IT expert simply so he could fire her for the multitude of ensuing malfunctions.

Many of Mr. Mackey's issues seem to stem from childhood trauma; he was victimized by bullies at school and was also molested by Woodsy Owl, a character designed to teach children of the 1970s not to litter with the phrase "give a hoot, don't pollute." But overall he's a nice guy.

Mr. Mackey also enjoyed relationships with the late Diane Choksondik (he may have been instrumental in her death) and Liane Cartman, mother of pupil Eric Cartman; a keen role-player, he took on the identity of the promiscuous Liane's sex slave and on at least one occasion (which happened to be discovered by Eric) drank her urine.

The Marsh Family

The Marsh family is, too all outward appearances, one of South Park's most upstanding, as befits their real-life genesis in the names of Stone's own parents and sister. But peep behind the respectable veneer and they emerge as a classic study in familial dysfunction that extends across at least three generations.

Randy Marsh is the son of Marvin Marsh, a suicidal geriatric and AARP activist; Randy himself is a hypochondriac alcoholic, porn addict, compulsive masturbator, pothead and living proof that the political idealism of the late 1960s is not necessarily the best tool with which to raise children of one's own.

A former member of the early 1990s boy band the Ghetto Avenue Boys, Randy Marsh has seen the top of the mountain—at the height of the band's fame, home was a mansion filled with willing nubile girls—and the bottom of the abyss; fired from the group when he hit the age of nineteen, he found himself millions of dollars in debt to the band's creators. He would later attempt to revive his musical career as the tween singer Steamy Ray Vaughn.

Marsh minored in Mongolian while working toward a PhD in geology. Employed by the United States Geological Survey, he is a Nobel Prize winner (for his theory on moderation) and is well versed in chemistry, biology, physics, and mathematics.

His science background frequently permits him to pronounce upon other issues too. It was Marsh who suggested the town combat a threatened rash of spontaneous human combustion cases by passing wind at every opportunity; Marsh, too, who led many South Park males to purposefully contract testicular cancer, in order that they might receive medical marijuana.

Marsh lost his job with the USGS following a political dispute with one of his coworkers; since that time, he has drifted through a variety of career choices, including WalMart employee, proprietor of a post-Blockbuster video store, school chef, and the host of a popular cable access cookery show, *Cafeteria Fraiche*.

Marsh shares with his father membership in the secretive Hare Club for Men; he is also the current *Guinness Book of World Records* holder for

"Biggest Crap," having defeated a drawing of U2 vocalist Bono with his 100+ Couric crap.

Fiercely devoted to his family, a quality he regularly proves at Little League baseball matches, Randy possibly met his wife Sharon at the Woodstock Festival in 1969, but equally possibly in a tree fort while playing Truth or Dare.

Widely regarded (at least among the sixth graders) as having "the sweetest boobs ever," Sharon is the most level-headed member of the family, although the marriage has not been without its troughs. Indeed, she briefly divorced Randy at one point so that she might marry a bearded dude named Roy. The liaison was short-lived, however, and she and Randy swiftly reunited.

The Marshes have two children. Shelley, the eldest, appears to be a borderline Tourette's sufferer whose natural inelegance is only exacerbated by the outsized dental braces she wears, and which have the effect of distorting her voice in an equally unattractive manner.

Stan, her younger brother (and favorite punchbag), is, despite his young years, a former head of the Scientology movement. His secret superhero identity is Toolshed.

Father Maxi

Catholic Priest Father Maxi is the generally pious but occasionally tempted Father of the South Park flock, a fierce advocate of Hellfire but a vociferous opponent, too, of the Holy Vatican law that permitted his fellow priests to molest children.

The McCormick family

Staunch supporters and long-time residents of the wrong side of the tracks, the McCormicks are unquestionably South Park's poorest family, but might also be one of its happiest.

Subsisting primarily on a diet of frozen waffles, canned fruit, microwave pizza, and bread sandwiches (two slices of bread with a slice of bread in-between), while struggling with a family budget that is frequently assailed by the need to continually bury their death-prone son Kenny, Stuart and Mrs. McCormick live a life of quiet alcoholism on his part; fiery but loving rage on hers.

It is with a healthy dose of affection that Mrs. McCormick is most frequently seen wearing a T-shirt proclaiming "I'm with Stupid" and pointing toward her husband (wherever he might be), although rumors that this is her only item of clothing have been disproved.

The level of the McCormicks' poverty has been demonstrated on many occasions, most notably when Kenny won a can of green beans in a competition, only for the family to be too poor to own a can opener. However, there is never any shortage of alcohol or drugs around the family home (at one point they operated a meth lab), while Kenny is always up to date on the latest electronic and computer games. He is also allegedly fluent in Romanian.

"It's funny that people care so much for Kenny," Matt Stone once reflected. "He's not even a character, he's like this orange blob that just moves around. People projected a lot of love on him."

Trey Parker has since claimed that Kenny is based on one of his childhood friends, also named Kenny, also renowned as the poorest kid in the neighborhood, and also married to an outsized orange parka whose voluminous depths made it difficult for anybody to comprehend a single word he said. This Kenny was also prone to regular deaths, at least according to his school friends who seized on his every absence from school as an excuse to say he died.

Kenny's secret superhero identity is Mysterion.

Two further McCormick children are seen but seldom heard.

Mayor McDaniels

Although many other municipalities would fiercely disagree, Mayor McDaniels has numerous claims to being America's most inept elected official, with even a suicide attempt (following the events of an ill-judged Hippie Jam Fest) proving an abject failure.

Jerome "Chef" McElroy

The son of Nelle and Thomas McElroy, residents of a Scottish villa close to Loch Ness, the hard-living, hard-loving school chef was the one adult in South Park the town's children could always rely on in times of crisis or danger.

The fact that most of Chef's advice revolved around sundry seduction and advanced love-making techniques did not dissuade the children from turning to him; nor, strangely, did it dampen the efficacy of his advice.

A talented songwriter as well as an excellent cook, Chef sadly fell under the sinister spell of the Super Adventure Club, a quasireligious cult whose brainwashing techniques ultimately (and convolutedly) led to Chef's tragic death.

Dr. Alphonse Mephesto

South Park's resident mad scientist lives in a sinister laboratory at the top of a hill, where his experiments have included cloning, cross-breeding, and the addition of extra posteriors onto various animals.

There is no denying the value of his experiments. It was Dr. Mephesto who perfected the cheesemunk, a slice of slick splicing that ensured man would never again need to look in two different places if he happened to want both a chipmunk and a piece of cheese at the same time. But it was for his work in the field of superfluous sphincters that Dr. Mephesto was nominated for the Nobel Prize, his "seven-assed Galapagos Turtle" proving the sensation of the scientific community. However, he was narrowly defeated, with astonishing irony, by one of his own neighbors, Randy Marsh.

Dr. Mephesto has a son, an arrogant lad named Terrance, but is more frequently found spending time with his assistant, Kevin.

Billy Miller

A fourth-grade drug kingpin, it was the thuggish-looking Miller who first introduced Cartman to life as a KFC dealer.

Peetie the Sexual Harassment Panda

Not a South Park resident per se, but a character who did impact heavily on the life of the town, if only for a brief moment of sue-me sue-you madness. And a stark warning to all of what can happen when public safety announcements go bad. Peetie was stripped of all authority and exiled to the little-known but (among people who make their living dressing up as absurd animals in order to put across a particular message) much-feared Island of Misfit Mascots.

There he was imprisoned alongside such putatively informative but ultimately pointless guardians of sense and sensibility as Jimmy the "Don't Hold Onto a Large Magnet While Someone Else Uses a Fan Nearby" Falcon; Willy the "Don't Stare Directly at the Sun" Worm; and Hoppy the "Don't Do Stuff That Might Irritate Your Inner Ear" Badger.

It's getting mighty crowded there, too.

Pip Pirrup

English-born and unmistakably Dickensian, Pip Pirrup was an aspiring dodgeball champion and the butt of every anti-British joke in creation. First sighted in the show's unaired pilot, then reintroduced deeper into season one, poor Pip was wildly unpopular among his classmates, all the more so since nothing ever seemed to ruffle that characteristically English stiff upper lip of his.

His suffering was brief, however. Pip was tragically killed during the Mecha-Streisand's rampage through South Park.

Chief Runs with Premise

The head of the local Native American tribe, the Chief is also the ruthless founder of the Three Feathers Casino, on the outskirts of town. Wildly ambitious, the Chief has made several attempts to acquire South Park itself, thus opening up a direct superhighway route from the casino doors to the city of Denver. He just needs to demolish the town first.

Scuzzlebutt

Tibet has its Yeti, the Pacific Northwest has its Bigfoot, and South Park has Scuzzlebutt, a terrifying, giant hairy humanoid with a piece of celery as an arm and actor Patrick Duffy for a leg. Initially believed (by Cartman) to have been invented to scare campers (by Cartman), the basket-weaving man-ape then appeared from deep in its wilderness home to save a party of hunters cut off by an erupting volcano. It was then shot by Stan.

A second Scuzzlebutt has also been sighted, however. This one weaves ice cream and has Brent Musburger for a leg.

Skeeter

A fiercely patriotic redneck, the distinctively flame-haired Skeeter is a bar room regular whose conversation usually begins with the words, "We don't take too kindly to . . . ."

Mr. Slave

Sadomasochist Slave was for a long time employed as Mr. Garrison's teaching assistant, in which role he regularly updated the children on his personal life, while demonstrating the remarkable flexibility of the human anus. Among the manifold objects whose insertion Mr. Slave was able to demonstrate were the class gerbil Lemmiwinks and a crude representation of heiress Paris Hilton.

His romantic ties to Mr. Garrison ended following the latter's sex change; Mr. Slave subsequently married Big Gay Al.

Bebe Stevens

The first of the fourth-grade girls to develop breasts, an attribute that was to cause a great deal of disruption among her classmates, Bebe Stevens is the class's fashion barometer, frequently responsible for introducing new crazes and fads to her classmates.

The Stotch Family

Linda and Stephen (aka Chris) Stotch are firm but fair parents, frequently disciplining their son Leopold for misdemeanors that may seem trivial, but that are nevertheless unbecoming in a well-brought-up young man. And for the Stotches, upbringing is everything, because that alone can camouflage the often dark side of the family dynamic.

For Stephen Stotch, discipline is an obsession that borders on the psychopathic, with young Leopold, or "Butters," as his friends call him, often grounded for weeks at a time. Weeks that Stephen is as likely to while away visiting gay bathhouses—the White Swallow Spa is a particular favorite—and the adults only movie house, the Studcat Theater. Indeed, it was his penchant for these establishments that led his wife to attempt to kill both herself and their son, by driving the family car into the river.

On another occasion, Stephen attempted to sell Butters to heiress Paris Hilton for $200 million.

Despite this, Butters remains a cheerful, good-natured, and generally naive boy, most of whose misadventures are due purely to childlike curiosity and innocence. However, he has a dark side, exemplified by the supervillain Professor Chaos. Fortunately for the universe, the professor's evil deeds are generally as inept as everything else Butters does. Or attempts to do.

Butters is generally popular with his fourth-grade classmates; indeed, following the death of Kenny McCormick (or one of them, anyway), Butters was promoted to "best friend" status by the traditional gang of

Cartman, Kyle, and Stan, although it swiftly became apparent that his primary purpose was to serve as the butt of his new friends' cruelty and jokes. Finally he was "expelled" from the group for being lame, although he has remained on the periphery of their activities and adventures, even forming an alliance with Eric Cartman.

Butters has a beloved aunt and uncle, Nellie and Budd.

Scott Tenorman

Scott Tenorman was an eighth grader who tricked Cartman into purchasing his pubic hair for $10.00, a price that ultimately rose to $16.12.

Enraged, Cartman plotted a complicated but exquisitely effective vengeance, involving the murder of Tenorman's parents, the transformation of their corpses into chili, and a delicious meal for the unsuspecting Scott.

It was only later that Cartman discovered that, far from being the only son of a hermaphrodite porn star, as he believed, he was actually the late Jack Tenorman's illegitimate love child. Add patricide to the boy's voluminous rap sheet (see chapter eight).

Wendy Testaburger

The vivacious Wendy is the most outspoken and determined of the fourth-grade girls, best friends with Bebe Stevens, and determined pursuer of the not-altogether-unwilling Stan Marsh. The course of true love, however, is not only rocky, it has also been known to be slippery, courtesy of Stan's early habit of nervously vomiting whenever Wendy got too close. Or spoke to him.

Craig Tucker

An aspiring sumo wrestler, fourth-grader Craig is also the host of the cable access TV show *Close-up Animals with a Wide Angle Lens*.

Tweek Tweak

The heir to the Tweak Brothers Coffee empire, overseen by his parents Mr. and Mrs. Tweak, Tweek is a grotesquely overcaffeinated, ADD-engorged fourth grader whose entire diet appears to comprise coffee. Highly susceptible to even the mildest stress, Tweek's youth has also been deviled by underpants gnomes, creeping into his bedroom at night to steal his briefs.

Timmy and Jimmy: South Park's most special children.

His parents' attempts to calm him down have included masquerading as a child abductor. It was not a success.

Jimmy Valmer (aka Jimmy Swanson)

Fourth-grader Jimmy is what some people like to refer to as "handi-capable," a disabled youth who actually uses his handicaps to his advantage—most notably, the ability to laugh at his own ailments in his career as a stand-up comedian. Indeed, Jimmy was responsible for creating what is widely regarded as the funniest joke ever told, the legendary Fishsticks routine, while he has also competed in the Special Olympics.

Principal Victoria

The Principal of South Park Elementary.

7

Who's Who?

An A–F of *South Park* Celebrities, Nonentities, and Random Stuff That Fits the Difficult Letters

A

A is for A Drawing of Alanis Morissette, and while few Canadian celebrities have, or ever will, eclipse Terrance and Phillip as ambassadors for all that makes their country great, Ottawa-born Alanis Morissette might at least eclipse them in any Dave Grohl Look-alike competition.

A domestic superstar long before the album *Jagged Little Pill* brought her to the attention of mid-1990s America, the woman *Rolling Stone* dubbed "the Queen of alt-rock angst" had just released her long-awaited follow-up album, the marvelously titled *Supposed Former Infatuation Junkie*, when controversy arose and threatened to devour her altogether.

Among the multitude of hits that both the real and the imitation Ms. Morissette enjoyed that year was one whose authorship was . . . to put it mildly . . . disputed. "Stinky Britches," declared former songwriter and latter-day school chef Jerome McElroy, was a song he had written some two decades before, back in the days when he believed his long-dreamed-of musical career had a chance of succeeding.

How "Stinky Britches" came to Ms. Morissette's attention, he did not know. Nor did he understand how the song's composer credit had somehow changed from his name to hers. Perhaps she simply became confused because the accompanying music video so resembled the one she'd made for an earlier hit, "Ironic."

Either way, Chef was certain that a single phone call to a top music business executive would put matters straight.

Or not. Despite Chef being able to produce a twenty-year-old recording of himself performing the song, Morissette's label not only refused to allow him his moment in the correctly credited sun, it also arranged for a cartoon of top showbiz lawyer Johnny Cochran to sue Chef for harassment.

It was an open and shut case. The Cartoon Cochran won a $2 million judgment against McElroy, and the chef was allowed just twenty-four hours in which to pay up. If he missed the deadline, he faced four years in prison.

McElroy could see just one way out. He became a male prostitute.

Oh, and his friends put on a huge benefit concert, her lawyer saw the error of his ways, Morissette surrendered the songwriting credit, and the copyright for "Stinky Britches" journeyed back to where it belonged.

B

B is for Boiled Bunnies, while begging the question, who could possibly want to kill Mr. Twig?

That was the conundrum that held the whole of South Park . . . or at least that part of South Park that is named Mr. Garrison . . . in its thrall.

Clearly the felon had a firm grip on popular culture. A movie buff, perhaps? In a scene terrifyingly reminiscent of the infamous horse's head highlight of *The Godfather*, Mr. Twig was found broken in half in Mr. Garrison's bed.

In a scenario surely inspired by the nightmarish killing of a pet rabbit in *Fatal Attraction*, Mr. Twig was also discovered submerged in a pot of boiling water.

Who knew what dire cinematic assassination attempts might be next in the pipeline for poor Mr. Twig?

Not that Mr. Twig had avoided making a lot of enemies over the years; or, rather, the weeks, since he first entered South Park society. Summer was sucking that dark day when Mr. Garrison mourned the sudden, apparently inexplicable, departure of his long-time teaching assistant Mr. Hat.

But Mr. Twig, literally a small wooden twig clad in a fetching purple shirt emblazoned with a pink triangle, entered his life and filled the void with a temper and tendency to tantrums that his predecessor could only aspire to. Anybody in Mr. Garrison's class could have been scheming Twig's demise. So could Mr. Hat.

It is very simple, and very simple-minded, too, to describe Mr. Hat as a puppet. He was a puppet, yes; a childhood toy that had accompanied Mr.

Garrison throughout what had clearly been a very hard life. But he was more than that. In psychological terms, Mr. Hat was the personification of all the aspects of Garrison's own personality that he found it difficult to live with. His racism, his bigotry, his homosexuality, all integral aspects of Garrison's personality that he was unable to express except through Mr. Hat.

He had his brighter side, though. Sometimes, Mr. Garrison once revealed, "Mr. Hat liked to pretend he was in a sauna with Brett Favre, and a bottle of Thousand Island dressing."

And then came the dark day when he disappeared. The dark day when Mr. Twig slipped effortlessly into the void. But Mr. Hat had not departed forever. Behind the scenes, he was biding his time.

And, possibly, watching a lot of movies.

C

C is for Chicken Pox. C is for Cootie. C is for the cacophony of afflictions to which the human flesh is treacherously heir. Head lice. Tonsillitis curiously misdiagnosed as HIV.

But C is also for Cause, and if you know the cause of an illness, you are on the road to discovering its Cure. So, when Stan Marsh contracted male vaginitis immediately after becoming a vegetarian, the physicians treating him simply drew a straight line from Cause to Cure. But not, first, without marveling at the appalling changes that were devouring the boy's body, as it erupted into a mass of small, perfectly formed vaginas.

There was only one thing that could save him. A massive infusion of 100 percent beef blood that didn't simply restore him to health. It also prevented his entire body from being transformed into "one great big giant pussy."

Skilled at administering to easily avoidable afflictions, Hell's Pass Hospital

A teacher's best friend is his puppet. Mr. Garrison and Mr. Hat.

has curative medicine down to a fine art. But it is also skilled in another field, remedying the rampages of attempted cures—such as those that threatened to become a local epidemic following the arrival on Main Street of Miss Information's Holistic Healing emporium.

Nobody doubts the validity of many traditional healing methods. Well, doctors and big pharmaceutical companies do, and so do the various authorities and organizations that they pay to agree with them. But the average person is smart enough to look back to a time before modern medicine began mixing sundry chemicals together and asking how folk cured their ailments back then?

Miss Information specialized in Native American medicines, a far-reaching litany of trusted cures and panaceas that she received direct from the horse's mouth. Without ever wondering why the horse sounded ever-so-slightly Mexican. Nor why it bore a startling resemblance to a badly drawn caricature of the comedians Cheech and Chong.

Her customers were no more curious than she; not even Sheila Broflovski, when she discovers that her son Kyle is suffering from a rare kidney ailment, and only one thing can possibly save him.

Cherokee hair tampons?

It takes a lot of courage to admit this, but Miss Information finally reveals that no amount of holistic healing is going to prevent young Kyle's life from ebbing out of his body. He needs a transplant, and Hell's Pass is where he'll get one.

Mrs. Broflovski gets the boy straight up to the hospital, where a kidney transplant does indeed save his life. It also permits us to see a side to Eric Cartman that few of us expected ever to witness. True, he was tricked into donating the life-saving kidney. But how strange that he has never mentioned it again. You'd think this was the kind of thing that he would go on about forever.

D

D is for Disasters, and there's been an awful lot of them, over the centuries. From the extinction of the dinosaurs (well, it was a disaster for them), through the sinking of Atlantis and the burial of Pompeii, ancient history was littered with calamities of Biblical proportions, and let us not forget the Bible's own shattering cataclysm, a rainstorm that simply didn't let up.

Since then . . . London, 1666; Lisbon, 1755; Peshtigo, 1871; Krakatoa, 1883; Mount Pelee, 1902; San Francisco, 1906; Three Mile Island, 1979;

the Indian Ocean, 2004; and South Park, Colorado, 1997, 1998, 1999, 2000 . . . . disasters can strike anytime, anyplace, and unlike lightning, any number of times. And nowhere gets struck as often as South Park.

The citizens of this small mountain town may not have lost count of the number of times they have been forced to resurrect their community following its latest razing; nor, like those hardy souls who build and rebuild their mega McMansions every time another wildfire sweeps through a secluded area of natural beauty that is . . . oh, what a shocker . . . historically regarded as pone to wildfires, would they ever consider living someplace else.

For the people of South Park, natural disasters are just something that happens every year or two, and a few days or weeks of untold terror are a small price to pay for the joy of the days when nothing at all goes wrong.

Neither do they bemoan the sheer unlikeliness of so many of the cataclysms that have befallen them; any more than the people of Boston scratched their heads at the absolute preposterousness of their city's great molasses flood, back in 1919.

There were molasses. They flooded. It took a lot of cleaning up. End of story. South Parkers were the same following the great urine flood precisely ninety years later. There was pee. It flooded. It took a lot of cleaning up.

Or the great poo explosion a year earlier. There was poo. It exploded. It took a lot of cleaning up. South Parkers are stoic, South Parkers are determined. Friendly faces remain everywhere.

At the same time, however, South Park does seem to have suffered more than its fair share of calamity, beginning back in 1997 when Mount Evanston, one of the most picturesque of the peaks that overlook the town, rumbled into volcanic life, trapping a party of schoolchildren in the path of its imminent eruption.

Not to be confused with either Mount Evans, elsewhere in the Rockies, or Mount Trashmore in Evanston, Illinois, an artificial skiing slope created on the site of a former landfill, Mount Evanston is not the only volcano in the Rocky Mountain range. Twenty-nine million years ago, the entire range was blazing fire and magma. It is, however, the only one to have erupted during the last few millennia, and only the fast thinking of local seismologist Randy Marsh—whose son Stan was a member of the endangered party—enabled the town to divert the lava flows away from civilization.

South Park was less fortunate eight years later, as another of the area's most popular tourist attractions, the world's largest beaver dam, apparently shattered as a consequence of global warming. Or because two fourth graders crashed a borrowed speedboat into it, although that's not quite such a dramatic explanation. Misbehaving juveniles were not a hot topic that week. Global warming was, however, and immediately in the path of the onrushing floodwaters, the nearby town of Beaverton had already been completely inundated.

South Park now lay directly in its path, and the phrase "Two Days Before the Day After Tomorrow" suddenly took on fresh and horrific meaning as the townspeople, again led by geologist Randy Marsh, counted down to zero hour. Two days before the day after tomorrow, after all, meant today.

News teams from across the country hastened to the disaster zone, each one vying to outdo its competitors in terms of relating and relaying the horrifying detail. Soon, a death toll several times higher than the town's entire population was being speculated on, while the more sensationally minded networks painted grisly portraits of the unprecedented nightmare that must now be gripping the survivors, a veritable orgy of looting, raping, and murder.

Other pundits weighed in, one side blaming terrorists, the other condemning the president. Suddenly, the human side of the disaster was completely forgotten (and with it the rescue efforts that should have been taking place), as media coverage instead focused wholly on finding a scapegoat for the disaster. For that is always far more interesting than another long shot of dead cats and stranded grandmothers.

But Mother Nature does not take kindly to being upstaged. An aborted rescue mission into beleaguered Beaverton resulted in the ignition of a lake of oil, adding flames to the nightmare engulfing that town. Geologist Marsh, meanwhile, was predicting ever greater calamity as his own findings predicted the dawn of a new and sudden ice age. Into which mix, government scientists cast the result of their own researches, an attack by a hitherto unknown race of Crab People.

All of which was conveniently forgotten as the waters receded and the fires were extinguished, and life in the tiny Colorado town returned to normal. For a time.

E

E is for Erectile Dysfunction. So is ED. ED is also for "Emergency Department." Should you take your ED to the ED?

Probably not.

"Erectile dysfunction is a fact of life. You want to show her you love her, but you're old, and so is she. The next time that special moment comes, don't let your sex drive fail you just because your wife looks like a shriveled prune. Fake it, with Cialis. It won't make her any hotter, but it will make you not care for up to three hours."

So says a mock commercial enjoyed by so many South Park connoisseurs toward the end of season sixteen. But erectile dysfunction is no laughing matter.

More marriages have been ruined, more self-esteem has been shattered, more famous soccer players have been enriched, more . . . etc., etc. . . . by erectile dysfunction. No, ED is nothing to laugh about.

The extremes to which sufferers might resort in order to cure it, on the other hand, are. Take crucifixion, for example. When Kyle inadvertently discovered that his father, Gerald Broflovski, was writhing nightly in the maw of the disorder, he thought nothing of arranging for one of his classmates (Cartman) to be crucified during a school reenactment of the Passion. Which makes perfect sense, because once the fat boy died, Kyle would be able to offer his father a res-erection.

Well, it's no stupider, or less effective, than most of the other treatments, pills, herbs, internal animal by-products, and powdered rhinoceros horns with which pseudo-science has attempted to succor sufferers for thousands of years.

When next we join the Broflovskis in the bedroom, however, a cure does appear to have been effected.

The United Parcel Service is an American institution. Reliable, regular, and absolutely trustworthy, the company's distinctively liveried big brown vans and their similarly besuited occupants are as familiar a sight on the streets of America as the mailman, the garbage man, and, in days gone by, the milkman. Which is why, murmurs the old-timer mechanic in one corner of the bar, we should watch them very, very closely indeed.

"There's a price to be paid with having things convenient," he says. "Used to be . . . a man had to go to the store to buy himself a pitcher of milk. Hyeah, but men got lazy. They wanted that milk delivered right to the door. Only problem was, the guy deliverin' that milk ends up fuckin' your wife. Sure, you had your nice cold milk delivered right to your doorstep, but your wife was gettin' pounded out like a mallard duck. And now you got your Amazon. And the milkman's come back."

His warning falls on fertile soil. Although, as with so much else in life, it is all a gross misunderstanding.

Realizing that Gerald's erectile dysfunction was as much a psychological problem as a physical one; realizing, too, that it was boredom with their current sex life as opposed to a lack of interest in sex itself that lay at the root of the issue, the Broflovskis have taken to role-playing. Sheila is the housewife in a state of seductive undress, interrupted during her morning ablutions by a nattily clad deliveryman; Gerald is that delivery man, bearing what we shall euphemistically describe as a package.

It is just unfortunate that their youngest son, Ike, should witness their activities and, failing to recognize his father in such unfamiliar clothing, sketches the scene with all the attendant misunderstandings in place.

Ike shows the picture to his brother Kyle. Who shows it to his friends. Who are overheard by Randy Marsh. Who passes the news onto the guys at the bar. And, before you can say "somebody who would have sex with Kyle's mom would have sex with just about anything," two very separate but peculiarly intertwined scenarios are unfolding across the sleepy streets of suburban South Park.

In the first, a gang of armed and masked vigilantes who bear a distinct resemblance to the guys in the bar are lying in wait for the hapless (and, let us not forget, utterly innocent) UPS guy, prepared to mete out the beating of his life; and in the other, with personal protection utmost in everybody's mind, sales of home security installations are booming. The resultant chaos, with every alarm in the town being activated at the same time, is both predictable and preposterous.

As is the idea that anybody could get turned on enough by a Cialis commercial to forget one vital truth. Erectile dysfunction is nature's way of saying "yes, your ass does look big in that."

F

F is for Fuck, and fuck is one of the seven dirty words that comic George Carlin, back in 1972, decreed were the worst things you could possibly say. On television, on stage, on record, in public, in private. It didn't matter what one's justification for deploying them might be. It didn't even matter what the Supreme Court declared to be freedom of speech. There were words that simply couldn't be used.

Needless to say, most of them have since been heard on *South Park*, and a wide variety of other shows as well. Some of which are even considered quite arty. A far cry from the days when Carlin was arrested for performing the monologue in public and, perhaps, one of the reasons why the forces of moral rectitude insist that the very notion of good, clean family entertainment has been pissed right down the fucking shitter by an army of depraved cocksuckers masquerading as social commentators when they're really just a bunch of motherfucking cunts.

There, wasn't that t*tillating?

8

Is Juvenile Delinquency a Problem in South Park?

Crime and a General Absence of Punishment

L aw and order in South Park is the responsibility of the Peak County Police Department, dedicated, loyal, trustworthy, and upright, and willing to undertake any task, no matter how distasteful, in order for justice to prevail.

Such as the time when Sergeant Harrison Yates went undercover . . . deep, deep, deeeeeeeeep undercover . . . as the dirty, filthy whore Yolanda, for the benefit of a prostitute sting.

On the frontline of the battle, however, stands Officer Barbrady. Borderline stupid, possibly illiterate, and certainly very easily confused, Officer Barbrady is nonetheless governed by a ferocious sense of right and wrong, a startling gift for unconventional interrogation methods, and a God-given aversion to what he calls the "lookie loos" who accumulate around any accident or incident he might have cause to investigate.

It's just a shame that he is rarely around when the real perps are perpetrating.

The undisguised embodiment of the secret wishes of many a town, South Park has never been truly forthcoming with its criminal statistics, although the possibility that they were lost on any one of the many-and-varied occasions on which the town has been destroyed should not be overlooked.

It is clear, however, that South Park's crime rate, when measured per capita, is at least several times higher than the national average, with all major, most minor, and a number of frankly absurd offenses being registered on a weekly, if not a daily, basis. Juvenile crime and delinquency in particular run far above the norm, as this snapshot of five randomly selected rap sheets clearly demonstrates.

Leopold Stotch aka Butters

Easily led and desperately susceptible to peer pressure, the majority of "Butters" Stotch's transgressions have been less the product of a true disregard for the law than they are the result of naïveté and gullibility.

Nevertheless, fantasies that portray him in the role of the wholly imaginary Professor Chaos reveal him to possess both the intelligence and the cunning to enact crimes of awesome seriousness, the majority of which fail only due to the boy's natural gift for ineptitude.

An only child, parental abuse might also play a part in the boy's psychological makeup. The father, Christopher Stotch, is stern and often unreasonably disciplinarian, with a pronounced interest in male pornography; the mother, Linda, has been diagnosed as a borderline psychotic and on at least one occasion has attempted both suicide and to kill her son.

It is recommended that these factors be taken into consideration when evaluating Butters's criminal past. The following litany of offenses may also be explained by his association with a peer group of proven dubious morality.

Blackmail: In April 2004, the accused did knowingly, and for purposes of future personal profit, videotape one of his classmates, namely Eric Cartman, privately dressing himself as the performer Britney Spears and dancing with a cardboard cutout of Justin Timberlake. Stotch then threatened to allow others to view this videotape unless Cartman acceded to a series of demands.

Consorting with prostitutes: On two occasions, in October 2009 and March 2010, the accused was witnessed in the intimate company of known prostitutes and strippers. In a related case, in 2004, the parents of the accused witnessed their son's inappropriate behavior with an unconscious drawing of celebrity Paris Hilton.

Deceptive Trade Practices: As the creator and distributor of the purported energy drink Butters' Creamy Goo, the accused was subsequently discovered to be selling his own semen, which at least accounted for the thick viscous liquid's bleachy flavor.

Hostage Taking: In 2008, the accused allied himself with the locally formed hate group the American Liberation Front, dedicated to the intimidation of America's Chinese population. In the course of one action, involving the occupation of a Chinese restaurant, the accused shot two male hostages, including a police officer, in the crotch.

Incitement: The accused was author of *The Poop That Took a Pee*, a book that was subsequently blamed for the shotgun murders of a drawing of the Kardashian family. The accused himself had previously expressed the desire to murder both John Lennon and President Ronald Reagan, these tragedies being averted only by the victims' own fortuitous earlier demises. He is also known to have associated with a group dedicated to the assassination of Sarah Jessica Parker.

Piracy: The accused was a known member of a feared Somali pirate crew

Threatening Behavior: Among innumerable instances, the accused was responsible for a hate video threatening a Colorado town with global flooding and all accompanying apocalyptic scenarios, said flood to be delivered via garden hose.

Treason/Anti-American Behavior: The accused was a known member of a rogue Civil War enactment group representing a breakaway southern "confederacy," implicated in a series of violent and murderous rampages.

Vehicular Homicide: The accused and one associate stole and subsequently crashed a Nascar, causing the deaths of eleven bystanders.

Stanley Marsh

A committed ecoterrorist, Stanley Marsh is that most dangerous of juvenile criminals, a left-leaning moral crusader who justifies his disregard for law by convincing himself (and, on occasion, others) that what is "right" is of greater importance than what is "legal." Possessed of considerable powers of persuasion that he has proven regularly willing to employ, the majority of Marsh's crimes are rooted in ecological concerns and include (but are not limited to) the following:

Arson: While engaged in underage smoking, Marsh was partially responsible for a major fire at South Park Elementary, having discarded a lit cigarette butt into a pile of flammable material.

Criminal Damage: As a crew member aboard the Greenpeace vessel Sea Shepherd, Marsh employed a variety of pyrotechnic devices, including flare guns and Molotov cocktails, against Japanese fishing vessels.

Criminal Trespass: In 2002, Marsh led an attack on agricultural premises owned by Carl Denkins, a farmer, and removed a number of calves. His subsequent demands included the insistence that the meaty delicacy veal be renamed "tortured baby cow."

Crucifixion: Marsh and an accomplice, Kyle Broflovski, were responsible for the attempted crucifixion and death of school colleague Eric Cartman.

Grand-patricide: Marsh has made several attempts to murder, or at least abet the suicide of, his grandfather, Marvin Marsh.

Illegal Downloading: Marsh was among several juveniles arrested for illegal downloading in 2003; among the alleged hapless victims of his heinous criminality were the crude renderings of the entertainers Lars Ulrich, whose intended purchase of a gold-plated shark tank bar was delayed for several weeks by the ensuing loss of income; and Britney Spears, who found herself forced to downgrade her private aircraft.

Incitement to Arson: A disastrous arson fire at South Park preschool, while set by another student, was planned by Marsh.

Mass Murder: Marsh was partially responsible for the Beaverton flood in 2005 and the ensuing deaths of "hundreds of millions" among the town's population of eight thousand.

Piracy on the High Seas: Marsh was one of two felons responsible for stealing and destroying a privately owned speedboat following a collision with a beaver dam. (See above.)

Possession of Firearms: In 2011, Marsh assaulted several local restaurant owners with an Uzi. At different times, the accused's arsenal has also included a deadly laser gun and numerous martial arts weapons.

Underage Drinking: While undergoing treatment for suspected Asperger's syndrome, Marsh frequently indulged in alcoholic beverages.

Eric Cartman

The lynchpin of any investigation of juvenile crime in South Park and its environs, Eric Cartman is the archetypal product of a broken home.

Raised single-handedly by a mother who for many years made her living from the vice trade, psychologists might argue that, far from compensating him for their predicament, her indulgence of her son only exacerbated the loneliness and deprivation her lifestyle forced on him.

Or they might say he is just an obnoxious, opportunistic, and thoroughly self-centered little boy who will certainly come to a very bad end. A thorough investigation of local records reveals that Cartman has been arrested just six times, including once while overseas. The seriousness of

Cartman. So much malice. Such heavy bones.

his crimes, however, can never be overestimated; neither can his refusal to consider any path beyond that of instant self-gratification.

Animal Cruelty: Cartman broke the leg of Kenny McCormick's cat; he has also regularly abused his own pet, Mr. Kitty.

Armed Robbery: Armed with a gun in readiness for an imminent apocalypse, Cartman attempted to relieve a Hebraic school friend of what was described as his "Jew Gold," a reference to an antiquated belief that all adherents to the Jewish faith were phenomenally wealthy, and which Matt Stone has explained thus: "I only have half a bag of Jew gold because my father is not Jewish. Rabbinical law states that half breeds are only entitled to half a bag and they must keep it behind their balls. Unless they're a half breed girl and then they can keep it in their purse or other pre-approved gold container."

Cartman also threatened two boys with a laser gun, demanding they surrender their Prank Time Phones. Other firearms violations involve possession of a Glock pistol and a stolen taser.

Arson: Although the boy has frequently been on the scene of accidentally caused fires, or fires set by external forces (volcanic eruptions, spontaneous human combustion, etc.), he destroyed his own bedroom in a blaze purposefully intended to immolate his Peter Panda plush.

Attempted Murder: Cartman has made numerous attempts to kill his school friends, most notoriously with a wiffle bat. He also made an attempt on the life of the president of Fox network.

Breaking and Entering: Taking advantage of a night of drunken revelry elsewhere in the town, Cartman broke into every house he could and stole the television set. He also burglarized the Broflovski household, making off with three triangles of Zinthar.

Cannibalism: Although it could be considered accidental, Cartman did once mistake a deceased friend's ashes for chocolate milk powder.

Child Abuse: As founder of the Crack Baby Athletic Association, Cartman distributed crack cocaine to the infant members of the organization. Footage of the consequences was then posted to the Internet, an act of rash stupidity that nevertheless appears to be the default setting for so many juvenile (and adult) lawbreakers. Commit a crime, film it on your phone, and then put it up on Facebook. Seriously, where do they find these people?

Conspiracy to Matricide: After his mother recruited a Dog Whisperer to attempt to deal with her son's behavior, Cartman plotted her death.

Credit Fraud and Identity Theft: Cartman used his mother's credit card without her authorization to purchase airline tickets.

Criminal Damage: Cartman's lack of respect for the property of others has oft been demonstrated, most notably in the destruction of "Butters" Stotch's bedroom; and, on another occasion, the entire Stotch residence. He has also been implicated in several widespread outbreaks of TP-ing.

Cyberbullying: Having been enrolled in an anger management course, Cartman sent a series of increasingly abusive text messages to the doctor's wife, inciting her to commit suicide.

Drug Dealing/Distribution/Manufacture: As part of a membership drive for his Crack Baby Athletic Association (see above), Cartman supplied crack cocaine to pregnant women. He also operated a meth lab out of his own home, leading to the mistaken arrest of his mother before his own guilt was determined.

Embezzlement: As the self-proclaimed spiritual leader of his own evangelical church, Cartman regularly misused donations to the church for his own private purposes.

Fraud: By the simple expedient of replacing the word "love" with the name "Jesus" in a number of songs (thus establishing himself also as a serial plagiarist), Cartman falsely represented his pop group as being a Christian Rock band—although, in fairness, there's a lot of groups you could say the same thing about and nobody has arrested them yet. Sadly.

He has also pretended, for financial gain, to be mentally disabled.

Gang Membership: Cartman founded and, for some time, led a shadowy underworld cartel involved in the black-market smuggling and sale of fried chicken, following rumors that KFC had been forcibly closed down. A similar situation was also a major part of the comic book Chew, written and illustrated by John Layman and Rob Guillory. Although in that instance, both the criminalization of chicken consumption and the resultant black market were actual events.

Graverobbing: Precipitating a rash of rumors regarding necrophilia in South Park, Cartman was among a small group of adolescents who exhumed the remains of Sheila Broflovski's late mother for use as a Halloween decoration.

Hate Crimes: Cartman has been at the forefront of hate groups dedicated to the extermination of Jews, ginger-haired people, non-ginger-haired people, hippies, the population of San Francisco, and Token. Among myriad others.

He has also proven intolerant of a wide variety of other groups, both uttering and causing to be uttered slurs against their condition. Although sometimes it is funny. Like the time he forced a midget to repeat the words "Carol Ann, don't go into the light."

Hit and Run/Vehicular Homicide: At the wheel of a stolen race car, Cartman lost control and killed a total of eleven people, including spectators, one driver, and trackside officials. He then left the racetrack and caused further mayhem in a nearby trailer park.

Hitchhiking: Hitchhiking is illegal in the state of Colorado. Therefore, Cartman's trip to Washington, D.C. (in order to force Kyle to suck his balls) was conducted in an illegal manner.

Kidnapping: Among the most serious instances of kidnapping and false imprisonment for which Cartman can be held responsible, authorities unreservedly number the confinement of sixty-three hippies in his basement and the locking of Butters in a bomb shelter for three days.

Butters was also the victim when Cartman removed him unlawfully from the mental hospital to which he had been confined.

Manslaughter: Cartman has accidentally killed his friend Kenny on several occasions, most notably with a frying pan while attempting to squash a bug.

Medical Terrorism: Having been diagnosed with HIV, Cartman deliberately infected his friend Kyle by squirting his own blood into the boy's mouth.

Murder: There are mass murderers and there are serial killers. And then there is Cartman. The scope and variety of his victims alone is remarkable, ranging from actor Rob Reiner to a Revolutionary War period messenger boy; two members of the Chinese Mafia and an undisclosed number of Mexicans.

   Cartman was also implicated in the killing (and subsequent cannibalization) of Mr. and Mrs. Tenorman, and an attempt to assassinate Sarah Jessica Parker.

Piracy: Cartman was briefly leader of a feared band of Somali pirates.

Poisoning: Cartman's love of pharmaceuticals led to the attempted suicide of classmate Jenny Simon, after he spiked a cupcake with industrial-strength laxative, setting in motion a chain of shaming events that prompted the girl to try and kill herself.

   He also poisoned another classmate, Billy Turner, by introducing a foreign substance to the boy's lunchtime milk. Finally, he fed Scott Tenorman the ground-up remains of his own parents in the guise of a tasty chili. Which, in fact, it was.

Prostitution: Whether actively soliciting in the guise of Vietnamese prostitute Ming Lee or more passively playing the part, Cartman has regularly displayed a sexual precocity quite unbecoming of a youth of his age.

Shoplifting: While visiting a local drugstore, Cartman ingested an unknown quantity of unpurchased Vagisil and then left the premises with no intention of paying for the goods.

Slander: Infuriated by his mother's refusal to buy him an iPad, Cartman appeared to accuse her of having sexually abused him on national television. On another occasion, he accused classmate Wendy of embezzlement and complicity in war crimes—namely the genocide of the Smurfs; and falsely accused the Hakeem family of being terrorists.

Terrorism: Cartman issued threats against the makers of the *Family Guy* television series; he was also involved in a violent assault on a FedEx facility following his committal to anger management courses.

Torture: Having secretly infected classmate Billy Turner's lunchtime milk, Cartman then chained the boy to the school flagpole and informed him that he would die unless he could find the antidote—which he could only do if he cut his own leg off first.

Unlicensed Surgery: Operating a weight loss scam, Cartman instigated the performance of an unauthorized liposuction procedure on Butters.

Violation/Obstruction of the Pure Food and Drug Act: Cartman was responsible for the unlicensed selling of hamburgers seasoned in his own anus, causing a major outbreak of food poisoning, while purposefully misaligning the true and unimpeachable reality of ass-burgers disease.

War Crimes: As commander-in-chief of the Drunken Southern Civil War army, Cartman waged all-out warfare on the civilian population of these United States, inciting his troops to loot, burn, rape, and plunder. Several members of his army were also child soldiers, in direct contravention of international law.

Kenny McCormick

Having been born into grinding poverty on a scale seldom seen outside of telethons and Bob Geldof's scrapbook, it is easy to assume that much of Kenny McCormick's criminality is the product of environment, as opposed to any deep seated antisocial tendency. In addition, many of his purported crimes were reactive as opposed to proactive, possibly allowing for a justifiable claim of self-defense, or at least misadventure. Assuming anybody could understand a word he says. Nevertheless, the following offenses have been added to his permanent record.

Attempted Infanticide: Kenny attempted to abort his unborn little brother with a sink plunger.

Attempted Murder: Believing he was acting to avert the destruction of the hitherto pristine and unsullied reputation of NASCAR racing, Kenny was only narrowly prevented from killing Eric Cartman.

Blackmail: Although not considered a crime on Earth, Kenny committed blackmail on the Planet Fognl after photographing the two-headed Joozians sucking one another's jagons while inserting digits into their thrushers.

Breaking and Entering: In search of an illicit "high," Kenny broke into Cartman's home, believing that the urine of the household pet, Mr. Kitty, could be employed as a euphoric. On another occasion, he was one of four boys who illegally entered Cartman's home and stole his kidney.

Conspiracy: Alongside Cartman, Kenny was implicated in a plot to murder actress Sarah Jessica Parker.

Drug Abuse: Kenny was a user of unknown cocaine-like alien drugs. He is also a habitual paint sniffer.

Fraud: Masquerading as a talent agent, Kenny attempted to collect money from Token.

Indecent Exposure: Kenny appeared in the school photograph standing on his head and wearing his parka upside down, with his bare posterior visible through the hood.

Kidnapping: Kenny was involved in kidnapping Cartman from the hospital, in an attempt to enter him into a rodeo bull riding contest.

Pedophilia: Having possessed the body of the actor Rob Schneider, Kenny attempted to kiss fourth-grader Milly.

Prostitution: As the host of the Krazy Kenny Show, Kenny instigated a competition (with Johnny Knoxville and Tom Green) to determine which of them would charge Howard Stern the least amount of money for a hummer. Kenny's bid of ten dollars won, but he was jailed before he could follow through. (A look-alike was recruited for the task and died as a result of it.)

Underage Sex: Kenny and girlfriend Tammy Warner indulged in oral sex after removing their purity rings.

Unlicensed Firearms: Kenny is known to have possessed an unlicensed sniper rifle.

9

What Came from Outer Space?

Lots of Stuff

South Park entered our universe with a bang. Or at least with a very loud fart. Accompanied by flame. A little-known and seldom documented side effect, it seems, of that most common manifestation of extraterrestrial curiosity, the anal probe.

The date was August 13, 1997, and American television viewers, themselves curious as to what this new Comedy Central animated half hour might be about, found themselves witnessing the most significant alien encounter since Roswell: "Cartman Gets an Anal Probe."

These aliens knew every trick in the book. They announced their presence with a series of extraordinarily graphic cow mutilations—so thorough that many of their victims had physically been turned inside-out. And while the town sheriff, Officer Barbrady, strove desperately to alleviate local concerns by insisting that there is nothing whatsoever unusual about a cow turning itself inside out, even he could not explain away the presence of several clearly other-worldly beings in the field, calling to the beasts and offering them fresh hay. So, in common with certain law enforcement practices the world over, he ignored them altogether.

Other townspeople, however, already had their suspicions; Chef, the singularly named school cook, had not only seen a UFO in the area, he had also bought the T-shirt; gloriously emblazoned with the lifelike image of a so-called visitor and the single word "believe."

Eric Cartman, a pupil at the local South Park Elementary, too, had encountered these beings, although, until he heard of Chef's experiences, he had convinced himself that it was a dream. And that despite his friends Kyle Broflovski, Stan Marsh, and Kenny McCormick doing their best to convince him otherwise. Quite correctly, Eric believed they were simply trying to frighten him.

Chef's story, however, caused all four boys to reconsider their stance. As did the terrifying sight that greeted Kyle when, once aboard the school bus, he happened to look out of the back window and saw his little brother Ike being held by two more of the visitors.

Eric's story was not dissimilar to many other tales of alien encounters reported over the years. Neither did his aliens particularly differ from those encountered and described by other victims of their curiosity; elongated humanoids, all but featureless bar wide eyes, hairless and gray—hence their most common designation as Grays.

It is this constant factor in the tales of alien witnesses that convinces so many people that the stories are true. Likewise, it is the sheer mind-numbing repetition of the same "experiences" that convinces others to believe it's all hooey.

Whatever. Human history is not only littered with so-called alien encounters, it may also have been shaped by them. Monuments Stonehenge and the Pyramids are among those mysterious ancient arti-facts that could, according to certain scientists and researchers, only have been constructed with extraterrestrial aid, while a History Channel docu-mentary screened in the South Park region in November 2011 made it clear that the first Thanksgiving feast was certainly engineered by creatures from another world, the inhabitants of a planet in Canis Major, peopled by a race of beings resembling traditional American pilgrims.

Not only that, but stuffing might well have been the product of extra-terrestrial technology; while Plymouth Rock is almost certainly a gateway to this other world, safeguarded by the Keeper of the Portal, Natalie Portman.

By the time of these revelations, however, the people of South Park, if not inured to the existence of aliens, at least possessed a weary compla-cency about them, an attitude that dates back almost fifteen years, to the night when all hell broke loose around them. The night when Cartman got an anal probe.

Forgotten today, and barely considered at the time, 1997 marked the fortieth anniversary of what is generally regarded as the first-ever case of alien abduction; or at least the first to grasp the popular imagination. Others had been reported in the past, dating back centuries. But not one had the same impact as the experiences of a farmer named Antônio Vilas-Boas, who lived and worked close to São Francisco de Sales, in Brazil.

In common with many farmers, Vilas-Boas was in the habit of doing much of his farm work at night, when the temperatures were cooler than during the day. This particular evening, October 16, 1957, he was plowing a field when he glimpsed what appeared to be a red star in the sky. A red star that was growing closer with every passing moment until it was poised above him, a circular craft with a rotating cupola, a red light, and three legs, which were suddenly extending outwards as the saucer prepared to land.

Vilas-Boas gunned his tractor into life, preparing to flee, only for the vehicle's lights and engine to inexplicably fail. Leaping to the ground, he started to run, but was grabbed by a short, five-foot, humanoid wearing gray overalls and a helmet. Its speech was a series of yelps, its eyes were small and blue, and it was not alone. Three other of its kind emerged from the saucer, subdued the wildly struggling farmer, and hauled him inside their strange vehicle.

Once inside, Vilas-Boas was stripped naked and coated in gel, then hauled into a vast, semicircular-shaped room, where the inspection began. Blood was drawn from his chin, before he was taken to another room and, seated alone, was subjected to a gas that made him violently sick. After which another of the aliens joined him, female, naked and beautiful, with platinum hair and bright red pubes. They had sex, following which Vilas-Boas was handed back his clothes, and after a quick tour of the spacecraft, he was released. The saucer departed and Vilas-Boas went home. The entire experience had lasted four hours, but his story has intrigued for more than fifty years.

Natalie Portman, Keeper of the Portal.

Cartman was not forced to have sex with his captors. He was, however, subjected to an anal probe, an intimate and humiliating invasion that hit the headlines just four years after Vilas-Boas's strange experience, when the aliens struck again.

This time, their victims were the strangely Flintstonian-named Barney and Betty Hills, an American husband and wife who were returning to their home in Portsmouth, New Hampshire, following a vacation in Montreal. It was September 19, 1961, around 10:30 p.m., and they were a little south of Lancaster, New Hampshire, on Route 3, when Betty Hills spotted what she thought was a falling star. A falling star unlike any she had ever seen before, because it appeared to be moving upwards.

Barney, driving, stopped the car at a picnic area, and they watched the glowing orb through their binoculars. Flashing multicolored lights confirmed that it was no ordinary star; reminded Betty, in fact, of a story her sister had told her a few years earlier, about having seen a UFO. Could this be another one?

Returning to their 1957 Chevy Bel Air, the Hills decided to follow the craft's course as much as they could, passing through Franconia Notch, watching the craft pass over Cannon Mountain, and drawing closer as it passed the Old Man of the Mountain. And then it happened. About a mile south of Indian Head, the craft suddenly descended toward their car. Barney slammed on the brakes, and the mysterious object also halted, hovering about a hundred feet above them, so vast that it filled the windshield.

Barney stepped out of the car, clutching his revolver, and this is where things went hazy . . . so much so that it was only later, under hypnosis and further examination, that he and Betty were able to piece together everything that happened to them: how up to a dozen humanoids, wearing shiny black uniforms and caps, were visible, communicating with them telepathically; how the craft emitted a series of buzzes and beeps that seemed to shake the entire car.

"They're going to capture us," Barney warned Betty, and he was correct. But they would not initially remember any of what befell them. The couple's own next waking memory found them around thirty-five miles farther down the road, with just a vague sensation of unease and discomfort to alert them to anything untoward having occurred.

Their wristwatches no longer worked. The strap of the binoculars had torn, Barney's shoes were scraped; Betty's dress was torn and covered in a strange pink powder. There were odd, concentric circular marks on the trunk of their car. Barney had an overpowering urge to inspect his genitals.

Betty phoned the air force to report a UFO sighting, and the following day, the pair sat through their first official interview. She devoured the available literature purporting to examine the UFO phenomenon and contacted the author of one such book, a retired Marine Corps Major named Donald E. Keyhoe.

He passed her onto another expert, but in the meantime, Betty had started having vivid dreams about what had happened. The five-foot-tall hairless gray humanoids with enormous eyes, tiny ears, and minuscule noses. The medical examination that began with her hair and proceeded down her entire body. The needle that was thrust into her navel. The star chart that one of the aliens showed her, when she asked where they were from.

Then it was Barney's turn. Under hypnosis, he recalled the aliens inspecting his mouth and ears . . . scraping samples from his skin . . . collecting a sperm sample with the aid of a cup-like device that was laid over his genitals. And the anal probe.

Here, Cartman's experiences differ considerably from Barney's. And from any other even remotely feasible victim of alien investigation. The aftereffects of his probe not only include flammable farts; he also had a cycloptic robot inserted into his anus, while it became increasingly obvious that the Grays had also taken over his mind. Obvious, that is, to everybody apart from Cartman. So far as he was concerned, he simply enjoyed singing "I Love to Singa." And farting fire.

Far more pressing, of course, was the need to rescue little Ike Broflovski. Approaching the aliens' spacecraft, Kyle initially hoped that simply asking for his brother's return would suffice. He was wrong; in response, the aliens blasted his friend Kenny with a star-shaped object, leaving him for dead in the street. In fact, he was merely stunned, in which state he was then killed when Officer Barbrady, pursuing a herd of stampeding cattle, ran him over with his police car.

But Stan and Kyle responded to the first assault, regardless. With a cry of "Oh my God! They killed Kenny!" . . . "You bastards!," they prepared for war. Alone, because Cartman continued to deny that anything unusual was taking place, and took himself home.

A plan was drawn up, luring the aliens back by using Cartman as bait, tethered sacrificial-goat-style to a tree. That accomplished, Stan, Kyle, and their school friend Wendy watched in astonishment as an eight-foot-wide satellite dish emerged from the bound boy's behind. The spacecraft returned, Ike leaped to freedom, and the aliens snatched up Cartman again. Before they departed, however, they had one final message for the inhabitants of Earth.

Cows are the most intelligent beings on the planet.

Cartman was not lost. The following morning, while Stan, Kyle, and the miraculously revivified Kenny awaited the arrival of the school bus, their absent friend fell from the sky to land alongside them. He had news, too, of a new dream, one in which he contracted pinkeye from *Charles in Charge* actor Scott Baio while imprisoned on an alien spacecraft.

His school friends were unimpressed, and the aliens were patient. Very patient. The universe beyond teems with life. But viewed through the telescope at the South Park Planetarium it seemed peaceful, almost silent. Although the establishment's director, Dr. Adams, would have his own fiendish schemes to perform in later months, the Grays remained strictly noninterventionist. They did not even become involved when Cartman was among a party of boys who hijacked a crashed but still serviceable spacecraft belonging to another race entirely, the Marklar.

No, they were playing a longer game, albeit with shorter invaders. Like the terrifying creature whose mighty spaceship burned through the

Charles. He's in charge, apparently.

planet Earth's atmosphere, came to a gentle landing, split open to reveal a nightmarishly ferocious monster . . . who was promptly squashed like a grape by a passing South Park school bus.

Earth's luck could not hold out forever. And it ended the day Cartman first astonished and then horrified his friends by appearing to relive the trauma of his original encounter with the Grays. A flashback that, in the process, trapped them all in that most horrifying vortex that any television character can be subjected to.

A repeat.

Suddenly, the quartet discovered the awful truth about the whirling globe that they, and we, call home. That the entire history of the planet has, in fact, been nothing more than a television reality show being broadcast for the entertainment of an alien race called the Joozians, pale greeny-yellow piggy-parrot-faced creatures who control all of the media in the universe. Including the Earth.

Reactivating the eighty-foot satellite dish that was implanted so long ago in Cartman's anus took a matter of moments. Or it would have had Cartman not insisted that Kyle be the one who digitally operated the device, and then farted every time the boy came close.

Finally, however, the dish was operational, and a patiently waiting scientist named Jeff (aren't they all?) was at last able to communicate with the Joozians. Whose chosen means of communication and science turned out to be word association, and who were very unhappy to learn that their existence had been discovered.

There was just one solution to their dilemma. The show would be canceled. The Planet Earth would be canceled.

Far from home, abducted by the Joozians, Stan, Kyle, Kenny, and Cartman found themselves in a race against time to persuade the aliens to give the show a reprieve. A task that proved easier than anybody expected when two of the head aliens get drunk and start indulging in what their society would consider extremely inappropriate sexual behavior with one another. Behavior that Kenny photographed and used to blackmail the Joozians.

Earth was saved, with everybody's knowledge of the Joozians' existence wiped from their memories to preserve the alien's valued anonymity; only the photograph survived, in Kenny's possession, but nobody could remember what it actually depicted.

Perhaps it was better that way.

10

Do Blow-Up Dolls Dream of Inflatable Sheep?

Sex in South Park

It is one of the modern parent's most impassioned laments. The knowledge that, via the eternally pervasive influence of television, advertising, celebrities, and fashion designers, children are becoming increasingly sexualized, at increasingly tender years.

A golden age has dawned in their minds, one in which expressions and deeds that are now allegedly common currency in middle school were once unknown to anybody under forty. And another, in which the very act of demonizing certain behavior did not automatically push it to the top of the average adolescent's "must do" list.

Neither is this golden age a crock of rose-tinted spectacled hogwash. How could it be? Today's parents' own moms and dads remember it with equal clarity. So do theirs. And theirs too. In fact, for as long as parents have been worrying about their sons' and daughters' sexual curiosity, there has always been an earlier age in which such concerns were unimaginable. And they've always had someone, or something, to blame.

Curse that William Shakespeare, with his liberal plays and potty-mouthed characters.

Maybe these golden ages did once exist. Maybe, in the deepest, darkest recesses of history, there was an era when kids did not sample cigarettes because they thought it looked adult; did not sneak a nip from their parents' liquor cabinet, just to find out what being drunk felt like. When they had no curiosity about their own bodies, and those of their friends. When they weren't adolescents at all, merely little adults who had all sense of joy, experimentation, and the thrill of the unknown sucked from their souls while they were still in the womb.

Maybe.

But not in the twenty-first century, and certainly not in South Park. For it was there, just a few short years ago, that a highly respected research team determined that positively nobody was safe from the scourge of sex addiction. Not even fourth graders. With or without apologies to Marvin Gaye (it really doesn't matter), the entire squalid affair was published under the title of "Sexual Healing." And it does not make pretty viewing.

News headlines across the preceding weeks had been filled with the somewhat sordid saga of golfer Tiger Woods' extramarital activities, behavior that resulted, it appears, in an especially violent confrontation with his wife. None of which was particularly newsworthy; none of which, really, was anybody's business but the Woodses'.

In a world, however, where twenty-four-hour television news coverage and wall-to-wall celebrity nonsense have decreed that there is no problem on earth that does not have a battery of experts waiting to fix it; and, equally, one in which nobody can be held responsible for their own actions without another battery of experts on hand to pronounce a medical reason for it, Woods became just one more in a growing coterie of men—usually rich and successful men, because otherwise why would we care?—to be diagnosed with the affliction of sex addiction.

An uncontrollable appetite to indulge their lust at every possible opportunity. To act, in other words, like almost any guy who has just discovered that he is considered absolutely irresistible by the opposite sex and doesn't feel the need to hide that particular light beneath a bushel.

That's no answer, though, is it? Because, if it was, then nobody could get rich diagnosing sex addiction as a genuine medical complaint. As real as alcoholism, obesity, and compulsive shoplifting.

Investigate! Where does sex addiction come from? How does it begin, how can it be cured, and what, beyond the size of his bank balance and the talents of his publicist, determines that this man should be a registered sex addict and that man's just a horny slut?

The study begins in childhood, a sample group of seemingly normal schoolchildren who are interviewed, analyzed, and finally diagnosed. South Park Elementary was selected as the host for the investigation, and very quickly the results came back. No less than three South Park students were discovered to be suffering from sex addiction: Kyle Broflovski, Kenny McCormick, and Butters Stotch.

They needed treatment, they needed counseling. Gently, at first, but with increasing vehemence, the boys were warned of the consequences that an untreated sex addiction may . . . no, will . . . result in.

An unrestrained sexual appetite.

A lifetime of meaningless encounters.

And, ultimately, death by autoerotic asphyxiation—a concept that so entranced Kenny that he promptly rushed off to try it. With inevitable, tragic consequences.

Shocked by such vivid evidence of their affliction's potential consequences, Kyle and Butters checked themselves into the Karne Institute for Sexual Addiction, a center that specialized in treating their ailment.

There they found themselves in the animated company of some of America's most notorious alleged fellow sufferers: the Michaels Jordan and Douglas, David Duchovny and Charlie Sheen, Billy Bob Thornton and David Letterman, Kobe Bryant and Tiger Woods, Elliot Spitzer and former President Bill Clinton.

But they also discovered the somewhat unusual, but certainly controversial, nature of the addiction's treatment; which is not to cure the man of his philandering ways, but to advise him on better ways of not getting caught indulging them.

Because, as a drawing of Clinton's Oval Office successor-but-one Barack Obama declared when he studied all the findings, there was only one truly effective cure for sex addiction. The disease must be killed at its very source—which was the Roswell Alien, who released a sex addiction virus when it crashed into the New Mexico desert all those decades before, and who was now holed up in Independence Hall, Philadelphia.

Only with his death, or at least that of a soldier disguised as a wizard alien, could the scourge of sex addiction be placed back into the Pop Rocks packet from which it emerged, as a cultural craze that had now run its course.

And it seems to have worked. Either that, or the media realized that nobody really cared.

Such well-meaning meaninglessness notwithstanding, of course, juvenile sexuality is a minefield, an obstacle course of biological jack-in-the-boxes that leap out at the unsuspecting passerby with increasing, and ever-more perplexing, regularity as he or she approaches and then passes through the teenaged years.

Stan Marsh's sister Shelley, for instance, was just thirteen years old when she started dating Skyler, a rough-and-tumble twenty-two year-old whose membership in the band Lords of the Underworld established him as something of a prize catch. Or so Shelley believed until she discovered that he only wanted one thing, and wasn't too fussed about where he got it from. The attentions that he paid to Cartman's mother proved that.

Not that anybody would ever suggest that adult concern for childhood sexual awareness can occasionally step beyond the realms of reality. That it can, in fact, serve only to alert the kids to something they may not normally have discovered for several years to come.

Such as the day that Peetie the Sexual Harassment Panda arrived in town with the highly laudable intention of warning those same fourth graders of the dangers of sexual harassment. Which, with just a little misunderstanding, swiftly developed into a mass of lawsuits as everybody sued everybody else under for committing that crime, often without even understanding what they were complaining about.

The school was bankrupted, the town was at war with itself . . . and the only people who appeared to be making any profit from the melee were the lawyers. Remember that, next time you spill hot coffee on your crotch.

It was *Cabaret* author Christopher Isherwood (okay . . . he wrote the short stories on which *Cabaret* was based, but let's just go with the catchall title that everybody has heard of, okay?) . . . Christopher Isherwood who declared that the true measure of a country's sexuality can be judged by the number of laws it has prohibiting its citizens from actually exercising their own sexuality. And another author, erotic scribe Chrissie Bentley, who countered that an even truer measure can be gauged from how many people ignore those laws and carry on.

Certainly any law book combining the statutes of the fifty states will overflow with prohibitions that, regardless of whether or not they are actually enforceable, apparently have no place whatsoever in modern society.

Both oral and anal sex are still illegal in one out every four or five states. There are (or, until recently, were) state-enforced prohibitions on the number of vibrators one person could reasonably own. And in terms of what you allow into your own home, definitions of "obscenity" don't vary merely from state to state, they can alter radically from town to town.

Colorado is one of America's more enlightened states. Maybe it's the year-round influx of all those cock-sucking, ass-fucking, z*****-x*************g outsiders descending on the hiking, climbing, and skiing resorts for which the state is so justly renowned. Maybe not.

True, it is still against the law to kiss a sleeping woman anywhere in the state, and the town of Cattle Creek continues to enact a prohibition on people making love in rivers, streams, or lakes. It also remains a Class

2 misdemeanor for any innkeeper, anywhere in the state, to knowingly rent a room to an unmarried couple if he has reason to believe they are intending to have sex in there.

But there are a lot worse places than that to live.

One law that almost all the states agree on, however, is a prohibition on the sale of sex. Prostitution might be the oldest profession in the world, but it is also one of the most legislated against. Which means, no matter what age he was, or had waited to attain, Butters was in for a world of hurt the day he hired a prostitute to . . . .

Actually, kissing is not one of the things that a prostitute is prohibited from doing in Colorado. She can't . . . well, you don't need them to be spelled out for you, do you? But a simple kiss, an innocent peck, a momentary pucker, there's no earthly restriction against that, even if money is exchanged beforehand. So when one of the schoolgirls let it be known that she is selling kisses for five dollars each, no laws have been broken, no regulations have been breached. Sally Darson can keep her five bucks, and Butters can hold his head high among his school friends. Of course he has kissed a girl.

Ah, but Butters doesn't stop there, does he? Talking with Sally, he realizes that she is onto a good thing, and he's in on the ground floor of that good thing. With Butters assuming the role of her "business manager," promoting her services far and wide, Sally is soon raking in a small fortune, one five dollar bill at a time. Indeed, soon she is so busy that Butters needs to recruit more girls simply to meet the demand.

By the time he returns from a local Players Ball . . . or, in the common vernacular, a pimps convention . . . Butters is firmly in the thrall of his new occupation. Which, in turn, puts him firmly on the radar of a man with a mission.

Sergeant Yates of the South Park Police Department is determined to rid his town of the scourge of prostitution. So determined that, despite possessing a lush mustache, a hairy body, and a shockingly deep voice, he has no hesitation in dressing up as a prostitute and taking to the streets in order to catch the johns in the act.

Neither, oddly (or maybe not . . . it takes all sorts, after all), do the johns have any hesitation in handing their twenty bucks to the resultant vision of decidedly unfeminine unloveliness.

Yates is dedicated. If a man offers twenty dollars for oral, he will receive oral. And then be arrested. If a man wants anal, he will get anal. And then be arrested. Somewhere in the police handbook, there is surely a page that states that the john need only pay in advance for the required act in order to be handcuffed, but Yates wants to make sure that his convictions stick. Either that or the page was missing. Or . . . no, let's not go there.

In fact, let's not go anyplace else at all. Yates is so consumed by his work that soon, he has his own pimp and is working under the nom-de-street of Yolanda . . . and he often even forgets to arrest the men he has serviced. Butters, meanwhile, is so successful that he now controls every whore in South Park, including Yolanda, while still laboring under the misapprehension that all they do is kiss the client. And it all ends happily, without anybody we know even getting arrested. Because when Butters retires, he frees all his girls to return to the streets without pimps watching over them, and Yolanda is happy with the man of her mustachio'd dreams.

Hurrah.

Butters is unusual because he is so naive. Other kids his age have at least a glimmering of what all the fuss is about. Eric Cartman is aware enough of the significance of pubic hair that he happily pays ten dollars for a handful. He is conscious enough of the importance of penis size that he protests furiously when the school takes to publicizing measurements. Kenny McCormick's rap sheet includes at least one instance of underage sex, and all the boys are well versed enough in at least the rudiments of sexuality to understand that Mrs. Cartman's past glories as a star of German *scheisse* movies and *Crack Whore* magazine covers is not an especially conventional career.

Translating those rudiments into concrete awareness, however, is another matter entirely. And one whose initial broaching was spawned from the most unexpected, and decidedly nonsexual, source. *The Lord of the Rings.*

When John Ronald Reuel Tolkien originally wrote *The Hobbit*, some years before its 1936 publication, he intended it simply as a story for his own children. He certainly never considered that public acclaim and demand would require no less than three volumes of sequels some twenty years later (*Lord of the Rings* was first published as a trilogy in 1954–55); nor that his fantasy world of Dark Lords and dwarves, wizards and wonder, Rings of Power and Middle Earth was destined to become one of the three best-selling novels of all time; would fire an entire subculture of late sixties hippie idealism; would birth a new genre of fantastic literature; and would, by the early twenty-first century, be established among the most successful movie franchises of all time.

Indeed, he might even have balked at imagining a time when his stories were billed as "a franchise," as though Gandalf and Frodo and Peregrin Took were simply servers in a burger bar, presided over not by a being of immeasurable mystery and magic, but a board of rapacious businessmen whose vision stretched no further than the next delicious dollar.

Nevertheless . . . .

"The Return of the Fellowship of the Ring to the Two Towers" is the story of three boys and one supernatural entity who possesses the body of one of them (you can guess who . . . whose frame is large enough for at least two people?), righteously clad in the costuming of the movie's heroes, attempting to deliver Mr. Marsh's rented VHS tape of *The Lord of the Rings* to Butters's house, so that he can watch it before it has to be returned.

Caught up in the all-pervading excitement and imagination of the movie itself, the three (or four) adopt the simple delivery as their own sacred quest, journeying "to the house of Butters," and wondering only whether they should proceed "through the mines of Endor or over the mountains of Grog."

All of which would have been fairly straightforward had Randy Marsh not then made a terrifying discovery. We all remember how easy it was to mix up our videocassettes, to put one movie in another's box, and then file it away without realizing. Most of the time it's a harmless error, and one that will lead to much merriment (and frantic searching through the entire library for the correct tape) at some future date.

Not so harmless, or merry, however, when you suddenly discover that the copy of *Lord of the Rings* that Butters is now sitting down to watch is, in fact, *Backdoor Sluts 9*, unanimously regarded as "the hottest porno ever." A movie that makes *Crotch Capers 3* look like *Naughty Nurses 2*. A movie so disturbing that even *People* magazine commented on it. Or so Gerald Broflovski tells his wife when she asks how he could possibly know that it is "the single most vile, twisted, dark piece of porn ever made."

A fresh quest! Having safely delivered it, the boys must now reclaim the VHS from the house of Butters. While simultaneously avoiding the attention of a band of orc-like sixth graders, who have also stumbled on the Secret of the Shellcase. And ultimately the boys are victorious.

But there are casualties, gallant souls whose wounds will linger long into adolescence.

Butters, transfixed by just a few moments of *Backdoor Sluts 9*, and then transformed into a clinging, crawling, Gollum-like character, forever demanding to be reunited with his "precious."

The dark wizard Talangar the Black. Or Token, as his parents prefer to call him. Charged by his fellows to watch the movie, to discover what strange magic has descended on this particular tape that people should act strangely at the mere sight of it. For the boys, still oblivious to the true nature of their cargo, can comprehend only that there is something especially mysterious, and possibly even magical, about this particular copy of *Lord of the Rings*, and Talangar is the most powerful wizard they know. Or he was, before trauma and shock left him unwilling to play the game any longer.

And Randy Marsh, who instantly summarizes the latter situation, but probably isn't the exact person one would hope to recruit to explain to your child about the birds and the bees. Particularly birds and bees that have just sat through *Backdoor Sluts 9*.

When a man and a woman are in love, Marsh begins, they make love. The man puts his penis into the woman's vagina . . . and Token pauses, then asks, "and when the woman has four penises in her at the same time, then stands over the men and pees on them, is that part of being in love too? Five midgets, spanking a man . . . covered in Thousand Island dressing. Is that making love?"

Other parents have gathered, other parents add their own wisdom to the sexual train wreck that is piling up around their children's shattered psyches. Wisdom surrounding the things beyond a penis that a lady might like to insert into her vagina. "Telephones, staplers, magazines," ventures Sheila. "Now onto double penetration," begins Gerald. "Going number one and number two," intercedes Randy. And maybe we should leave the rest of it there and allow the concerned parents of South Park to explain the secrets of sex to their offspring in private.

But it's a good thing Cartman's mom didn't open her mouth as well.

Although, come to think of it . . . rewinding the tape to an especially depraved sequence . . . maybe she did. Maybe she did.

As a final observation, however, please do not start thinking the whole episode is obsessed by sex. Because it also provided the initial impetus for *South Park*'s "The Stick of Truth" role-playing game, as Parker and Stone explained shortly before the RPG's 2013 release.

"I really loved RPGs growing up, and even now I really love them," Parker explained. "We started kicking around the idea of a *South Park* RPG . . . when we did [this] episode . . . . I think since then we've talked about how cool a big, real RPG with the kids playing a game within the game could be. We had been kicking around the idea since then." And on the subject of kicking, "the *South Park* game will be a brilliant cross between Elder Scrolls: Oblivion and FIFA. You gotta go kill a bunch of monsters . . . but you can only use your feet."

Who's Who? (Continued)

A G–P of *South Park* Celebrities, Nonentities, and Random Stuff That Fits the Difficult Letters

G

G is for Guitar Hero, because for as long as man has been unable to play a real guitar, he has played air guitar.

It is a devilishly simple concept. No equipment needs to be purchased, no music needs to be played. In a silent room, a deserted space, an air guitarist can earn as many cheers and plaudits from a grateful music industry as any so-called top performer. But put an air guitar maestro in a room with that top performer and the showmanship really begins.

The air guitar might well be the greatest musical instrument ever made.

So, of course, somebody had to think of a way of marketing it and selling it back to the people who'd been playing it for free for so long.

Karaoke for instrumentalists was coming.

Conquering the youth of South Park as effortlessly and efficiently as it swept up the musically ambitious of every other town and city, Guitar Hero can forge lifelong alliances, or shatter lifelong friendships. Together, Kyle Broflovski and Stan Marsh were a mighty force in the realms of the game. Which is when Stan's father Randy suddenly asked them a most profound question.

Well, Randy thought it was profound. Rather than exert all this effort on a game, why not become a Guitar Hero for real? Why not actually learn how to play the guitar?

The boys laughed in his face. Guitars are gay. A point they apparently prove when Randy, himself once regarded a wizard guitarist, had his own go on Guitar Hero and wound up with precisely zero points. His son, without any grasp whatsoever of playing the instrument (as proved by his membership in an incompetent band called Moop), was regularly approaching 100,000 per game.

The lesson was hammered home even further when the Kincade Talent Agency scooped the two boys up to become international Guitar Hero superstars, endorsed by sundry celebrities and set for imminent fame. There was, the agency quietly whispered to Stan, just one drawback. Kyle was holding him back. Stan needed a new partner, and, blinded by the riches that now flashed before his eyes, he agreed. Exit Kyle and enter Thad, a Guitar Hero so heroic that he doesn't even need to plug in to play like a maestro.

Stan's dream was within reach. But with it there came a wealth of pressures that he had never even dreamed of. The need to constantly be at the top of his game. An inability to relax, to kick back with his friends, to shoot the shit with the boys in the old gang. Beaten down and broken up, he took refuge in the one game that seemed to offer him relief from the agony of his aspirations.

Heroin Hero.

The slippery slope starts here.

H

H is for Honey Boo Boo. H is also the second letter in "the Learning Channel," and the Learning Channel is one of American television's most august institutions.

Originally launched in 1972 as the Appalachian Community Service Network, and overseen jointly by NASA and the Department of Health, Education and Welfare, this devoutly informative broadcaster became the Learning Channel in 1980, following its privatization, and it positively reveled in educational content.

Documentaries were its forte, casual erudition that brought the wonders of nature, science, history, medicine, and current affairs into every home. To a nation growing increasingly starved of informed and informative content, the Learning Channel represented a beacon of light, hope, and education in the ever more turbulent morass of lowbrow television that swamped American viewing as the twentieth century approached its apogee.

The advent, in 1997, of a crudely animated cartoon featuring foul-mouthed schoolchildren and poorly impersonated celebrities was just one of the manifold nadirs with which the Learning Channel's rival networks fought for ratings; the revelation, the following year, that the President of the United States had received oral sex from an intern in the Oval Office was just one of the cultural watersheds that—in the words of a crudely animated and poorly impersonated James Cameron—"lowered the bar" of what society considered to be acceptable.

The Learning Channel rose above all of this. *Ready, Set, Learn* was the umbrella beneath which a host of worthy children's programs were aired. *Paleoworld* remains one of the finest explorations of prehistoric life ever broadcast. *Captain's Log* with Captain Mark Gray instructed would-be boaters on seaboard safety.

Clearly something had to change.

In 2001, the Learning Channel followed the example of numerous other hitherto sensibly named brands and organizations and reduced its title to its ultimate abbreviation, TLC, in the oddly popular but utterly misinformed belief that this somehow made it more attractive to . . . people who can't read?

And with the new name came a new range of programming, reality shows that drew on ever more elastic interpretations of the word "reality," and that fascinated audiences far removed from any that the fusty old Learning Channel could ever have dreamed of.

I Eat 33,000 Calories a Day; *Brides of Beverly Hills*; *My Big Fat Gypsy Wedding*; and delving into a world of preteen beauty queens and contestants that really does bring a new meaning to the nineteenth-century concept of carnival freak shows, *Toddlers and Tiaras*. From which there spun, with ruthless efficiency, *Here Comes Honey Boo Boo*.

Or, as Token reenvisioned her when seeking his own mega-bucks earning cable television concept, *Here Comes Fatty Poo Poo*.

The young entrepreneur's vision was simple. As simple, some critics might complain, as his target audience. In an age when political correctness decrees that nobody should ever suffer anything that even remotely resembles the censure of disapproval from their peers, no matter how much they may deserve it, *Fatty Poo Poo* investigated the cult of self-inflicted obesity in modern America.

All manner of uncontrollable factors can create obesity—genes, disease, medication, big bones. They cannot be helped. But an imprudent diet, and a refusal to remedy it, is not outside of a sufferer's control and, as such, should be as open to opprobrium as society's distaste for smokers. As another crudely drawn and poorly impersonated celebrity, First Lady Michelle Obama, declared, "obesity is an epidemic, but it is not a disease."

Into this certainly thought-provoking scenario lumbered Fatty Poo Poo, but behind the scenes and before them too, as rudely impersonated as any crude impersonation could be, Honey Boo Boo's real-life counterparts—six-year-old Alana Thompson, her mother Mama June, her father Sugar Bear, and her sisters Pumpkin, Chubbs, and Chickadee—were not amused. So unamused that Mama June had no hesitation in standing up and soundly berating the minds behind the mischief.

To the sound, surely, of an uncountable quantity of pots commenting on the color of innumerable kettles, Mama June told *TMZ*, "Me being a big person, I didn't take offense . . . that show is just not a show that I would want to be on to begin with. Just the way they portrayed [Honey Boo Boo's] show . . . it was kinda trashy."

An accusation that she apparently felt should not be leveled at her own program, and one whose veracity (or lack thereof) will not be remarked on here. You have a television. You have cable. Switch on the Learning Channel and watch the show for yourself. Just remember that the real Honey Boo Boo did not really have a pig's heart transplanted into her body after one cholesterol binge too many caused her own heart to give up the ghost. But . . . okay, I'll stop now.

One final, and perhaps irrelevant, observation, however. The Beatles were right when they sang "all you need is love." But they were seriously out of whack when they said there are eight days a week.

I

I is for Issues, and the late Lou Reed once said, "Give me an issue and I'll give you a tissue. You can wipe my ass with it." But that was a different kind of issue. The issue we should be examining is the fourth album by Korn. Issues.

Bakersfield-based Korn had been tearing up American eardrums for six years, since 1993, when they approached Trey Parker and Matt Stone with a unique marketing deal. The crunchy, crashing nu-metal band were on the eve of releasing their new album, and already they were looking at an instant number one smash. Their last disc, *Follow the Leader*, had smashed into the chart at the very top in its first week of release, and since then, Korn had only grown hotter. It would have been so easy to sit back and let the publicity machine do all the work for them. Instead, they asked to become a part of *South Park*.

James Shaffer, Reg Arvizu, David Silveria, Brian Welch, and Jonathan Davis had never taken the easy way in. Supporters of their earliest sound described them as the herald of a whole new genre in rock, an entire new approach to noisemaking. It was metal, but not as we know it. And not, a lot of writers wrote, as we especially wanted to know it.

Korn would not be discouraged, though. Poor reviews for their self-released debut album did not deter them; neither did the mainstream music industry's apparent belief that if this nu-metal stuff was just ignored, it would very soon go away. How often does the mainstream music industry really get things right to begin with? Gigging around California, Korn found fans, made friends, even saw the first bands come along who directly proclaimed Korn's speed-punk-through-a-wind-machine-wringer sound as a formative influence. Their debut album landed them a tour with Ozzy Osbourne; their second, *Life Is Peachy*, went double platinum.

They co-headlined Lollapalooza and launched KornTV. Now they were set to premiere their new single, "Falling Away from Me," on national television, but no traditional guest slot for them. They would be performing it on *South Park*, in the midst of an adventure that portrayed them not as the nu-metal Gods of a million studded armbands, but as a modern-day *Scooby Doo* gang, drawn into a spine-chilling mystery that battled to deduce, among other things, whether the town of South Park was being haunted by pirate ghosts—that is, ghosts who had taken it on themselves to become pirates? Or by ghost pirates—pirates who, after death, had become ghosts?

Into this already perplexing thriller were introduced Niblet, the band's possibly extraterrestrial bird companion; an apparent outbreak of Satanic lawbreaking; the exhumation (and subsequent consumption by a stray dog) of Kyle Broflovski's late grandmother, Cleo; a public demonstration of what sex with a corpse both looks and sounds like. And a misguided priest attempting to turn people away from the soul-frying mythos of Halloween by wreaking even greater havoc with cotton swabs and squirrels.

Plus, and possibly most nightmarish of all, the life-size Antonio Banderas Love Doll that poor Liane Cartman had mail-ordered for herself, but that was opened and claimed by a spoiled-rotten son who found it impossible to even consider the possibility that any package delivered to the house was not intended for him.

The loincloth-clad Love Doll's presence, bobbing behind Cartman throughout the goofball hijinks that unfold, ensures that the debut of the new Korn single will always be remembered. At least by people who have forgotten everything else about one of the finest Halloween specials ever aired on American television.

J

J is for Jay Leno, actor, comedian, and all-round funny guy, the erstwhile James Douglas Muir Leno who became the face of the nightly *Tonight Show* in 1992 (when he replaced Johnny Carson), and was still its face following his departure in 2009, when his replacements in the studio hot seat ultimately included himself.

Presiding over an age during which the face of American popular entertainment changed beyond all recognition, Leno—with his oddball monologues, crooked smile, and killer chin—remained one of the few constants that we could rely on.

Unless we happened to be Kenny McCormick.

Matt Stone and Trey Parker's *The Jay Leno Short* was created for *The Tonight Show* with Jay Leno himself. *South Park* was just a few months beyond its televisual debut; already, however, it had impaled itself on the popular imagination, and Leno was more than happy to become the butt—and, indeed, the voice of the butt—of one of its jokes.

Thanksgiving was mere days away, and the cartoon Leno had agreed to speak on the subject of the holiday's history with the third-grade kids at South Park Elementary.

What followed, however, could never have been a part of his own prepared script.

"Believe me," he declared as the first volley of chin jokes erupted from the classroom. "There isn't a chin joke you can tell me that I haven't already heard, okay?"

"I bet you go through about forty razors when you shave, huh?," responded a nonplussed Kyle.

"Did you have to check that into 'oversized baggage' on the plane?," demanded an unconvinced Cartman.

"If the Pilgrims would have had Jay Leno's chin, they could have plowed their fields with it!," concluded a disbelieving Stan. At which point an enraged Leno stormed out of the classroom, his chin knocked over a flagpole ... dislodged a heavy bust of George Washington ... and Kenny was killed.

"You bastard."

But *South Park* had not finished with Leno, nor had Leno finished with it. When the school bus driver Ms. Crabtree discovered a new career as a stand-up comedienne, an appearance on *The Tonight Show* with Jay Leno marked the apex of her career. By which time, incidentally, Leno's chin reached down to his knees.

Who helped popularize the Fishsticks joke? Jay Leno.

Who threatened to shoot Kenny through the head? Jay Leno.

Whose name, fortunately for critics of his humor, is an anagram of "lean joy"? You've got it.

His chin killed Kenny.

K

K is for K13, and visitors to Aspen, Colorado, are already quivering with fear.

Yes, we all know that Aspen, for all its trendy appeal and moneyed status, is no stranger to tales of the supernatural.

The Little Red Ski Lodge, reputed to be the town's oldest extant lodge, has long been reputed to be haunted.

The Hotel Jerome on East Main Street, a one-time morgue and home to the legendary Prohibition-era Aspen Crud drink, boasts a drowned boy, a lovelorn silver broker, a bullied maid, and, for no apparent reason at all, a spectral sink full of soapy water.

Every slope has its sinister legend, every snowfall is reminiscent of an ultimately doom-laden past storm.

But not one of these phantoms can match the horror of K-13.

The boys encounter the terrible mystery of K-13 when their parents, taking advantage of what they believe is a free trip to Aspen, deposit the boys on the slopes while they attend a thirty-minute seminar on time-shares. Challenged to race by a local bully and ski champion, Stan—who has been indulging in the pastime for less than a day—is mortified to discover that the chosen course will be K-13.

Mortified because, as a conveniently passing old-timer explains, K-13 is the most dangerous ski run in America. Towering above the other, gentler runs, its crooked peak and foreboding slopes resemble nothing so much as a witch's hat. But even that is tame when compared to the true terror of the mountain.

Ignoring the lessons taught by countless horror movies and novels; ignoring, too, the experiences even of nearby South Park, where a pet shop built on an old Native American cemetery found itself specializing in the most bowel-loosening pets imaginable, the ski run on K-13 was erected on what had been a Wichicaw Indian tribal burial ground.

A vampire Wichicaw Indian burial ground.

Vampire Wichicaw Indians who ate children with no eyes.

Thirty-five people have died on the run, and their ghosts still stalk the frozen wastes. It was here that a group of students on a skiing vacation were slaughtered by a wolf-boy escaped from a nearby mental institution; it was here . . . . but ah, we're modern men and women here. We have no time for superstitious nonsense and old wives' tales.

But we still shiver and shake at K-13's very mention. Let's move on.

L

L is for Leia. Princess Leia. And just as *Star Wars*, the movie series that brought her immortality, can never be described as "just a movie," so *South Park* is not simply a cartoon. It is also a potpourri of cultural oddities, drawing both inspiration and dialogue from a wealth of outside sources. Song lyrics, advertising slogans, overworked catchphrases, and even celebrity deaths have all been referenced and drawn into the weekly action, together with a wealth of half-or-more-forgotten one-liners drawn from the seething subconscious of a generation.

One such one-liner emerged from a viewing of the CBS network's 1978 *Star Wars Holiday Special*, a Christmas one-off that included such delights as Carrie Fisher, as Princess Leia, singing "A Day to Celebrate" to sundry Wookies and droids; Diahann Carroll serenading Chewbacca's dad through the Mind Evaporator; and Jefferson Starship stepping in as the Holographic Band for a rocking take on "Light the Sky on Fire."

In truth, it is one of those shows that has lingered in the public consciousness more as a nostalgic tour de force than for any actual quality it may have possessed, a bitter summation that the online existence of sundry clips (including, regretfully, all of the above) only confirms.

But *Star Wars* was bigger than big business in 1978, already on its way to becoming the highest-grossing movie of all time—in an age when that kind of statistic did not seem to change every time theater ticket prices were increased in time for the next blockbuster release.

Its cast and characters alike were as familiar to the public as any television star; and for many of the millions who sat enraptured through the *Star Wars Holiday Special* that festive evening, there could have been few who did not wish for their own chance to snag some of the purported zillions of bucks the movie had made, so that they might pick up one of those newfangled video recorders that had recently made their debut on the high-end marketplace and capture the unspooling festivities to watch and watch again.

It seems scarcely credible today to remember a time, within living memory of anybody over the age of thirty or so, when television programs could not be recorded for later, or repeated, viewings; an age when, once a show had been broadcast for the first and often only time, it could never be seen again.

The first video recording machines hit the market in 1972, and the next few years saw sufficient sales and developments to assure the various

Princess Leia, galactic beauty and potential Frizzie Fighter.

manufacturers that there was a market for such devices. But prices in
the four-figure range deterred all but the wealthiest, or most dedicated,
purchasers, and so the *Star Wars Holiday Special* passed into memory, to be
filed away with every other show of the age. Gone, but not forgotten.

And if popular (and it was exceedingly popular) entertainment
was drifting into the oblivion of memory and nostalgia alone, other

programming was passing away even faster. Television commercials would blink into life and then fade; news broadcasts would be consumed and then forgotten; news readers . . . well, you get the picture.

Sometimes, though, the fates would conspire, and what was once regarded as ephemeral and erasable would buck all the odds and come up fighting again. That same December night, WCBS-TV 2 (New York) news anchor Rolland Smith found himself trailing the eleven o'clock news with a brief break in the midst of the *Star Wars* special . . . and somebody, somewhere in Channel 2's catchment area happened to own one of these newfangled video recordy machine thingies.

Happened to be taping the show.

Happened not to be editing out the commercials.

And, in later years, happened to allow copies of the tape to make their way out into the vast underground network of collectors and fans for whom no *Star Wars* ephemera is too ephemeric.

Even when it involved a newsreader discussing hair care.

"The frizzies" was a term that shampoo advertisers loved to throw around in those days, referring of course to that oddly unfortunate look of . . . well, frizziness . . . that can sometimes accompany hair washing. Fight the frizzies with this, fight the frizzies with that . . . and here comes newsman Rolland Smith, popping up to bumper his broadcast with the words "fighting the frizzies . . . at eleven."

A clip that, were we to fast-forward to December 1, 1999, to *South Park's* own Christmas special, "Mr. Hankey's Christmas Classics," would inspire a news anchor of the show's own devising to promise, somewhat enigmatically, that he too would be "fighting the frizzies at eleven."

A feat that he then proceeded to perform, in a boxing ring.

All of which is an extraordinarily long-winded way of saying *South Park* remembers things so you don't have to. But it's true.

Oh, and as for Princess Leia . . . don't you think Wendy Testaburger looks a little bit like her? When she's not dressed up as a Wookie, of course. (Wendy, that is. Not Princess Leia.)

M

M is for Malcolm McDowell, one of the finest living actors of our age and, as he informs us during the opening sequences of a *South Park* episode called "Pip," a self-proclaimed "English person."

He was also an utterly unexpected guest star when *South Park* revisited one of the greatest classics of English literature, Charles Dickens's *Great Expectations*.

It is the story of a young man named, indeed, Pip and the life of poverty from which he is rescued by an unknown benefactor—whom he assumes to be the eccentric Miss Havisham, for whose adopted daughter Estella he was recruited as a playmate; but who turns out to be Magwitch, an escaped convict whom Pip once assisted.

In *South Park*'s hands, many of these rudiments remained the same. Of course, there was also the matter of the Genesis Device that Miss Havisham has invented, fueled by the tears of heartbroken young men and designed to allow the elderly Miss H. to take possession of Estella's sweet young bod. And the twenty-five baby bunnies that Estella messily slaughters. And the robot monkeys. And Malcolm McDowell.

But aside from these, it was a very faithful adaptation, all the more so since McDowell himself is the consummate upper-class English actor, and the star of some of that nation's most coruscating movies. *If…* , in which he plays a public schoolboy who makes Eric Cartman seem well-adjusted; *Clockwork Orange*, in which he plays a gang leader who makes the public schoolboy seem well-adjusted; *Caligula*, where he personifies the titular Roman Emperor who etc., etc. . . . . . And *Cat People*, in which he is sometimes a cat.

Yes, a great actor, a great man, and a great English person.

N

N is for Stevie Nicks, a singer, an icon, and such a fabulous force of nature that the military, her audience, even her own Fleetwood Mac bandmates are unable to tell her cartoon counterpart apart from a goat.

So, she stays at home and sends the goat out to work in her stead. Brilliant.

O

O is for O'Pray . . . Bird O'Pray, an independent record label set up by the rock group Ween, on which they released their debut album *Live Brain Wedgie*, among sundry other juvenile prolusions.

Founder members Dean and Gene Ween were just fourteen when they adopted those names (their true identities are Mickey Melchiondo and

Aaron Freeman) and not much older when their first recordings squeaked out on cassette tape. Yet Ween were, and remained, perhaps the closest rock music has ever come to recreating the *South Park* experience for the ears—one reason why the band was such a natural inclusion on the bill for Chef Aid.

That and the fact that the members confessed that everything they knew about songwriting they owed to Chef . . . because they stole it from him. Although maybe that confession had perhaps already been confirmed by a string of early singles that included such notable titles as "Long Legged Sally Was a No-Necked Whore" and "I'm Fat," and all released on record labels that, in those delicious days at the tail end of the 1980s, were regarded as the few oases of sanity in a music industry otherwise obsessed with records and performers that sounded exactly the same.

Sounding the same is something Ween never did.

They've made a rap album, a prog album, a country album, and more, collections of genre-hopping music that balance so neatly on the thin line between parody and purity that by the time Ween appeared at Chef Aid (performing "The Rainbow"), beforehand it was anyone's guess what form of music they'd be playing.

Which is one of the reasons why we love them so. The other, of course, is that Parker and Stone's DVDA band performed several times on the same bill as Ween, while the duo also directed the video for the band's "Even If You Don't" single.

P

P is for the Ghost of Elvis Presley, and P is for Pity, as in pity poor Elvis. The King of Rock 'n' Roll . . . the Quiff that Stiffed the Fifties . . . the guardian of the last horde of alcohol on the embattled island of Hawaii . . . reduced to this. A cheap joke about his legendary consumption of unhealthy food, a proto-Honey Boo Boo with a pelvis instead of a pig's heart.

But P is also for Pubic Hair, and P is for pathetic, because that's how Cartman appeared the day he declared himself the first kid in his grade to get his own pubes. Because he genuinely didn't realize that you were meant to grow them yourself, as opposed to buying them for ten dollars from eighth-grader (and future Ginger Kid ringleader) Scott Tenorman. A miscalculation that set off a whole chain of P-shaped reactions. Such as . . . .

P is for Pony, the animal that Cartman intended training to bite off Scott's wiener (a la Hannibal Lecter's infamous p-is-for-pigs), after the eighth grader not only refused to give the boy back his money, but then set it on fire in front of him.

P is for Parents, poor Tenorman's parents, whom Cartman set up to be slaughtered by the shotgun-wielding owner of the pony, and who were then ground up into chili and fed to their unsuspecting son.

But, best of all, P is for Poetry, to which Cartman turns his attention as he gazes victoriously on his victim's tearstained face.

"Nyah nyah nyah nyah nyah nyah, I made you eat your parents."

12

How Many Deaths Can One Man Take?

The Manifold Demises of Kenny

An unflatteringly affectionate rendering of late-night television talk show host Jay Leno probably summed it up best, shortly after he killed Kenny (see last chapter). As the boy collapsed to the ground, fatally injured, Stan and Kyle set up their traditional lamentation. Or a slight variation thereof.

"Oh my God! Jay Leno's chin killed Kenny!"

"You bastard!"

To which a distinctly nonplussed Leno responded, "Oh, who cares? He dies in every damn episode!"

Give or take the occasional escape, he was correct, too. Poor Kenny has been sacrificed on more occasions, to more graphic passings, than the entire cast of the unrated slasher version of *It's a Wonderful Life*.

Yes, like them, he has been devoured by rats, blown up by a tampon, and mistaken for a duck-billed platypus. But he has been devoured by rats, blown up by a tampon, and mistaken for a duck-billed platypus with style. With panache. And with one inevitable consequence. Sooner or later, and generally sooner, he will return.

Kenny McCormick enjoys a distinctly ambiguous relationship with the Grim Reaper. The first time he died, which was more or less a few minutes after the first time we met him, the assumption is that that was the end of him. He was kaput.

The second time, we began to wonder.

The third time, we saw the joke.

The fifty-second time . . . even his mother was beginning to grow weary, although whether it was the funeral expenses that were wearing her down or the freakish rebirth of the child is unclear.

On at least one occasion (oddly, around the same time as Cartman was signing himself up for NAMBLA), it was suggested that his every death is immediately followed by his return to his mother's womb, a swift incubation, and an even swifter eight-or-nine-year growth spurt that enabled him to be back at the bus stop on his way to school before his friends have even had a chance to start missing him.

Kenny, on the other hand, believes he is laboring beneath a mysterious curse, and he may well be correct. "I've experienced death, countless times," he once revealed. "Sometimes I see a bright light. Sometimes I see Heaven. Or Hell. But eventually, no matter what, I wake up in my bed, wearing my same old clothes. And the worst part? Nobody even remembers me dying. I go to school the next day, and everyone is just like, 'Oh hey Kenny.' Even if they had seen me get decapitated with their own eyes."

Even if they see him burst into flames.

Death by Spontaneous Human Combustion

Spontaneous human combustion, or SHC, is one of the most widely documented yet altogether inexplicable phenomena to which the human body is allegedly heir. It is over six hundred years since history recorded what it regards as the first-ever case, when a fifteenth-century Italian knight, Polonus Vorstius, first vomited fire and then exploded into flame after consuming a couple of ladles of strong wine. According to Danish doctor and mathematician Thomas Bartholin, who published details of the case in 1641 (that is, 171 years after the original incident), SHC was the only reasonable explanation.

Thereafter, fresh incidents came . . . not exactly fast and furious, but considerably more frequently. In 1725, a Parisian innkeeper was woken by the smell of smoke and discovered his wife, Nicole Millet, reduced to ashes in their kitchen, lying on a straw pallet which itself was untouched by the flames. Other wooden items around her were likewise undamaged. The innkeeper was promptly charged with her murder, and he was initially declared guilty. On appeal, however, the judges agreed with his defense of "spontaneous human combustion," and Nicole's death was declared to be the consequence of "a visitation of God."

That same century saw Countess Cornelia Di Bandi meet a similar demise, her remains discovered midway between her bed and a window, with all but her lower legs and three fingers consumed by flame. The room was smothered in soot, and two nearby candles had been partially melted by the heat. But no other damage was discovered, and a verdict of SHC was inescapable.

Kenny goes to Hell.

These cases were curios, to be speculated over by scholars and medical students, but scarcely a part of the common vernacular. That situation altered dramatically in 1853, after Charles Dickens included an incident of SHC in his novel *Bleak House*. There, a rag-and-bone merchant named Mr. Krook erupts into otherwise inexplicable flames, and Dickens professed himself a firm believer in the phenomenon.

Critics of his books disagreed, of course, regarding the cause of death as utterly implausible and accusing Dickens simply of indulging in cheap sensationalism. And there, although many other cases have been recorded and many theories have been advanced, modern science rests today. There are believers and there are disbelievers.

The theories, though, pile up. Excessive alcohol consumption is a favorite, the idea being that the victim's body is so pickled in flammable spirits that it takes a mere spark to ignite it. The fact that the fire is generally concentrated to the victim's body alone, leaving surrounding objects (including chairs and, as in Paris, straw) untouched, is not necessarily addressed by this theory; neither is the belief, held by some researchers, that the fire burns without causing its victim any pain or suffering.

Natural human energies—the kundalini of mystic Eastern renown—have been fingered; so has the subatomic pyrotron theory, which is rooted in the existence of a tiny but high-powered particle that travels through the spaces between the quarks that comprise the atoms, which compose the molecules of the human body. Every so often, one of these pyrotrons strikes a quark and the whole shebang explodes. Quantum physics, don't you just love it?

A third theory, advanced by the early twentieth-century paranormal researcher Charles Fort (from whose name the term "Fortean" was derived), insisted that human bodies themselves did not spontaneously combust, but rather suffered the attentions of "things and beings that, with a flaming process, consume men and women."

A fourth, suggested by Soviet parapsychologist Genady Sergeyev in 1976, pointed to telekinesis and described a medium, Nina Kulagina, who only narrowly escaped a fiery death while channeling kinetic energy. A fifth considers ley lines, the mysterious (and themselves fiercely debated) energy lines that naturally run across the planet. And a sixth, developed by South Park geologist Randy Marsh, blames the societal distaste for farting in public and the ensuing buildup of flammable gas. This, incidentally, is in stark opposition to the insistence of an unnamed blond man from the same town that "it usually only happens to fat people near open flames."

South Park itself became obsessed by the subject of SHC following the otherwise inexplicable char-broiling of (perhaps unsurprisingly) Kenny McCormick. Anxious to ward off panic, and to prevent other citizens from succumbing to the same ghastly fate, Marsh set to work, eventually coming up with a theory that would see him receive the Nobel Prize.

"The little boy combusted because he had a new girlfriend," he explained. So enamored was he with his new paramour that he refused to pass gas when he was in her company. Instead, he bottled it up, causing a massive buildup in the bowel area. "Normally a person would expel this byproduct in the form of a pleasant fart. Should the gas not be expelled, the methane can build up and then ignite, leading to . . . disaster.

"Kenny combusted because he held his farts in for too long."

Mystery solved.

Death by Evil Goldfish

Creatures from evil parallel dimensions are a constant hazard, not only in South Park but elsewhere. Mythology, psychology, and lunatic fringe theories abound with beings that slip between the dimensions to whet their horrific appetites on human flesh; science fiction and fantasy rejoice in their existence; and the horror movie industry would be a lot less healthy without them.

Where are these dimensions? We do not know. But their portals are everywhere, and in South Park, Colorado, the locals still speak of the one that unleashed a terror so terrifying that its name still causes grown men to shudder.

It was called Spookyfish.

At least six deaths are attributable to the so-called Spookyfish, among them Kenny McCormick, Stan Marsh's Aunt Flo, an unknown man whose Missing Person photograph bore a startling resemblance to William Shatner, two men found dead in the Marsh boy's bedroom, and a third savaged to death on the street while Spookyfish's fellow denizens of a dark dimension (Spookypig, Spookygoose, and Spookybird among them) rampaged through the town.

Of the deaths, Kenny's was, perhaps inevitably, the most graphic, as Spookyfish leaped from his bowl, dragged the boy in by the head, then spun him around and around in a manner not unlike a food blender, before spitting him out to be consumed by nonspooky rats.

Less predictably, this was one of the very few occasions on which Kenny's mother expressed any true concern and regret over the boy's disappearance. However, she had been drinking.

Death by Rock Star

Pity poor Ozzy. One day, he's just another hard-rock idol, touring the world and blasting out his music to a legion of devoted followers. And the next, he's the bat-biter supreme, the maniacal metal monster who devours flying rodents for fun, and who knows what else for an encore? Happily married as the Ozmeister is, you may not need to lock up your daughters when his circus rolls into town. But you should certainly count their heads when they get home from the show.

In January 1982 in Des Moines, Iowa, Ozzy found himself holding a rubber bat that someone had thrown onto the stage. At least, he thought it was a rubber bat. It looked like rubber, it felt like rubber . . . quite understandably, Ozzy wondered whether it tasted like rubber.

Out in the auditorium, meanwhile, the kid who threw it onstage thought it was a dead bat. It looked like a dead bat, it felt like a dead bat

. . . and, oh look! Ozzy's going to find out whether or not it tastes like a dead bat.

He bit off its head.

At which point, *Rolling Stone* magazine revealed that it was neither rubber nor dead. The bat was very much alive, if not quite kicking, and Ozzy later revealed that he had to go get a rabies jab immediately after.

End of story?

Not quite.

"It's amazing people remember all the crap," the once-and-future Black Sabbath front man remarked a few years later. "But it's not anyone's fault but mine, and the amount of mileage I've had out of it has been amazing. It just gets a bit tedious when someone goes, 'So Ozzy, tell me, what do bats taste like?' The amount of times I've been asked that question in America—'Now we have the infamous bat-biting rock 'n' roll freak, Ozzy Osbourne!' Sideshow, sideshow . . . I tell 'em it tastes like a good McDonald's."

Besides, it's not as though he'd not done something similar in the past.

The previous year at a record company convention, he got it into his head that he should release a dove into the auditorium during his performance. But of course, things didn't quite go according to plan.

"I was at a CBS Convention, right? You don't realize what these business things are like. All the old codgers are there and they don't give a fuck about you, it's just a sham. They play your album while you're there then forget you. Well, I wanted to make a real impression.

"The scam is, the bird was dead. We were planning to release it there, but it died beforehand. So rather than waste it, I bit its head off. You should have seen their faces. They all went white. They were speechless. That girl in the pictures was screaming. Eventually a bloke came up and said 'You better go.'

"The dove's head landed on the PR chick's lap in a splatter of blood. To be honest with you, I was so pissed it just tasted of Cointreau. Well, Cointreau and feathers. And a bit of beak."

So you probably still don't need to lock up your daughters. But if you have an accident-prone son . . . .

According to the chronicles of South Park, it was Chef who suggested Ozzy do it, of course. Well, sort of. As the Birmingham-born bat-beheader announced from the stage of Chef Aid, "we're all here to help our good friend, Chef, who has touched our lives in the past. I remember when I was just starting out, Chef suggested I buy a pompadour hat. I thought he said, 'Bite the head off a bat,' so I did. And the rest . . . oh, it's just history. Now, let's go crazzzzyyyyyyyyy!"

Crazy enough to perform "Nowhere to Run."

Crazy enough to reach down from the stage and pick up the nearest child, who just happened to be little Kenny.

And crazy enough to . . . well, Stan said it best.

"Oh, my God! Ozzy Osbourne bit Kenny's head off!"

Death by Falling Space Junk

It is estimated that there are currently over three hundred thousand separate pieces of debris in orbit around the planet Earth, all of them one chunk or another of the vast quantity of probes, satellites, rockets, capsules, and so forth that humankind has flung into the heavens over the past six decades.

Most of these pieces are tiny, smaller than one centimeter. But around twenty thousand of them are bigger, and a few are a lot bigger. Entire satellites, disused or decommissioned, bump around up there. Large chunks of rocket, the "stages" into which the old moon shots were divided. There's a toothbrush, lost by one of the astronauts aboard the MIR space station. A tool bag. A wrench and a pair of pliers. And a whole bunch of bits and bobs left over after China launched a successful antisatellite missile test in 2007.

Of course, most of this stuff is safely floating around, a hazard to other spacecraft, of course, but of no concern to us down here. Occasionally, a piece might reenter the atmosphere and begin its long descent to the ground, but it will usually have burned up long before it poses a risk.

Usually.

In 1969, chunks of a Soviet space project rained down onto a Japanese ship, injuring five sailors.

In 1979, when Skylab fell to Earth, debris was scattered across western Australia.

In 1997, a woman in Oklahoma was hit on the shoulder by a wallet-sized fragment from the fuel tank of a Delta II rocket.

In 2002, a Star 48 Payload Assist Module came down into the Saudi desert.

And then there was the long and protracted death of the MIR space station, which officially deposited just one piece of debris on dry ground, in a backyard in Amesbury, Massachusetts (the rest fell into the South Pacific), but which unofficially . . . .

Unofficially, MIR claimed two victims.

The first was Seattle college student Georgina Lass. Temping downtown one sunny day she was enjoying her lunch break when she sensed something approaching her from above. Something very large, very fast and very fiery. And before she could even think of moving, she was struck by the space station's toilet seat.

Seriously deceased by the incident, she was recruited to a shadowy organization known as the Grim Reapers and became the effervescent star of *Dead Like Me*, truly one of the shining glories of mid-2000s American television. So incandescent that, if *South Park* had never existed, Kenny would have been a shoo-in for the male lead role.

Instead, Kenny was busy being dead elsewhere, because—with perhaps crushing inevitability—he was the space station's other victim. Tragically flattened while waiting at the bus stop and, as if that was not horrible enough, subjected to further indignities when his corpse was inadvertently filled with Worcestershire sauce instead of embalming fluid at the mortuary. Worcestershire sauce being a little-known but highly effective means of creating zombies.

Reanimated with a voracious appetite for human flesh, Kenny escaped the morgue, savagely biting several morgue workers as he did so. Who themselves were transformed into zombies, only for their condition to be misdiagnosed as pinkeye. A common mistake, of course, but one that was to have lethal consequences, especially as Halloween was just around the corner. The one time of year when few people would even look twice at a herd of living dead shuffling through the darkened streets.

Only the school chef, Chef, seemed to appreciate the enormity of the situation; only the late Kenny's closest friends, Kyle, Stan, and Cartman, were in any fit state to tackle the problem. Visiting the mortuary and swiftly discovering the Worcestershire sauce mix-up, they make a call to the manufacturer's helpline to learn their next step. They must kill the original zombie.

Kenny must die.

Again.

And so he did.

Again.

The townspeople returned to normal; South Park returned to normal. For now.

Death by Video Game

It sounds like it should be an urban myth, the story of the devoted gamer who spent so long glued to the screen of his whateverbox that he (or she) completely failed to notice their life force ebbing away, before being discovered in a crumpled heap, dead fingers still clutching the joystick as the action on the screen continued undisturbed around them.

It should be, but it isn't.

For whatever reason, video games are compulsive in a way that few other pastimes are. A sportsman knows when he is at last too tired to pitch that last ball, or kick that final goal. The most devoted chess player is well aware when his mind is too tired to make that next decisive move. Even Snakes and Ladders freaks have their limits.

But video games . . . . one more level, one more killing, one more item, one more crop. In 2013, the children of South Park even braved the perils of Black Friday at the mall just to score a sweet deal on the latest Xbox. Or PlayStation. And the fact that the whole adventure was enacted to a theme of *Game of Thrones*, HBO's award-winning adaptation of George R. R. Martin's medievalesque fantasy of knights, damsels, dragons, and (according to a fascinated Butters) wieners only added fresh peril to the mission.

Which is exactly how it ought to be.

One more level, one more killing, one more crop.

In 1982, in Calumet City, Illinois, a teenage devotee of Atari's Berzerk arcade game racked up the two highest scores on a machine and then dropped dead of a heart attack. Thirty years later, an eighteen-year-old Diablo III player was found dead in a Taiwan Internet café after racking up a marathon forty hours of nonstop play. In South Korea, a couple was charged with murder after allowing their baby to starve to death—because they were too busy caring for the baby they'd had in a virtual world.

And, in-between times, the Grim Reaper himself has had a high old time snatching the last breaths of anyone so bound up in whichever artificial existence they are visiting that they forget to attend to the needs of the real world in which they actually live.

One deceased gamer was actually discovered to be suffering from malnutrition.

Others were simply in serious need of a good bath.

Perhaps the best-known illustration of the manifold ill effects that video can wreak on the human brain did not, thankfully, result in death. But no less than 685 people were hospitalized after watching "Dennō Senshi Porygon," a 1997 episode of the popular Japanese television anime series *Pokemon*. Seizures brought on by an anime technique called "paka paka" ensured several victims remained in the hospital for weeks as their brains recovered from exposure to a six-second sequence of brutally bright strobe lights, flashing at a rate of about 12 Hz.

In the real world, the program went on a four-month hiatus, and televised anime found itself subject to a raft of new, stringent controls.

In South Park's world, on the other hand . . . .

The fiendish head of Chinpokomon toys and video games, Mr. Hirohito, watched that lethal episode and believed he had discovered a way, at long last, of avenging Japan's defeat at the end of the Second World War.

All of the tricks that landed Pokemon in trouble were dragged out and revised. Chinpokomon would not simply cause children to seize. It would completely and utterly brainwash them, and, with the company's marketing strategy targeted specifically at the United States, Hirohito dreamed of creating a vast juvenile army that would rise up and topple the American government.

Of course, his plot would ultimately fail. But still it was not without its victims. A parka-clad kid in South Park, Colorado, was stricken by a seizure as he played the game, and just to make double-sure that his friends all appreciated his sacrifice, rats burst from his body as he lay on the ground and proceeded to devour his lifeless flesh.

There's a famous scene in Andy Warhol's *Bad* when a watermelon is dropped from a very high place and explodes with a splat on the sidewalk below. A woman walking past with her child stops, points, and gently declaims, "That's what will happen to you if you're bad."

Kenny's death here was a little like that. So just unplug the thing now, and go read a book.

Death by Life Support Machine

But talking of unplugging things . . . . and still talking about video games . . . remember the episode where Kenny becomes the first kid in town to get the new PlayStation Portable? The one that was designed by God and his Heavenly Hosts, to aid them in their quest to locate the one human being capable of leading a mere ten thousand-man army of angels against a tide of evil ten billion strong?

That stuff's all true. Where we step into the world of sheer fantastical nonsense is what happens after Kenny gets crunched by an ice cream truck. Hovering on the edge of life and death, his battered body lies unable to communicate, eat, or even breathe without the aid of a life support machine.

But how long should he be left that way? How long is too long for any caring society, let alone family, to leave a loved one lying in a state of permanent and irreversible vegetation? And even if the family and friends are split down the middle as to whether or not the plugs should be pulled, should the entire affair really be fought out in the full glare of the media spotlight?

A final, tasteless blurring of the already precariously fine line between private tragedy and mass entertainment that even *South Park*'s staunchest supporters murmured might have been a comment too far. For while Kenny's clan contested what the dying boy's wishes might have been, far away in Florida, the real-life relatives of a real-life person, Terri Schiavo, were embroiled in a brutal and brightly spotlit legal battle to decide whether or not she should be allowed to slip away. A battle that ultimately lasted fifteen years.

Yes, maybe this particular episode of *South Park* was tasteless. But for once, the real-life events that inspired the story outdid even the parody.

Death by Boomerang

A simple one this. Boomerangs are thrown, boomerangs come back, and Heaven help anybody who doesn't keep a close eye on their trajectory and either duck or catch them when they return. Because otherwise . . . .

Sherlock Holmes was faced with a boomerang mystery in an episode of the twenty-first-century *Sherlock* TV series. A man standing alone in a field by a river is apparently scanning the skies for something unseen. A nearby car backfires. The man impulsively turns his head to investigate the sound and then drops dead to the ground.

It was an easy case for Holmes to solve, even after the cream of the local police force professed themselves baffled. There was no such mystery surrounding Kenny's death, however. It was Mrs. Choksondik's fault.

Mrs. Choksondik had recently been assigned the role of sex education teacher at South Park Elementary. An unusual choice because, despite the certainly supercharged relationship that she was currently enjoying with school counselor Mr. Mackey, Mrs. Choksondik liked neither sex nor men. And it was her task, she believed, to convince her charges to share her dislikes.

Most schools, at least those that admit they are living in a multicultural, multisocietal, twenty-first-century environment, will advise their pupils that unprotected sex can result in any one of a variety of unpleasant sexually transmitted diseases.

Mrs. Choksondik went a little further. She advised her pupils that sex itself wasn't even a prerequisite for sickness. Nothing more intimate than unprotected proximity to a boy was sufficient to leave a young girl's body addled with infection. And so South Park Elementary found itself divided into two warring factions—the girls, desperately striving to protect their health and bodies from the diseased, disgusting boys, and the boys who want only to put an end to the foolishness.

The girls will not be dissuaded, however, and they arm themselves for a fight to the death.

Kenny's death.

Struck on the head by a viciously sharpened boomerang, hurled by the precocious Bebe.

Sherlock Holmes was unavailable for comment.

Death by Autoerotic Asphyxiation While Dressed as Batman

Death by autoerotic asphyxiation is one of those demises that everybody seems to have heard rumors about . . . very specific rumors involving well-known Australian pop stars, for example. Famous actors. British politicians. Ohio kidnappers. But which few reliable sources will ever come out and admit to having actually occurred.

You can't blame them, of course. Sexually inspired deaths, particularly those that involve a degree of . . . shall we say deviation from the norm . . . are never going to be truly comprehended by the masses; plus, there is a very understandable societal reluctance to publicize, or even demonstrate, the procedure for fear of inducing further cases.

It was bad enough back in the seventies, when kids started hanging themselves (successfully or otherwise) in emulation of Alice Cooper's then-current stage act. Nobody wants to walk in on their INXS-loving son and find him in a similar position of overzealous hero worship, with or without his pants on.

It certainly isn't something to make light of, which is why the sexologists who visit South Park Elementary to screen the kids for sexual addiction are very, very careful when raising the topic with the boys, and even more careful about explaining it.

"I don't want to go into too much detail but . . . you choke yourself with a belt around your neck while masturbating dressed up like Batman or something, then you pass out from lack of air and apparently it makes your orgasm super awesome."

No. That would never encourage a kid to take off his orange parka for perhaps the first time in his life, don the garb of the caped crusader, and . . . .

Death by Death Cult

Technology and education notwithstanding, mankind has always sought guidance from the heavens. Astrology, cloud forms, eclipses, bird flight, rain showers . . . and comets. Especially comets. The most volatile of all the astral messages, comets have fascinated and frightened mankind for millennia.

To the ancient civilizations of the Near East, through the Greek and Roman periods, into the first millennium of the Christian era, the sighting of a comet portended imminent disaster. The first Viking assault on England in the eighth century was preceded by sightings that ranged from a simple moving object in the sky to full-scale representations of fire-breathing dragons. The Norman invasion three centuries later was witnessed, and apparently predestined, by the appearance of Halley's Comet. And the fear has never truly dissipated.

In 1773, the French astronomer Joseph Jerome Lefrancais de Lalande predicted that a total of sixty-one comets were about to have a close encounter with the earth. Of course, he did not say how close, so the city of Paris assumed the worst. In purely emotional terms, the ensuing panic arguably did as much damage as an actual comet strike would have. Had there been one. Which there wasn't . . . .

Seventy years later, a cult called the Millerites gained both strength and numbers as a passing comet apparently lent gravity to founder William Miller's belief that the entire planet was about to be consumed by fire. All life would be extinguished on April 3, and when April 4 doomed bright and sunny, well, the Millerites weren't the first, and they certainly wouldn't be the last, prophetic cult to admit that maybe they got it wrong. Or, better still, that God changed his mind as a result of their prayers. Ha, you can't argue with that one, can you?

Neither is this all redundant superstition, crushed by the enlightenment in which modern society dwells today. In March 1997, the Heaven's Gate cult exterminated itself, so that its membership might catch a ride on the passing Hale-Bopp Comet, and who is to say it was coincidence alone that decreed, less than a month earlier, that American television viewers should be gripped by the two-part TV movie *Asteroid*, in which great swathes of the south were wiped out by another such astral body.

Heaven's Gate was not a one-off, either. The decade had already seen three major cult-oriented mass suicides, and several more were threatened. The Order of the Solar Temple even did it twice, perishing by their own hands at sites as far apart as Switzerland and Canada, in 1994.

And so to David Blaine, an immensely gifted illusionist and endurance artist whose feats have included being buried for a week beneath Trump Plaza, spending sixty-three hours in a block of ice in Times Square, and another thirty-five hours balancing on top of a pillar in Bryant Park. And, in-between times, an animated look-alike visited South Park, performing conjuring tricks on Main Street and inviting passersby to attend the camp and seminar he was hosting nearby. Where they would be inducted into Blaineology, a fast-growing religious cult that was set to go head to head with Jesus Christ, to see who can perform the most miraculous miracle.

Jesus did his best, but the water-into-wine routine is old hat now. His rival could eat his own head.

Jesus followed up with the loaves and fishes, and then produced a playing card from behind his rival's ear. The illusionist levitated, spun, and then vanished into a deck of cards before cutting it in half, tracing a circle, creating a bigger circle, erupting into a veritable storm of whirling cards—and then stepping out of the maelstrom unharmed. That, even Jesus had to admit, was an impressive trick.

"Jesus," said Jesus.

The cult grew. Soon the Blaineologists were camped out on the National Mall, petitioning the government for tax-exempt status. Recognized as a true religion, they believed, they would be unstoppable. There is just one drawback. Nobody believed they were actually a religion.

So the cult members did what cult members do. They began drowning themselves in the Reflecting Pool. Some of them were saved. Others were not so lucky.

Kenny, hardly surprisingly, was numbered among the latter.

The Fishsticks Joke

The funniest joke in the world, according to *Monty Python*, is so funny that nobody can hear, read, or even contemplate it and expect to live to tell the tale. It was developed, they say, during the Second World War, when one Ernest Scribbler scribbled it down—and promptly died laughing.

His mother walked in and discovered his body. She picked up what she believed to be a suicide note. She, too, died laughing.

A Scotland Yard detective made a gallant attempt to secure the joke. He died laughing as well.

The War Department got hold of it and weaponized it for deployment against the Nazis. A team of crack translators was set to work translating the joke into German, one word each, for fear that further exposure might prove fatal. One of them mistakenly read two words and was hospitalized. But finally their work was done, and the funniest joke in the world was deployed for the first time in the Ardennes in June 1944. It was ruthlessly effective.

"Wenn ist das Nunstück git und Slotermeyer?"

"Ja! Beiherhund das Oder die Flipperwaldt gersput!"

Maybe you had to be there.

There is no reliable evidence for anybody having ever died as a direct result of exposure to the Fishsticks joke, and that despite it, too, being reliably described by authorities as far apart as exaggerated caricatures of Conan O'Brien, Jay Leno, David Letterman, and Ellen DeGeneres as the funniest and most all-inclusive joke ever told.

Nobody at all. Apart from one. A drawing of Comedy Central comedian Carlos Mencia, beaten to death and then decapitated by similarly rendered rapper Kanye West, who not only believed Mencia's outlandish claims to have created the joke in the first place, but was also convinced that it was targeted at him.

But he didn't. And it wasn't.

"Magst du Fischstäbchen?"

"Ja."

"Mögen Sie setzen Fischstäbchen in den Mund?"

"Ja!"

"Was bist du? Ein Homosexuell Fisch?

The Many Deaths of Kenny

Potentially Fatal Injuries: Incidents That Kenny Visibly Survived, Whether by Luck or Continuity Error

- Apparently dies at the bus stop.
- Apparently dies while attempting to play "the brown note."
- Apparently killed by a "big, black, scary monster."
- Apparently killed by a misfiring rocket during an assassination attempt on wrestler Vince McMahon.
- Apparently run over by the Fonz's motorbike.
- Arms torn off by two Middle Park Cowboy players.
- As Mysterion, impales himself.
- As Mysterion, is stabbed in the heart by a member of the Cthulhu gang.
- As Mysterion, shoots himself.
- As Mysterion, shoots himself again and is seen being reborn.
- Autoerotic asphyxiation while dressed as Batman.
- Blasted by an alien spaceship.
- Carried away by a giant bird.
- Contracts but apparently survives the plague.
- Crushed beneath car but escapes through sunroof.
- Crushed by a volcanic bomb.
- Crushed by the Native American Hut during the school play.
- Drowned by urine.
- Flies into brick wall after falling off a swing set.
- Has his head bitten off by Ozzy Osbourne.
- Impaled by bull horns.
- Murdered by his newborn alien baby brother.
- Narrowly avoids drowning in river while clad in concrete boots.
- Run over by an ice cream van and placed on life support.
- Set on fire and again crushed by the volcanic bomb.
- Shot by a misfiring gun.
- Struck by bus.
- Trampled by a herd of cattle.
- Tumbles to certain doom from a Hawaiian waterfall.
- Turned into a duck-billed platypus by Damien.

Fatal Injuries That He Does Not Survive

- Accidentally shot by Mr. Garrison during a botched attempt to assassinate Kathie Lee Gifford.
- Accidentally shot by Ned.
- After a tampon gets stuck in his anus, the attendant pressure buildup causes him to explode.
- As a duck-billed platypus, shot by Jimbo.
- As a member of the Blaineologist death cult, drowns himself in the Reflecting Pool in front of the Lincoln Memorial
- Attacked by mutant turkeys.
- Battered to death by the Phonics Monkey.
- Blown up by a firecracker.
- Burned to death by a warning flare.
- Chewed up by the conveyor belt in front of the prehistoric man exhibit at the museum.
- Contracts a fatal dose of syphilis after experimenting with oral sex with his girlfriend Tammy Warner.
- Cooked to death in a microwave oven by Stan's mutant clone.
- Crushed beneath a derailed mining cart filled with underpants.
- Crushed by a chandelier.
- Crushed by a descending elevator at the mall.
- Crushed by a falling stage light.
- Crushed by a piano.
- Crushed by bleachers.
- Crushed by falling bricks.
- Crushed by falling tree.
- Crushed by gravestone after falling into an open grave.
- Crushed by the MIR space station.
- Crushed to death in a moshpit.
- Crushed to death when Cartman flings open his bedroom door.
- Decapitated by a Middle Park Cowboys player.
- Devoured by a prehistoric bird moments after learning he is no longer the poorest kid in South Park.
- Dies of boredom while ziplining.
- Dragged into a giant fan by a magnet.
- Dragged to death by Timmy's wheelchair while attempting to repair it.
- Drowned by Stan's evil Spookyfish goldfish.
- Electrocuted while switching on the hospital generator.

- Falls into a vat of lava.
- Fatally struck by a dodgeball.
- Frozen in carbonite by the CIA.
- Having overdosed on antacids in the belief they are mints, explodes following a drink of water.
- Having suffered a seizure and coma while playing the Chinpokomon video game, his body explodes and reveals itself to be full of rats.
- Head explodes during a visit to the planetarium.
- His head is sliced in two by a boomerang hurled by Bebe.
- Hit by locomotive after being dragged onto the tracks by a go-kart.
- Hit in face by a frying pan–wielding Cartman, during a Christina Aguilera–induced hallucination.
- Impaled on a pile of rusty nails.
- Impaled through the head on a metal pipe while riding a roller coaster.
- Inadvertently killed with an Iraqi sword being carelessly wielded by substitute teacher Ms. Ellen.
- Inadvertently strangles himself while playing solo tetherball.
- Killed by a bear while impersonating a deer.
- Killed by a fatal disease.
- Killed by a snow speeder.
- Killed by an explosion while in Afghanistan.
- Killed by a nonfatal disease (chicken pox).
- Laughs himself to death while watching Cartman's "I'm a Little Piggy" video.
- Life support machine is switched off.
- Pulverized by a succubus.
- Run over by a car.
- Run over by a motorbike.
- Run over by an ambulance. Mrs. McCormick later remarks this is the fifty-second occasion on which her son has passed away.
- Run over by Officer Barbrady's police cruiser.
- Sacrificed.
- Sacrifices himself to open the conch shell in which Moses is trapped.
- Shot by Bebe Stevens.
- Shot by police.
- Shot by the Chinese Mafia.
- Shot by airport security.
- Spontaneously combusts.
- Thrown against the ceiling.

- Torn to pieces by audience members during the filming of *Jesus and Pals*.
- Touched by Death.
- Trampled by a crowd leaving a theater.
- Vaporized by Saddam Hussein, posing as the Prime Minister of Canada.
- Vomits himself to death.
- While escaping from a river clad in concrete shoes, falls into a concealed underwater trench and drowns.

Postmortem Indignities

(proving, as Bob Dylan once came within ten words of writing, "Death is not the end of the crap that can befall your poor, shattered corpse.")
- As a zombie, bisected with a chainsaw-wielding Kyle.
- Decapitated by Kyle.
- Devoured by rats.
- Impaled on a flagpole.
- Now a disembodied spirit temporarily possessing the body of actor Rob Schneider, Kenny is "exorcised" after the actor is impaled on a flagpole.
- Still a zombie, crushed by a falling angel statue.
- Still a zombie, hit by a crashing aircraft.

13

That Chef Guy

What's His Story?

For many years, for many people, school cafeteria chef Jerome McElroy *was* South Park Elementary. Other faculty members might have considered themselves more valuable; others certainly behaved as though they alone were responsible for guiding their youthful charges into the sunlit uplands of adulthood. Some even had a hand puppet.

But Chef alone understood both what went on inside a child's developing mind and how to cultivate that activity toward its ultimate flowering.

His wisdom was unlimited, his instinct unfailing. No matter what problem his young acolytes were confronted with, a few words from Chef could point them toward the correct solution.

It was Chef who recommended that the Cure's Robert Smith be employed to battle the Mecha-Streisand; Chef who suggested the town ditch its traditional flag depicting a lynching and replace it with something a little less inflammatory; and Chef who occasionally gave the boys a far more explicit answer than their question may have required, as he took to singing slow-burning sexual funk songs when words failed him.

His musical talents were certainly not to be sniffed at. It was well known in South Park that their humble school chef had composed "Stinky Britches," an international hit song in the hands of Alanis Morissette. His influence over the music scene in general was proven when the very best of both classic and modern rock turned out to celebrate him at the Chef Aid charity event. And his super-suggestive ode to one of his favorite confectionary treats, chocolate salty balls, gave an utterly unexpected British number one hit to the one performer truly capable of standing in the same room as Chef, Texan-born funk behemoth Isaac Hayes.

Whose own story goes something like this.

Orphaned as a child and raised by his grandparents, the young Isaac Hayes moved to Memphis in his late teens, already a musical talent whose abilities verged on prodigious. A self-taught sax, piano, and organ player, the teenaged Hayes performed with such local acts as the Teen Tones, Sir Calvin and his Swinging Cats, and Memphis singer Jeb Stuart's backing band, the Doo-Dads. He also cut one single with producer Chips Moman, "Laura We're On Our Last Go-Round," in 1962, before he was recruited to saxophonist Floyd Newman's live group.

From there, Hayes became a regular musician at the Stax studio as it established itself alongside Motown as the heartbeat of American soul in the sixties, often standing in for the MGs' keyboard player, Booker T., after he began attending college in Indiana.

In 1964, Hayes cowrote the Mad Lads' "Sidewalk Surf" single, and in 1965 a songwriting partnership with another Stax sessioneer, David Porter, was debuted with Porter's own recording of "Can't You See When I Want To."

Over the next few years, the pair was responsible for a string of hits across the Stax spectrum, including Sam and Dave's "I Take What I Want," Rufus Thomas and Carla Thomas's "When You Move You Lose," Carla Thomas's immortal "B-A-B-Y," Sam and Dave's "Hold On, I'm Coming" and "Soul Man," Ruby Johnson's "I'll Run Your Hurt Away," and the Astors' "In the Twilight Zone."

Another project reunited Hayes with two of his former school friends, Eddie Harrison and Billy Moore, in the Premiers; Hayes and Porter's "Make It Me" would be their Stax debut. Hayes' own debut as a Stax recording artist, contrarily, was with a cover, the lazy sax-led instrumental "Blue Goose," cut with his old colleagues from the Doo-Dads, renamed Sir Isaac and the Doo-Dads for the occasion.

By 1967, Hayes was involved in virtually every aspect of the recording process at Stax, as a writer, a musician, and beyond. His arrangement for Otis Redding's "Try a Little Tenderness" seldom fails to bring a thrill to the ears, while he also cut a fabulous Christmas single with Booker T. and the MGs, a version of his own "Winter Snow."

Still, Hayes hankered for a recording career to call his own, and in January 1968, he was finally given the go-ahead to record what became his debut album. Taking over the studio following a company party, Hayes and the MGs rhythm section of Al Jackson and Duck Dunn relaxed into a late-night, laid-back jazz jam, released later in the year as *Presenting Isaac Hayes* and accompanied by a single of the improvised vamp "Precious, Precious."

Inaugurating a new Stax subsidiary, the jazz specialist label Enterprise, the album did little, but with Stax giving him the green light to continue, Hayes changed direction entirely for *Hot Buttered Soul* and emerged from the studio with one of the defining albums of the era. With the distinctively built front man accompanied by the Bar-Kays, *Hot Buttered Soul* featured just four cuts, the shortest, Charles Chalmers's "One Woman," coming in at five minutes; the longest, reenvisioning Jimmy Webb's "By the Time I Get to Phoenix" as the slow-burning mumblings of an erotic diarist, close to a marathon nineteen.

Somehow, "Phoenix" and the twelve-minute "Walk On By" were edited down for a double A-sided single. It became Hayes's first hit, but just as potently, it introduced Hayes's startling image to the world, shaven headed and bedecked in medallions, slow-rapping supercool sensuality

Chef, in the days when he funked the world.

over a landscape that slid from lush orchestrations to snapping guitar with barely a pause.

Hot Buttered Soul was the first of five consecutive R&B chart-toppers that Hayes would enjoy over the next two years; indeed, the forty-nine weeks that he spent at number one during that period was exceeded (by a mere three weeks) only by the combined efforts of the entire Motown family, including the Temptations, Diana Ross, and the Jacksons.

Hayes's next album, *The Isaac Hayes Movement*, followed, and even without any substantial smash singles, both it and 1970's *To Be Continued* were massive hits. But it was Hayes's next release, the soundtrack to the Richard Roundtree movie *Shaft*, that established the benchmark by which his career (and every other movie soundtrack of the 1970s) would henceforth be judged.

Shaft was Hayes's first attempt at writing a movie score; he worked, initially, from a 16mm copy of three scenes, basing what became the opening theme on a short piece of wah-wah guitar-inflected funk he'd written but had never found a use for in the past. Touring at the same time as he worked on the score ensured Hayes and his band remained fresh; so did the external influences he brought to bear on the project, "a lot of what happened in the '60s, the civil rights struggle, the Vietnam issues and so forth." Quoted in the blaxploitation movie history *What It Is, What It Was*, Hayes continued, "Society was more liberal and having more fun at that time. I tried to make the tracks like that."

He succeeded beyond anybody's wildest expectations. In 1972, Hayes became the first African American to receive an Oscar for Best Musical Score; he also picked up two Grammys and a Golden Globe, but he insisted that "one of the greatest compliments I ever got [was when] Dominic Frontiere, whom I respected so much and looked up to for what he had done in films, walked in and fell on his knees and kissed the back of my hand. He said 'thank you. Thank you for taking us out of the dark ages.'"

Shaft was unique, not in terms of its actual mechanics (a good movie soundtrack should reflect what's going on on-screen), but in its dynamics. "There was a lot of freedom," Hayes explained. "You were disciplined because you had to match a lot of dramatic cues on the film. But you had creative freedom to interpret how you felt they should be played against the scene. Since I did not have formal training, I was not restricted [in] what I could hear, what I could imagine. That's why the sound is so unique."

But even he never dreamed that "almost everything that followed for almost a decade had that same kind of sound, like *Shaft*. It revolutionized music in film and . . . television."

It also sent Hayes's own career skywards. *Black Moses*, his next album, went straight to number one despite its behemothic proportions—a double set, it included heavily stylized versions of "Never Can Say Goodbye," Gamble and Huff's "Never Gonna Give You Up," and Curtis Mayfield's "Need to Belong to Someone," alongside a Bacharach-David song, "(They Long to Be) Close to You," that had already become massive once that year, for the Carpenters.

Hayes toured through 1972, including the headline spot at the Stax label's Wattstax festival at the LA Coliseum. Unfortunately his role in the movie/LP documentary of the event was limited after MGM, distributors of *Shaft*, sued over the inclusion of great swathes of that soundtrack. Nevertheless, Hayes was represented by a gargantuan version of "Ain't No Sunshine," an all-but unrecognizable piano-led rap suddenly crashing into the signature theme.

A reissue of his debut album then kept the charts warm while America awaited his own next release, another double-album set, *Live at the Sahara Tahoe*. Augmented by an eight-piece horn section, the Hot Buttered Soul Ltd. vocal group, and the Al Trouti Orchestra, Hayes's show was super-slick, deliciously paced and arranged, incontinent with virtuosity and showmanship. As a physical experience, it was amazing; as a musical experience, on the other hand, it was maybe a little too much of a good thing. The album spent just two weeks at the top of the R&B chart, then slipped fast. Before the end of the year, Hayes responded with a new studio set, *Joy*—it peaked at number two, but still picked up a gold disc.

In 1974, Hayes moved into acting, appearing alongside Lino Ventura and Fred Williamson in *Three Tough Guys*. He followed up with a role in Jonathan Kaplan's *Truck Turner*, turning in competent soundtracks to both, and acting soon became at least as important to Hayes as his music. Indeed, by the mid-1990s, he was adamant that younger fans knew him more for his thespian abilities than for his records. *The Chocolate Chip* album in 1975 was to be his final number one, but Hayes was regularly appearing on television now, guesting in *The Rockford Files* and *Starsky and Hutch*; he also starred in John Carpenter's *Escape from New York* movie.

But he was also fighting a losing battle against mounting financial problems. At one point, he was said to be $6 million in debt, and in 1979,

Hayes filed for bankruptcy—ironically, around the same time he enjoyed his biggest hit in six years.

"When disco hit, I heard myself everywhere, in so many songs and styles, until I decided to chill. Finally, I took the unlikeliest disco song, an old Roy Hamilton tune, and gave it a new dance spin. It worked." Recorded with Millie Jackson, "Do You Wanna Make Love" returned Hayes to the R&B Top 20, while an accompanying album of duets made number

Isaac Hayes' 1974 acting debut.

nine. Two albums later, however, Hayes retired from music to concentrate on acting.

Hayes made his first musical comebacks in 1986, leading off with the latest in a long succession of recordings titled "Ike's Raps"—semi-lectures on the manifold evils of the day, beginning with crack cocaine (a long-time social crusader, Hayes had already established his own Isaac Hayes Foundation, set up to create low-income housing for the poor and elderly). The accompanying *U-Turn* and *Love Attack* albums were not a success, however, and Hayes returned to acting, resurfacing only to cut a 1991 duet with Barry White, the lascivious "Dark and Lovely."

The mid-1990s brought another outbreak of Hayes mania, at the hands of a rap and hip-hop community that never tired of sampling his work. Hayes released two new albums in 1995, a smooth vocal set, *Branded*, and a driving instrumental album suitably titled *Raw and Refined*, drawn from a stockpile of grooves and rhythms dating back to the late 1960s. The opening "Birth of Shaft" was itself drawn from the original sessions for that soundtrack.

Most remarkable of all, however, Hayes finally celebrated another #1 single. As one of the vocal stars of *South Park*, he topped the UK chart in December 1998 with the deliciously risqué "Chocolate Salty Balls." And for the next seven years, Hayes's mellifluous tones and "come to bed" suggestions were as much a part of the show's success as any other single character.

Nobody was as surprised by that as Hayes himself.

His recruitment to *South Park* itself sounds like a minor subplot in one of the episodes.

Watching the explosion in animated movies taking place at the time, Hayes had recently asked his agent to look into getting him some voice-acting work, and presumed that Disney, or one of the other major anima-tion studios, would be at the top of the queue. Instead, when the call finally came, his agent didn't even seem keen to tell him what it entailed.

"It was kinda nebulous. My agent wouldn't tell me what it was," Hayes told SF Gate. "He just said it was . . . 'different.'"

A meeting with the brains behind this nebulous difference was arranged in New York, and Hayes wasn't particularly interested in that, either. But he was in town, so why not at least hear the guys out?

"I showed up with attitude, too. They were polite. I said, 'What's the part, man?' They just said, 'You're perfect for it!'"

"What kinda part?" asked Hayes, and so Stone and Parker explained. "'It's this cook in this little town in South Park, Colorado, and you'll cook for and mentor these little foul-mouthed kids.'" Hayes admitted he took one look at the script, then demanded to know who put them up to the joke. Because this whole thing could only be a joke. Couldn't it?

"It's legit," they responded. "We're serious about it."

"I said, 'You all some crazy white boys!'"

Hayes decided to do it. It was a one-off story; the Chef would appear in this single episode and never be seen again. Or so Hayes believed. "It's some quick money. I'll knock this off, it'll last about six weeks and I'll be on my merry way." It was only as the pilot episode's airdate approached, and he faced the reality of being associated with a cartoon called "Cartman Gets an Anal Probe," that the reality of what he had agreed to set in. "What can I say to my friends about this show? I'm going to have to sneak out of town like a flasher."

Instead, he became Chef. Quite literally in some corners of his life. Interviewed by *Factmag*, shortly before his death, Hayes admitted, "At this time of my life I like cooking. I've done it all, now I like to cook." His favorite meal was turkey meatloaf, and his recommendation for a romantic birthday dish . . . "Let me see . . . make some barbecue. For dessert, take a banana, put some syrup on it—no chocolate—and heat it up good."

But then it was all over.

It was toward the end of the show's ninth season. "Trapped in the Closet" was the episode in which Stan Marsh encountered Scientology, at the same time he was revealed as the reincarnation of its founder, science fiction author L. Ron Hubbard. The problem was, Stan had difficulty believing many of the tenets of the faith. No. He had difficulty believing any of the tenets of the faith. A failure that, coupled with the on-screen antics of several of Scientology's best-known public figureheads, served to utterly disillusion the youngster.

Who, however, could he turn to for advice? On this occasion, not Chef. Isaac Hayes was himself a practicing Scientologist and, accustomed though he surely was to the show landing itself in the hot springs of controversy on a regular basis, on this occasion the controversy was too close to home.

Just days later, it was revealed that Hayes had resigned from the show. "There is a place in this world for satire, but there is a time when satire ends, and intolerance and bigotry toward religious beliefs of others begins," Hayes allegedly declared in a public statement. "As a civil rights activist of the past 40 years, I cannot support a show that disrespects those beliefs and practices."

Matt Stone, naturally, saw Hayes's motives a little differently.

"This has nothing to do with intolerance and bigotry and everything to do with the fact that Isaac Hayes is a Scientologist and that we recently featured Scientology in an episode of *South Park*. In ten years and more than 150 episodes, Isaac never had a problem with the show making fun of Christians, Muslims, Mormons, and Jews. He got a sudden case of religious sensitivity when it was his religion featured on the show. To bring the civil rights struggle into this is just a non sequitur. Of course, we will release Isaac from his contract and we wish him well."

Indeed, as the *British Guardian* newspaper put it, "Criticising the hit US television series *South Park* for being offensive is a bit like criticising *Antiques Roadshow* for focusing too much on old things."

The entire affair was muddied further by the knowledge that Hayes had proved such a staunch supporter of the show, and its intentions, back in the censorial aftermath of the *Bigger, Longer & Uncut* movie. "If we give in to [censorship] and allow [entertainment] to become a scapegoat, you might wind up living in who-knows-what kind of state . . . . If you believe in [your artistic vision] and you've got a moral conviction, take it to 'em!"

And muddied even further when another statement from the Hayes camp denied that the first one had even been issued with his permission, and that "Trapped in the Closet" had nothing whatsoever to do with his departure.

Fox News reported, "Isaac Hayes did not quit *South Park*. My sources say that someone quit it for him. Friends in Memphis tell me that Hayes did not issue any statements on his own about *South Park*. They are mystified." And a year on, Hayes himself told the *New York Post* that he left over money. "They [Parker and Stone] didn't pay me enough . . . . They weren't that nice."

Whatever the reality, Hayes's decision left the show facing one of the most serious creative dilemmas in its entire history. How best to say goodbye to a character who had been as much a part of *South Park*'s success as any of its leading preteens?

Stone explained to the *New York Times*, "We always had a really good relationship with Isaac. He was a really sweet guy. We were sitting there one day, trying to figure out what to do, and what another episode could be. 'We should do a show on Scientology.' 'Well, maybe we shouldn't because of Isaac.' And it was like, you know what, [forget] that, we've done everything else. My mom is Jewish, we've certainly done our share of making fun of Jews. It just didn't feel totally honest not to do it because of that.

"We thought Isaac would understand or be like, 'Oh, I didn't like that one, but whatever, that's your prerogative.' And we'll never know, but it seemed like he was getting pressure from other people around him. The little bit that we knew Isaac, he was a really mellow, cool guy. I don't think he really cared that much. I don't think he wanted to be in the middle of it."

Well now he was. And again, the question hung unanswered. How to handle his departure?

It had to be done sensitively. With calm and grace. It could not be seen as petty, bratty, or gratuitous. Chef should depart with the same majesty as he had lived.

Who are we trying to kid?

"The Return of Chef" opened season ten with a "previously on *South Park*" flashback that had, in fact, not previously been shown in any guise: Chef bidding adieu to his young friends as he sets off to join the Super Adventure Club, an organization that indeed promises its members the super adventures of a lifetime. He returned months later, but it was clear to all that he had changed. His voice seemed higher. His attitudes less wise. His sexuality more . . . bizarre.

Once, years before, Cartman had alarmed friends and guardians alike by joining NAMBLA, sensing in its exclusively male, adult membership a level of maturity and sophistication that he would not find among his companions.

Okay, so some of the members with whom Cartman consorted online were a little strange. One even boasted about being "eight and a half inches," as if his newfound cyber-friend could ever be impressed by such dwarfish stature. Still, Cartman was content. At no point did it strike him as even remotely strange, let alone inappropriate, that so many adult men should want to become close friends with an eight-year-old boy.

Nor did he sense anything at all sinister about the organization's full title, the North American Man/Boy Love Association. (Not to be confused with the North American Marlon Brando Look-alike Association, although it is a very easy mistake to make, as Mr. Garrison discovered.)

Chef had not joined NAMBLA. But the Super Adventure Club was scarcely different in its aims, and Chef, brainwashed though he certainly was, had taken to their teachings with a passion. Hypnosis offered a temporary respite from the strange sensations and urges that now coursed through his mind, but the Super Adventure Club has never given up one of its own without a fight. And so set the stage for one of the most remarkable, protracted, and ultimately, beautifully, spitefully deaths in television history, as Chef was:

- Struck by lightning . . .
- Set on fire . . .
- Thrown, still blazing, from a vertiginous bridge . . .
- Dashed against the rock walls of a steep ravine . . .
- Impaled on a tree branch . . .
- Attacked by a mountain lion . . .
- And a grizzly bear . . .
- Shot . . .
- And torn to shreds . . . .

Watching in horror with the rest of the gang, Cartman could offer just one slender ray of hope. Chef might still be alive because "the last thing you do before you die is crap your pants."

Chef duly crapped his pants.

Chef was dead. Or was he? Unseen by any of the former friends and colleagues who mourned his passing back in South Park, the Super Adventure Club were not so fast to say goodbye.

Inspired, no doubt, by a similar scene in the latest *Star Wars* movie, *Revenge of the Sith*, the club constructed a survival suit that could reanimate the battered, lifeless body and recreate all of the perversions of which they had ever dreamed. As this new Chef made clear with his very first words.

William P. Connelly, the leader of the Super Adventure Club, spoke first, simply asking the newly reanimated Chef to say something, anything.

"Hello there, children. How would you like some Salisbury steak?"

The procedure had worked! "Yes," slathered Connelly excitedly. "Go on!"

Chef's South Park Songbook

"I'm Gonna Make Love to You Woman"
"Oh Kathie Lee"
"Hot Lava"
"Loving the Football"
"Love Gravy"
"Pig and Elephant DNA Just Won't Splice"
"Make Love Even When I'm Dead"
"Christmas Lovin'"
"No Substitute"
"We're All Special"
"Waitin' on a Woman"
"Dodgeball Song"
"Chocolate Salty Balls"
"Love Bug"
"The Morning After" (duet with Veronica)
"What the Hell Child Is This?"
"The Menstrual Cycle Song"
"I Can't Wait Until I Grow Up"
"The Prostitute Song" (duet with James Taylor)
"Sometimes You Kill Your Teacher"

"And for dessert," Chef continued, "how would you children like to suck on my chocolate salty balls?"

Connelly adopted a child's voice. "Oh, you mean like a chocolate candy?"

"No," replied the dark and sinister voice behind the mask. "I mean my balls."

14

Sport and *South Park*

What's This Load of Balls About?

For as long as humankind has played sports, it has suffered sports-related injuries. Indeed, some sports were specifically designed to cause pain and suffering, and if boxing remains the last frontier in that respect, still the avid historian can look back on such merry pastimes as gladiatorial contests, Christians and lions, and Morris dancing and barely suppress a shudder of vicarious glee. All that blood. All that gore. It's better than a night spent watching Geraldo reruns.

Even among the sports that are considered more or less modern inventions, history can track back to a time before the rules were homogenized and codified, and thrill at the notions of, for example, medieval football, the parent from which American football, Australian Rules, rugby, and soccer all sprang.

Some researchers claim the game originated in China, where the severed heads of decapitated enemies were used as balls. Others credit the English, celebrating a victory over the Vikings by, again, separating heads from the bodies of the fallen and then hoofing them around a field. The winner, naturally, being the team who managed to kick the most heads into the goal mouth.

It was an energetic pastime, and a ball-breaking one as well. Even after human heads were replaced by more conventional spheres (pig bladders were a favorite), the game certainly had no problem with either high spirits or mean spirits. Boisterous competitors, roughly arranged in teams of more or less equal numbers but not at all limited in what those numbers might be, would kick, punch, bite, and gouge their way across playing fields that could stretch from one town to another, resulting in injuries that would make even the most bloodthirsty modern spectator wince.

Finally, in the year 1365, King Edward III banned Londoners from indulging in the pastime outright, declaring "there is great noise in the city caused by hustling over large balls from which many evils may arise which God forbid; we command and forbid, on behalf of the King, on pain of imprisonment, such game to be used in the city in the future."

Those evils naturally included injury and death.

Slowly, the game pulled itself together; slowly, some of the more outlandish methods of subduing an opponent were outlawed, and, by the late nineteenth century, the roots of the various games that are today called football (rugby, soccer, Aussie Rules, Gaelic, gridiron, and more) had taken recognizable shape.

Pain remained a key component of them all, however. Sometimes it's an accident. Sometimes it's deliberate. Sometimes it's a tactical necessity. But it was not until the early 1990s that medical research began taking a serious look at the kind of long-term damage being done to our sportsmen, often in the form of debilitating brain injuries induced by the succession of concussions that had hitherto been considered a vital and harmless component of many of the sports.

Indeed, a report on PBS's *Frontline* in late 2013 revealed that, of forty-plus former NFL players whose brains had been examined (postmortem) by researchers, all but one showed signs of chronic traumatic encephalopathy. A condition best developed by being repeatedly, over a period of years, hit very hard on the head.

The NFL's own research went even further, to reveal that former players were nineteen times more likely to develop Alzheimer's and similar disorders than the general populace. Oddly, the NFL then disowned these findings, but the genie was out of the bottle.

Every time another especially garish or gruesome wound was broadcast live on national television; every time another former sports star shuffled forward to mumblingly explain how a lifetime spent being hit on the head had not had any ill effects on his what-was-the-question-again, so the hue and indeed the cry went up.

Make sports safer.

So the NFL did. In March 2011, teams voted to move kickoffs from the thirty to the thirty-five yard line and prohibit a running head start of more than five yards for members of the coverage team. A key element, it was said, in the drive to reduce the potential for brain damage.

Other authorities went even further, however, as Randy Marsh discovered as he sat watching the Broncos with his son and his friends on TV one evening, and pointed out a particularly punishing play to the boys. They looked at him blankly. They weren't allowed to play kickoffs any longer. The school had decided they weren't safe.

Randy was . . . perplexed might be a nice way of putting it . . . to discover this, although there was, and is, a certain truth to the insistence that the kickoff is the most dangerous play in the game. At least inasmuch as it is the moment when you are most likely to watch players collapse like nine pins, heads cracking back, faces contorted with pain, and all accompanied by a sound that CBS Sports' Mike Freeman once compared to "large trees snapping in half. Except those are the skulls of humans making contact at high speeds."

The notion of eliminating the play even from pro ball was already floating around, with NFL commissioner Roger Goodell one of the forces lining up on the side of the abolitionists. Such a change would change the face of football as we know it, of course. But better that, argued the measure's supporters, than changing the brains of the players on an equally permanent basis.

Randy Marsh did not lose his temper. He did not rant, rage, and rave. Well, he did a little. But then, cool, calm control took over, and when he stood up at the next PTA meeting to voice his concerns about the partial emasculation of the greatest game on Earth, he eschewed anger, eschewed argument. He resorted instead to sarcasm. He was in a room full of intelligent adults, after all.

"Yeah, I'd like to talk about this genius new rule in the football program about no kickoffs?"

Mr. Mackey responds. "Uh, yes, we've decided to go without kickoffs because of the concerns raised over concussions, m'kay?"

"Oh yeah," Randy agreed. "We don't want our kids getting hurt playing football! But I think I have a way to make it even better! Why don't we have the players just wear bras? Yeah, the players should all wear bras! And instead of helmets, they should wear little tinfoil hats, 'cause, you know, it's the future and we shouldn't be so barbaric!"

Clearly, he was making it up as he went along. Equally clearly, his every word was dripping with sarcasm. But to his astonishment and horror, nobody seemed to realize that. Instead, he was asked how bras and silver hats would make the game safer.

Well . . . "we'll have a balloon instead of a ball, and whoever catches the balloon tries to run while all the other players hug!" And when he is asked, by the utterly credulous Mr. Mackey, whether the students would enjoy such a game, Randy can control himself no longer.

"Oh they'd love it! A sport where safety is all that matters? How about we call it 'sarcastaball'?"

A new game is born. A new national pastime. Sarcastaball swept the country. Randy was elected coach of the Broncos, and while a handful of voices were raised in protest, they too resorted to sarcasm as a means of making their points. So when Randy was invited one evening to appear on the CBS Sports Network, it was the easiest thing in the world to believe the host as he adopted his camera-best rictus grin and squeezed the words out like a constipated duck.

"We're gonna talk some sarcastaball. I can't wait. I can't wait to talk sarcastaball because it's really compelling. . . . it certainly makes for an exciting game. How about last night's nail-biter that ended zero to zero? That's a game I wanna watch twice. That's a game I wanna watch four times. Check that: I'll watch that game . . . five times . . . ."

Nobody can bring themselves to drop the demeanor; nobody, beyond the occasional dissenting voice back at South Park Elementary, is willing to admit that sarcastaball is quite possibly the lamest sport ever invented— and even they are suppressed when confronted by the game's most volatile cheerleader, young Butters.

A failure at every other sport he has attempted, Butters finds himself a budding sarcastaball superstar, his natural naïveté and niceness permitting him not only to utterly comprehend the game but to embrace its every tenet as well. In fact, if it wasn't for the fact that he credits his entire sarcastaball talent to the regular ingestion of his own sperm, the entire affair might well have ended with Butters triumphing over all the odds that normally assail him.

Unfortunately, he didn't actually realize it was sperm. He thought it was a magical energy drink that he just happened to be able to produce at night. And so he started marketing it to the sarcastaball community, and it was only when the secret ingredient was finally unmasked . . . an event that coincided neatly with Sharon Marsh finally tiring of her husband's now-perpetual sarcasm . . . that sarcastaball was unveiled for what it is.

A really stupid idea, adopted by a really stupid society that, with mind-numbing regularity, refuses to realize that sport, like every other ingrained facet of modern culture, already possesses sufficient safeguards to eliminate pain, suffering, injury, and loss from its remit. What is lacking is the backbone to actually enforce the laws and rules that already exist, as opposed to creating new ones to remedy freshly minted misinterpretations.

New laws rarely remedy old problems. They simply wallpaper over them with another lay of feel-good bureaucratic bungling. And new sports will never replace the ones we already love, because . . . well, because they won't.

Sport is an essential part of life in South Park. The surrounding Rocky Mountains offer some of the most beautiful and popular skiing in America, with the playboy's paradise of Aspen just a short drive away. Ziplining, NASCAR racing, peewee hockey, an all-conquering baseball team, the Pinewood Derby, physical fitness, and WWE wrestling have all enjoyed their day in the broiling sun of South Park fun and fantasy, and if the results of the locals' enthusiasm do occasionally slip away from the essentials of the event itself, then that is how sports evolve. Yes, even wrestling.

Still, controversy rages. Even confirmed atheists found it difficult to suppress a shudder of existential angst when Eric Cartman's birthday party was hijacked as the venue for a "winner takes all" pay-per-view prize-fight between Jesus Christ and Satan, the now legendary "Boutin' at the Mountain."

Neither has South Park been spared that one seemingly ineradicable blot on the sporting landscape, the heinous sin of doping.

Performance-enhancing drugs, like mindless violent, hideous injury and fans who insist on taking their shirts off on bitterly cold afternoons, have been a part of the sporting landscape for as long as competitive sports have been played.

Thousands of years before Lance Armstrong denied ever pumping himself up with sundry substances and cycling his way to glory, ancient herbalists were identifying the most beneficial properties of sundry bushes, shrubs, and weeds, and concocting potions that could help an athlete run faster, throw further, hit harder, jump higher.

The Olympics of classical Greece were a cornucopia of magic potions, herbs, and preparations. Sheep testicles, it was believed, enhanced testosterone. Wine infused with a touch of strychnine was a primitive stimulant. Imperial Roman gladiators would chow down on anything if they believed it would give them an edge over their opponents, and as we march into the modern era, we learn of the first recorded death from performance-enhancing drugs—a Welsh cyclist at the 1896 Paris-Bordeaux race, who perished from an overdose of trimethyl. Perhaps he should have stuck with the smack and coke speedballs that his competitors were sucking down.

German athletes allegedly devoured nitroglycerine at the 1936 Olympics; later in that same decade, the English soccer team Wolverhampton Wanderers were regularly injected with monkey glands in the belief that the treatment would improve their confidence and stamina. And so on, until a whole new competitive sport had been created, the battle between the sports authorities and their pharmaceutical opposites to keep ahead of one another's latest innovations.

Today's sportsman is best advised to avoid even the most basic household headache remedy for fear that nestled secretly somewhere within its ingredients is one of those dreaded banned substances. Today's drug tester, on the other hand, needs to know of every potion cooking in the basements of the world.

None of which was enough to deter Jimmy Valmer from adopting a steroid regime as he prepared for the Special Olympics in 2004, and he was simply fortunate that he had such a great friend in Eric Cartman, who feigned his own handicaps as a way of teaching Jimmy the error of his ways. Or so he said afterwards. More likely, the fat bastard was simply trying to cheat his way toward the $1,000 prize that waited at the end of the athletic rainbow.

Indeed, Cartman has little compunction about using either underhand methods or under-the-counter drugs as a means of advancing his personal quest for riches and glory.

Who but Cartman, after all, could have conceived the Crack Baby Athletic Association? He truly believed (and, sadly, he is probably correct) that a sport in which born-addicted babies battle one another for a ball of crack could scarcely fail.

Despite appearances, however, South Park's junior sporting community is not utterly devoid of morality or compassion. When PETA contacted South Park Elementary to complain about the school's use of a live and clearly terrified cow as mascot, the students were swift to step up to the plate and happily contemplate the authorities' suggestions for a replacement mascot.

Contemplate, but not concur with.

Dismissing their elders' choices, the children found themselves divided between just two potentials, a giant douche or a turd sandwich. Which, as a PETA activist informed Stan (shortly before the entire PETA compound was mysteriously murdered, thus allowing the cow to return to its lofty position unopposed), is the way of all elections.

"It's always between a giant douche and a turd sandwich. Nearly every election since the beginning of time has been between some douche and some turd. They're the only people who suck up enough to make it that far in politics."

Which is a point with which even the most devoted sarcastaball enthusiast could not disagree.

15

The *South Park* Songbook

For Little Kids and Grown-Ups Too

"Firstly, we consider ourselves a rock band because that's the coolest thing. Then we like to say that we're writers and we're storytellers because there definitely is a power to that: 'Star Wars' has done just about as much for mythology as a lot of the religions have."

—Trey Parker

It's not exactly sixties heartthrob Engelbert Humperdinck intoning "Lesbian Seagull" over the closing credits to *Beavis and Butt-Head Do America*. But from the moment Cartman, under alien control, launched into a rousing chorus of "I Love to Singa" (a song first heard in a 1936 Tex Avery cartoon), music has been of paramount importance to the inhabitants of South Park.

It has soothed souls, molded minds, influenced ideas, and changed entire situations. It has made people laugh, cry, and turn away in disgust. It has encouraged some of the biggest superstars in popular entertainment to visit South Park. And, of course, it has made us smile.

"We've had musical stuff in the show forever," Stone told Pitchfork. "That's mostly because Trey's a big musical fan, and he's a great songwriter. He's been writing songs his whole life. So, since the beginning, we've always put a lot of musical moments."

Moments such as "Ding Dong They Caught Saddam." Hot hits like "The Biggest Douche in the Universe." Tender (if, in these dark days, increasingly contentious) toe-tappers like "Sometimes You Kill Your Teacher." And before you shrug and write them off as just one more branch of a novelty rock 'n' roll family tree that reaches back through Spinal Tap, Weird Al Yancovic, the Heebeegeebees, the Rutles, and the Bonzo Dog Band, we should allow Stone to continue.

"Probably the best one from the early years, one good enough to be in a real musical, was 'The Lonely Jew on Christmas.' Trey can write songs you can't dismiss out of hand, [and this] wasn't a spoof. It was a real song about a real little kid, and it just had a great concept. That was one of those early songs that pointed out to us that, 'Oh, wow, there can actually be quality songs on this kind of show.'

"It's a really touching song, and I kind of know how it was because I was a Jewish boy growing up in Colorado."

And that is the secret of a great parody. The song needs to stand on its own two feet as well as those whose shoes inspired it in the first place.

Working closely with Parker and Stone in the musical department, Adam Barrett Berry completed the triumvirate of talent that lay behind the original *South Park* sound. Born in 1966, he was at the very dawn of his career when he joined the *South Park* team in 1997, yet his work as both composer, setting Parker's lyrics to music, and performer would become as integral to the show's early identity as any other component.

Berry departed *South Park* in 2000, after sixty-five episodes; Jamie Dunlap and Scott Nickoley of the Los Angeles-based Mad City Production Studios succeeded him; Dunlap alone has handled the scores since 2008, and is one of the very few members of the team not to be working out of the show's own production offices.

But these are not the sole musicians to have soundtracked the show. Parker and Stone, together with staff members Bruce Howell and D. A. Young, were also regularly heard, in the guise of their own band DVDA. A name that might hijack the familiar term for an audio-only DVD disc, such as high-end audio buffs love to enthuse about. But it might also (and this is the correct answer) redeploy an abbreviation that is popular in the world of pornography, "double vaginal, double anal."

The best of DVDA's work fell into the realm of musical satire, taking an otherwise familiar song and twisting it into something new, yet still recognizable. Which itself is a talent that precious few writers and musicians are capable of pulling off. But the band was not simply a studio concern. Throughout their lifetime, DVDA gigged regularly around Los Angeles, and have played shows with those other masters of musical chicanery Ween and Primus. And therein lies a neat deviation.

Primus was the first band ever heard on *South Park*, performers of the show's so distinctively written and arranged theme tune, and no matter what else may have changed about the show in the years since then, that theme remains inviolate.

Bassist and vocalist Les Claypool and guitarist Tod Huth launched Primate, the band that would become Primus, in 1984 in their hometown of El Sobrante, California. Their early work saw the basic duo joined by a drum machine—largely because it was the first percussionist they met that did not complain about the already bizarre hybrid of funk, metal, and Frank Zappa-ish disregard that the duo intended making.

The return from the army of one of Claypool's old friends, Vince Parker; saw the machine packed away; and Primate recorded their first demos shortly after. Barely had the music dried on the tape, however, than disaster struck in the form of another band, called the Primates, who threatened all manner of dire legal retribution unless Primate changed their name.

The trio agreed, becoming Primus and celebrating by spending the next four years going through drummers at an almost Spinal Tappish rate. Neither local stardom nor the recording of a second demo could glue anybody to the drum seat for long, and when Tod Huth, too, quit—leaving Claypole alone to carry the Primus flag—it looked as though the band was at an end.

Claypole rejoined a band he had played with earlier in the 1980s, Blind Illusion, but he continued scheming future Primus sounds, in the company of Blind Illusion's guitarist Larry LaLonde and drummer Tim Alexander. The old band re-formed; a handful of live shows followed; and within a month, Primus were preparing, at last, to release their debut album, recorded live at a couple of shows in Berkeley.

Suck on This announced the band to the world of alternative rock; *Frizzle Fry* began hitting people over the head. In 1990, a tour with Jane's Addiction, then at the height of their wacked experimentalism, saw Primus nightly out-weird the headliners, a trio that made enough noise for a small army, and seriously did not appear to give a cuss for any musical conventions beyond their own.

That same year brought a deal with the Interscope label and the album *Sailing the Seas of Cheese*. MTV picked up on the first in a succession of Primus videos that were at least as distinctive as the band's music; Hollywood snagged them to appear in *Bill and Ted's Bogus Journey*; and suddenly innocent bystanders at a host of major concerts . . . fans of Rush, Public Enemy, Anthrax, and U2 among them . . . found themselves exposed to Primus before the headliners took the stage.

They scored a hit with a cover of XTC's "Making Plans for Nigel"; haunted dreams with the video for "Mr. Krinkel," Claypole in a

The journey ... not as excellent as the adventure, but not as bogus as many sequels.

tuxedo'd pig costume, playing upright bass before a carnival freak show; toured for two years and tasted the Billboard Top Ten with their 1993 album *Pork Soda*.

They headlined Lollapalooza and played at Woodstock '94, the twenty-fifth anniversary of the legendary hippie-fest where Stan Marsh's parents once claimed to have met. A new album, *Tales from the Punchbowl*, was as spectacular as those that preceded it ... and then, one day, Claypole's phone rang.

Claypole explained, "Matt and Trey were big Primus fans, and they called our office and asked us to do a theme song for the pilot of a show they were doing for Comedy Central. They sent us the original script for [*Spirit of Christmas*] and we were impressed."

In all honesty, he confessed, nobody could see the scheme going anywhere, "We didn't think they would be able to pull it off because we've seen the original and people who've seen the original know . . . . we didn't think they'd be able to water it down enough and have it still be effective. But obviously they did."

"I was a humongous Primus fan in college," Stone explained. "I went to see them every time they went to Colorado and thought they were great." Primus were the only artists considered as he and Parker began scheming the *South Park* theme tune, writing to the management company named on the sleeve of one of the band's albums, and adding a VHS copy of *The Spirit of Christmas.*"

"We said, 'We're doing a pilot for Comedy Central, and we'd love for you to do the song.' Two or three weeks later, I get this call. We're in the office, cutting out our stupid little construction paper and trying to do the show, and I get this call. It was like, 'Matt, Les Claypool's on line one.'

"He was my hero at the time. I was so into the guy. And he was on the phone like, 'What are you guys looking for? What do you guys need?' He was looking for some direction, and my direction was idiotic. It was like, 'Oh just do whatever you want to do, do whatever you want to do. It's a small town in Colorado.' That's about how much I gave him. And he came back with that song . . . such a perfect encapsulation of *South Park.*"

The theme was approved; Claypole was thanked with an appearance in the opening credits themselves, walking through the town playing his guitar, clad in a red long-sleeved shirt, blue jeans, purple socks, blue shoes, white hat, and shades. And Primus would become a part of the *South Park* mythos forever more, appearing at Chef Aid; releasing a record titled after everyone's favorite store on Main Street, Rhinoplasty; and, no matter how often the show's opening moments may be remixed and reenvisioned, Claypole remains the voice of reason around which the other characters squeak, squawk, and sing their own lyrics: Cartman's celebration of ample parking and welcoming neighbors; Stan and Kyle's warm embrace of friendliness and kindness; and Kenny's heartwarming declaration, "I like girls with big, fat titties, I like girls with big vaginas."

It was Kenny who, perhaps most surprisingly of all the boys, first demonstrated his musical talents when he picked up a copy of the best-selling paperback *Learn to Sing like Bocelli for Dummies* and accomplished precisely what it says on the cover.

His rendition of "Con Te Partiro" may or may not have been the most conventional ever performed, but it was certainly sufficient to establish him as one of Romania's biggest singing sensations ... at least until he was forcibly deported during a US raid and accidentally shot by one of the agents.

Once unleashed, however, the musical prodigies of *South Park* exploded into prominence, led—again surprisingly—by Timmy, a tragically handicapped child who had just been transferred to South Park and placed in Mr. Garrison's class.

There, despite the apparent disadvantages of the rest of his condition, he was diagnosed as suffering from ADD and loaded up with Ritalin—a chemical substitute for what Chef maintains has always been the most effective treatment for rowdy kids, a program called "You Can Either Calm Down or I Can Pop You in the Mouth Again."

Which may or may not be what transformed this hitherto mild-mannered, if severely disadvantaged, wheelchair-bound youth into the wild beast who auditioned for, and was accepted into, the Lords of the Underworld, a South Park garage band who were about to undertake the greatest challenge of their career so far.

Led by guitarist Skyler (Shelley Marsh's ex-boyfriend, gossip fans!), backed by his friends Jonesy and Mark, the Lords of the Underworld had already been through the mill, breaking up once as they tired of slamming their heads against the walls of commercial indifference, but re-forming when a local Battle of the Bands competition threatened to give them a real shot at the big time. The first prize was the opening support slot at the (imaginary) music festival Lalapalozoda.

They won the battle. They won the hearts of America. By the time the festival rolled around, Timmy and the Lords of the Underworld were so huge that the scheduled bill-topper, named for and strangely resembling Phil Collins, had no alternative but to accept that they were even more popular than him and allow them to replace him as headliner.

Well, we say he had no alternative. But, of course, he did. Indeed, he had no difficulty whatsoever in planting the seeds of jealousy among the Lords.

The band shattered in backbiting disarray and "Phil Collins" was restored to his rightful role as headliner, performing such monster hits as "Boo-Bodio" and "You'll Be in Me" before an audience that was so zonked out on Ritalin that they actually enjoyed the show. Or at least they were enjoying it right up until Chef managed to spike them all with the antidote to the drug. At which point they all came to their senses, howled Phil offstage, and the Lords spontaneously re-formed to save the day.

The Lords of the Underground were not South Park's only local band. Just weeks later, Kyle, Cartman, Kenny, and Stan were convinced—by an especially realistic dream of Cartman's—to form a boy band, Fingerbang. But a boy band with a twist. Wendy was also a member, on account of being the only one among them who could actually sing.

It was always going to be a fraught exercise. Randy Marsh, Stan's father, had his own flirtation with boy band fame back in the early 1990s, as a member of the Ghetto Avenue Boys. But he also flirted with disaster, too, as the entire edifice shattered in his face.

Taking Fingerbang to one side, he recalled how the fame of such outings is fleeting; warns that once the screaming stops, life becomes an empty facade.

But the boys (and girl) cannot be dissuaded. It was the age, after all, of 98 Degrees, 'N Sync, Take That, and the Backstreet Boys, so many utterly unique and easily distinguishable talents whose sweet sounds and sharp moves seemed to be dominating the pop charts throughout the Western world.

Nothing, the children were convinced, could prevent Fingerbang from conquering the universe.

Hiring Timmy as cameraman, Fingerbang shot a video and landed a gig at the South Park Mall. And when Kenny was accidentally killed in an unexpected escalator-related incident, Randy Marsh shook away his own years of denial and horror to step into the breach and perform with the kids.

All to no avail. Cartman's dream insisted that God had promised him $10 million if he formed a boy band. Once the show is over and the proceeds are counted up, Fingerbang found themselves precisely $9,999,998 short of the magic total.

The band broke up in despair and disarray. But Cartman would never stop dreaming of that $10 million, and soon a new musical sensation loomed high. Christian rock.

The disappointments of Fingerbang were locked securely away in the past, now. The boys had a new group called Moop, an adventurous fusion of hip-hop, R&B, and Latin jazz that Randy Marsh has already dubbed the sound of "a group of Vietnamese people having their intestines pulled through their mouths."

Into that frantic potpourri of rhythm and expression Cartman believed a new ingredient should be introduced. His love of God. Or, more accurately, his love of the riches that will undoubtedly accrue if Moop would only sing impassioned songs of praise.

Outraged at the suggestion, his bandmates disagreed. Cartman was out of the band, but not before laying a wager. He bet Kyle that the new group he intended to form, Faith + 1, would be awarded a platinum disc for record sales before the remains of Moop achieved the same lofty status. The stakes—ten dollars.

He was not simply blowing hot air, either. With Butters on drums and Token playing a bass, he found in the family basement, Faith + 1 had an apparently foolproof plan. While Cartman's erstwhile bandmates struggled to discover inspiration from the music they were downloading from the Internet (which would inevitably lead to a whole new heaping of hurt), Cartman simply took songs that had already been written, soft and successful love songs, and changed the lyrics to match his new cause.

The result—a number one album for Faith + 1, their popularity no doubt aided by a wildcat strike announced by the rest of the music industry, performer after performer downing tools until fans learned to join them in the fight against the cancer of downloading.

Faith + 1 appeared to have won the wager. The hits spun off the album: "I Found Jesus (With Someone Else)," "Savior Self," "Christ, What a Day," "Three Times My Savior." "I Wasn't Born Again Yesterday," "Pleasing Jesus," "Jesus (Looks Kinda Hot)."

A million records were sold. All that remained was for the band to receive the commemorative disc. At which point, Cartman's entire plan went awry. Christian record labels, it appears, only hand out gold, frank-incense, and myrrh records. There is no platinum in their awards system. There is no platinum disc.

Cartman lost it. He cursed the Lord, he cursed his bandmates. Token beat him to a pulp, Butters farted in his face. His humiliation was complete.

Or was it?

16

Is This the Greatest Show on Earth?

The Terrance and Philip Story

"If South Park had been cynical the whole time, it would not have lasted this long."

—Trey Parker

Terrance and Phillip are the finest, funniest comedians the world has ever known.

Born in Montréal on November 12, 1959, the suave blond Sir Phillip Niles Argyle began working with Toronto native Sir Terrance Henry Stoot (born January 18, 1959) while the pair were still young children, before graduating to their own prime-time television show, sensibly titled *The Terrance and Phillip Show.*

They are Canadian, blessed with the physical attributes that apparently characterize all Canadians. Or at least all Canadians in South Park. Small beady eyes, geometrically shaped bodies, and cute little egg-shaped heads, bisected at the mouth, that move up and down when they speak.

Characterized by a brand of high-brow, almost existentialist humor so advanced that the duo's critics frequently admonish them for working far above the heads of the majority of their audience, *The Terrance and Phillip Show* was in fact born of a happy accident.

Appearing with their original variety act on America's *Ed Sullivan Show* at the age of six, Phillip accidentally farted. Any embarrassment he may have felt, however, was instantly eliminated by the realization that it was the first thing he had said all evening that the audience understood.

A new career was born from within the resultant miasmic cloud.

Originally broadcast in the US on the Cartoon Central network, but later picked up by their homeland's own Canadian Network, the popularity of *The Terrance and Phillip Show* swiftly spread. In France, they are known as *Terrance et Phillip*; in Germany as *Terrance und Phillip*; and in Italy as *Trombino and Pompadour*, a guise that never fails to raise a smile among those wits who insist on altering it to *Trombare and Pompino*—*Fuck and Blowjob*, as a popular translation software softly puts it.

Everywhere their popularity can be gauged from the availability of a wide range of T&P merchandise, although to television watchdogs in the United States, the names of Terrance and Phillip equate to something else entirely. Of all the evils that a jealous outside world has perpetrated on the hearts and minds of innocent American youth, not one has proven so damaging, so dangerous, and so mindlessly puerile as Terrance and Phillip.

Such cultural clashes are normal, of course. In this instance, however, the resultant hostilities did not merely end in a few bad reviews and the premature cancellation of the show mid-season. This time, it threatened a complete breakdown in cultural relations between the United States and its northerly neighbor. And all this because Trey Parker and Matt Stone had finally had enough of the early critics of *South Park* complaining that the animation, the jokes, and the story lines were childish. To paraphrase those other great Canadians, Bachman-Turner Overdrive, "they hadn't seen nothing yet."

Terrance and Phillip first entered our consciousness just six episodes into *South Park*'s first season, in an episode otherwise concerned with Grandpa Marvin Marsh's 102nd birthday, and the old man's insistence that he'd have been happier if he'd died years before. In fact, he'd do it himself if he wasn't so old.

His mournful ruminations on the joys of suicide were interrupted at eight o'clock. Time for Stan's favorite show, one that Shelley promptly dismissed as "so stupid. That show's . . . for babies." And so, in American eyes, it might have been.

Who else, after all, could find fart jokes funny?

Nonstop fart jokes.

Repetitive fart jokes.

Farty fart jokes.

> Phillip: "Hey Terrance, I think I have to fart."
> Terrance: "Wait, before you do, pull my thumb."
> [Fart].

Or . . .

Terrance: "Hey Phillip, would you like a flower?"
Phillip: "I sure would, Terrance."
Terrance: "Alrighty then, here's a two-lip."
[Fart].

Or even . . .

Mrs. Cartman: "Eric dear? I just got a call from your friend
Kyle's mother. She said that this show is naughty, and might
make you a potty mouth."
Eric Cartman: "That's a bunch of crap! Kyle's mom is a dirty
Jew!"
Mrs. Cartman: "Ohhh, okay hon."

Sheila Broflovski was the loudest of Terrance and Phillip's concerned parental critics. Seriously, she was the loudest. Even when she is speaking softly, the woman has the voice of a distressed foghorn, and when she starts to shout, herds of wildebeest halt what they are doing and turn their heads in stark admiration. And these foulmouthed Canadians raised her voice to whole new levels.

Life's a gas for Canada's favorite fartists.

Not content with calling up all of Kyle's friends' parents to warn them against allowing their kids to watch the broadcast, she also contacted their school and swiftly brought the faculty around to her way of thinking, as well.

"Shows like *Terrance and Phillip*," a stern Mr. Garrison lectured his students, "are what we call 'toilet humor.' They don't expand your minds. You see, children, these kind of shows are senseless, vile trash.

"There's much more to life than two young men farting on each other. And throughout history, there have always been shows that have come and gone that have been very bad, and usually they get taken right off the air.

"You see, you should be spending your time enlightening your minds with more intelligent entertainment."

Of course, the kids ignore such wise counsel; of course, they carry on watching and adoring Terrance and Phillip, the same as they ever did. And so it came to pass that, as Stan, Cartman, and Kenny sat distractedly watching their heroes' latest air-form sculptures, Grandpa Marsh convinced them to hold the rope with which he was intending to hang himself.

Shelley Marsh entered the room, absorbed the scene with a single glance . . . and Terrance and Phillip were headline news, the disgusting Canadian import that drove three innocent third graders to attempt to murder a harmless old man.

That was it for the show. While the head of Cartoon Central attempted to quell mounting public unrest with a carefully worded official statement ("fuck you"), and the network went ahead with the scheduled broadcast of the Terrance and Phillip Thanksgiving Special, ultimately the suits had no choice but to bow to the pressure. The *Terrance and Phillip Show* was taken off the air, and its audience were left to find other diversions. Like breathing gas fumes or smoking crack. Or watching "some of those porno movie things."

Out of which, as the boys might say, we all learned something today.

Television in and of itself is not a bad influence on children. Parents who regard television as a cheap surrogate child minder, on the other hand, are.

Terrance and Phillip were down, but they clearly were not out. National heroes in Canada, they continued their mercurial rise with *Not Without My Anus*, an HBC movie of the week that, naturally, prompted even more complaints as American television preempted the previously scheduled concluding part of the previous season's "Cartman's Mom Is a Dirty Slut" cliffhanger finale in order to screen it. In real life. And people were upset. In real life.

"We thought people would love it," a chastened Parker admitted. "We thought of it as almost a meta-television joke. And people hated it. They were like, 'But who is Cartman's dad?' And we were like, 'Who the fuck gives a shit? He's not real. It's whoever we say it is!' But it was a big lesson that the audience doesn't like a joke on them."

It was April 1998. America's ongoing conflict with Saddam Hussein had settled into an uneasy state of semi-peace, a lull between the twin eruptions of Desert Storm and the post-9/11 assault. The menace of Hussein, however, remained alive for many people, and *Not Without My Anus* reached deep into the tremulous heart of that menace by portraying what might happen were Hussein's Iraqis to rise up and march against . . . Canada.

The movie opened with the last days of a highly publicized murder trial, Terrance standing accused of the heinous slaying of one Dr. Jeffrey O'Dwyer.

The evidence against him was impressive: hair fibers, blood samples, nail clippings, a piece of his shirt, a watch bearing his initials on it, a day planner on which the murder had been scheduled, and a haiku, in Terrance's handwriting, titled "Time to Kill Dr. Jeffrey O'Dwyer."

But the evidence stood no chance against Terrance's defense counsel, Phillip.

Armed with a wealth of contradictory material, including photographs of Terrance feeding llamas at the zoo and the fact that he would kill anyone who found him guilty, Phillip succeeded in winning a verdict of not guilty. And while onlookers wonder whether Terrance really had, as he put it, been saved from "the gas chamber," the pair headed home, apparently unconcerned about the entire affair.

It was not Terrance's first brush with capital crime, after all. In fact, the public prosecutor, a fierce lawyer named Scott the Dick, apparently charged him with a fresh murder every week.

Why? Could it be because he was jealous of Terrance's celebrity status, one of the two funniest men in Canada (and, therefore, the universe); one-time lover of beloved songstress "Celine Dion"; father of the adorable daughter Sally . . . .

Could it be because he didn't find fart jokes amusing?

Or could it simply be because he was a dick?

The two comedians are still mulling these questions when they learn the worst. Sally has been kidnapped and taken to Iran.

In a scene that could have been (and, in truth, was) borrowed straight out of Sally Field's 1991 motion picture *Not Without My Daughter*, in which her daughter is kidnapped and taken to Iran, Terrance and Phillip fly to Tehran . . . find Sally and bring her home. Only to learn that the whole thing was a diversion set up by Scott the Dick and, while they were out of the country, his newly acquired ally Saddam Hussein had invaded Canada. And, worse still, was about to force "Celine Dion" to sing the Iraqi national anthem before a CFL game between the Ottawa Rough Riders and the Vancouver Rough Riders.

Terrance and Phillip thought fast. There was one way of saving the day, of liberating Canada, of freeing "Celine." If everybody in the sports stadium should fart simultaneously, the gas might overcome the evil dictator and his fiendish henchmen.

Might?

No, it would! It did! Canada was free, "Celine" was free, and the movie ended, so heartwarmingly, with her leading the entire stadium . . . nay, the entire country . . . through a rousing rendition of "O Canada."

Not Without My Anus vindicated Terrance and Phillip in the eye of the American public. The uplifting message (up-lifting, not shirt-lifting), the triumph over evil, the affirmation of a shared foreign enemy, all of these things reminded the country that while Americans and Canadians will never be the same, underneath they will always be familiar. Some people even acknowledged that yes, even in the United States, farts can sometimes be funny.

Plus, the duo also used the movie to demonstrate to the stateside public that America's own television really wasn't much of an improvement. Scenes from what may have been Jerry Springer and what was certainly *South Park* played out on the duo's television screen, and Phillip surely spoke for many when he uttered, in absolute disbelief, "god damn, their TV shows are lame."

Restored to American cable, Terrance and Phillip's legendary "ass doctor" sketch brought them further fame as Terrance, playing the eponymous doctor, tried to convince Phillip that not only will his recently discovered ass cancer prevent him from farting any more, it will also prevent him from living.

Memorable, too, was their *Halloween Special*, in which the pair dressed up as ghosts and one especially ripe fart was described as "ghoulish." And just a short time later, their *Christmas Special* had millions tuning in to chortle as the duo's festive farts outraged even the hardiest of Santa's reindeer.

The success of the reborn *Terrance and Phillip Show*, however, was not to last. The parents and responsible citizens who opposed it during its original run had not changed their minds about it. When news broke that the pair was preparing to release their first full-length feature film, *Asses of Fire*, it was clear that a whole new line had been drawn in the sand.

17

Seventy-Five Further Celebrities

Just as Poorly Impersonated

1. Meat Loaf—the artist formerly known as couscous, until Chef suggested he think of something a bit meatier.
2. Carlos Mencia—top-rated Comedy Central comic brutally slaughtered by Kanye West.
3. Angela Merkel—the German chancellor joined then-president Christian Wulff in taking over South Park Elementary to protest the school's vote that Germany is the world's least funny country.
4. Cesar Milan—the dog whisperer became a Cartman whisperer.
5. Liza Minnelli—alongside Woman with Crablike Body and Man with Terrible Skin, a leading member of the Freak Union.
6. Alanis Morissette—top performer of "Stinky Britches."
7. Brent Musburger—unlike Patrick Duffy, Brent is only occasionally one of Scuzzlebutt's legs.
8. Randy Newman—humorous singer and satirist who opposes James Cameron in his gallant efforts to raise the bar.
9. Stevie Nicks—oddly, easily mistaken for a goat.
10. Nick Nolte—presented Randy with his Nobel Prize.
11. Elin Nordegren—one of the battling stars of the Tiger Woods EA Sports game.
12. Barack Obama—US President and confessed Tyler Perry fan.
13. Conan O'Brien—late-night talk show host who was complicit in the arrest of Terrance and Phillip.
14. Rosie O'Donnell—having protested the vote for class president in Mr. Garrison's kindergarten class, Rosie loses her life in a confrontation with Cartman's killer trapper keeper.
15. Jamie Oliver—English chef and a behind-the-scenes player in the fried-chicken black market.

16. Yoko Ono—the Beatle widow and performance artist was guest conductor for the Worldwide Recorder Concert in Oklahoma City.

17. Bill O'Reilly—television host whose guests have included "aging hippie liberal douche" and "pissed-off redneck."

18. Ozzy Osbourne—Chef Aid performer whose head-biting victims have included a dove, a bat, and a little boy in an orange anorak.

19. Brad Paisley—country singer who performs a duet of "I Swear" with Cartman.

20. Sarah Palin—level-headed political beauty and cat-burgling member of John McCain's jewel heist team.

21. Sarah Jessica Parker—the allegedly hideous heroine of *The Tale of Scrotie McBoogerballs* is led into the woods and disguised as a moose by Cartman and Kenny. They need only supply the antlers.

22. Dr. Phil—daytime TV host who introduces Cartman on his show as the "little boy whose mother constantly tries to fuck him."

23. Edgar Allan Poe—recalled from the grave to assist the Goth and Vamp kids in their battle against the Emos.

24. Sidney Poitier—as a giant turtle with fangs, the *To Sir with Love* star desperately battles the Mecha-Streisand, but is as easily vanquished as Leonard Maltin.

25. Pope John Paul II—aged, wrinkly subordinate to the Queen Spider.

26. Natalie Portman—keeper of the portal.

27. Maury Povich—talk show host.

28. Primus—performers at Chef Aid.

29. Vladimir Putin—Russian leader whose life is plagued by crank calls from George W. Bush.

30. The cast of *Queer Eye for the Straight Guy*—crab people.

31. R. Kelly—the third man in Tom Cruise and John Travolta's closet.

32. Radiohead—Scott Tenorman's favorite band laugh at him when they catch him crying.

33. Jon Benét Ramsey—the murdered child pageant girl star suggests Satan consult God for relationship advice.

34. Jon Benét Ramsey's parents—members of the club for people who have lost someone dear to them, but had absolutely nothing to do with their disappearance.

35. Rancid—punky stars of Chef Aid.

36. The cast of *Real Housewives of New Jersey*—relocate to South Park and generally cause mayhem.

The crab people eye up the straight guys.

38. Robert Redford—despite being saddled with a pockmarked pizza face, Redford brings Sundance to South Park with stinky results. And when DVDA played the "real" film festival, their repertoire included a song called "Robert Redford Fucks Babies."

37. Christopher Reeve—disabled former Superman with a taste for fetus juice.

39. Regis and Kelly —TV hosts whose show features the Queef Sisters.

40. Stella Reid—the star of *Nanny 911* abandons her attempts to modify Cartman's behavior after he suggests that her "uterus is slowly shriveling away, drying up, becoming totally worthless."

41. Rob Reiner—antismoking zealot who, when stabbed with a fork by Cartman, leaks a vile goo.

42. Janet Reno—captures the Romanian quintets by disguising herself as the Easter Bunny.

43. Michael Richard—he and Mark Fuhrman join Randy in petitioning Congress to ban the phrase "nigger guy."

43. Geraldo Rivera—talk show host who invites Cartman onto his show to discuss obesity.

44. Eric Roberts—prior to being eaten by hungry South Parkians, Julia's brother is reduced to reenacting crimes on *America's Most Wanted*.

45. Pat Robertson—prepares a missionary crusade to the planet Marklar as soon as he learns of its existence.

46. Jim Rome—one of a bevy of sports personalities who flock to Randy's sarcastaball dream.

47. Charlie Rose—TV interviewer whose chosen topics include the success of Timmy and the Lords of the Underworld, and why Stan persists in wearing his "What Would Jesus Do?" wristband.

48. Donald Rumsfeld—will support the president no matter what it takes.

49. Kurt Russell—leads the invasion of Imaginationland.

50. Pat Sajak—is genuinely astonished when *Wheel of Fortune* contender Randy Marsh chooses the wrong letter to complete the word "NAGGERS" in the category "People Who Annoy You."

51. Colonel Sanders—a ruthless black-market chicken dealer.

52. Rob Schneider—the star of *The Stapler*. Also the star of *A Carrot*. And also the star of *Da Derp Dee Derp Da Teetley Derpee Derpee Dumb*.

53. Arnold Schwarzenegger—the California governor and former Terminator doesn't care what New Jersey does.

54. Biggie Smalls—say his name three times into a mirror, and he will appear.

55. Robert Smith—crudely lipsticked, shock-headed Gothic moper (and that's in real life) who ultimately destroys the Mecha-Streisand.

56. Sonny and Cher—Terrance and Phillip guest on their show and fart on them.

57. Britney Spears—hapless victim of illegal downloading.

58. Steven Spielberg—George Lucas's partner in unmentionable perversions.

59. Sylvester Stallone—despite being as unintelligible as Kenny, nevertheless invites the City Wok guy's wife, Wing, to sing at his son's wedding.

60. Howard Stern—leads the debate on whether doing stupid and disgusting things on TV makes a person no better than a common prostitute.

61. Martha Stewart—knows how to decorate a queef. Can also eat a turkey ass-first. And that's her ass, not the turkey's. Although that as well. Probably.

62. Rod Stewart—wheelchair-bound and incontinent, the once proudly cockatoo-haired croaker is a special guest at Jesus's comeback concert.

63. Barbra Streisand—having already transformed herself into a giant mechanical dinosaur, Babs was also the terrifying inspiration behind Spooky Vision.

64. Sally Struthers—the well-nourished spokeswoman for starving African children.

63. Ed Sullivan—the first US broadcaster to invite Terrance and Phillip to appear on American television. Aged just six and cute as buttons, they sing a song about chicken and ham.

65. Taylor Swift—originator of the "Taylor Swifting" craze, which involves dragging your bare ass across the floor. Cats with poopy bottoms often do the same thing.

66. Mr. T.—leads the A-Team on a perilous mission to India, to take Mr. Garrison to rehab.

67. John Travolta—having failed in his attempt to lure Tom Cruise out of the closet, the *Greasey Pulp Fever* star instead joins him in there.

68. Lars Ulrich—Metallica pop star who cannot now purchase a gold-plated shark-tank bar thanks to illegal downloading.

69. Van Halen—while Kyle gorges himself on Cartman's farts and pre-serves world peace in the process, Eddie and the boys headline a massive, days-long concert in Jerusalem to celebrate the end of war forever. Or at least until Stan lets on that the ginger cow was not what everyone thinks it was.

70. Kanye West—the one man who does not get the Fishsticks joke. Nor does he appreciate rumors that Kim Kardashian is a hobbit.

71. Grant Wilson—alongside fellow *Ghost Hunters* cast member (and plumber) Jason Haws, Grant visits South Park to investigate reports of the celebrity specters who haunt the Broflovski house.

72. Oprah Winfrey—talk show host who invites Towelie onto her show to talk about his new book. Later she discovers he is a towel, so she has him on again in order to confront him about his lies. A lynch mob rises up to punish him, led by Oprah but opposed by her own heavily armed talking vagina.

73. The cast of *Yo Gabba Gabba!*—adorable Nick Jr. TV characters whose careers are endangered after the pubescent Ike awakens the rainbows-and-unicorns-loving Foofa's fascination with her dark, sexual side.

74. Tina Yothers—judging South Park Elementary's Halloween costume contest, she declares Wendy's Chewbacca outfit the winner.

75. George Zimmerman—he didn't do it. Well he did, but not in the way everyone thought he did.

18

Was It Really Bigger? Longer? Uncut?

South Park—the Movie

Yes it was.

South Park: Bigger, Longer & Uncut is one of those rare movies that wholly lives up to its title. It's a *South Park* movie. It's bigger than the television series, and longer too. And one presumes that it is uncut because, having sat through the barrage of violence and expletives that comprises the vast majority of its airtime, one is hard-pressed to imagine what could possibly have been excised before it reached the movie house.

Yes, it's that good.

The basic facts are easy to relate. An animated musical comedy, *South Park: Bigger, Longer & Uncut* was produced by Trey Parker and Matt Stone, directed by Parker, cowritten by Parker, Stone, and Pam Brady, and scored by Parker and Marc Shaiman with additional lyrics by Stone. It was produced by Paramount Pictures and Warner Bros. in association with Comedy Central. Blah blah. Oh, and it glanced back to two of the show's most important formative influences via the involvement of two very special guests. Mike Judge, the creator of *Beavis and Butt-Head*, was brought in to voice Kenny; and Eric Idle, one-sixth of the original Monty Python team, was recruited as Doctor Vosknocker.

Planning for the movie began in January 1998, while *South Park*'s first season was still underway—a lesson learned from the fate of the *Beavis and Butt-Head* movie, *Beavis and Butt-Head Do America*. Their parent show was three years old by the time its snorting, snickering heroes made the transition to the silver screen, and much of the duo's core audience, not to mention the show's original appeal, had apparently been lost by that time.

For aficionados of the delinquent deadbeats, the movie remained a riotous romp, but public interest had definitely declined. Or so said those industry people who have somehow contrived to get paid for uttering such pronouncements. *Beavis and Butt-Head Do America* made $20 million-plus in its all-conquering opening weekend, and its final gross of $63 million-and-change wasn't a bad return for a film that only cost $12 million to make.

But it could have been more, said those same "do you mean they really get paid to say this stuff" folk, and if you were inclined to take their whittering seriously, maybe there was a lot to be said for making the *South Park* movie at a time when critics and audience alike could scarcely talk of anything else.

Mike Judge, creator of *Beavis & Butthead*, and the voice of the big screen Kenny.

Maybe there was some truth in those pronouncements, too. Parker and Stone were preparing the second season, and it was not going too well ... in fact, Parker later admitted, the writing process was "disastrous." So disastrous that, by the time the movie was ready for release and *South Park* was into its third series, there was mounting cause to believe that they had already waited too long.

In the week the movie was announced to the media, in 1998, the second episode of season two, "Cartman's Mom Is Still a Dirty Slut," earned an 8.2 rating—the highest Nielsen numbers that any basic-cable programming had achieved all year. Admittedly, it was only April, but that still wasn't bad.

Twelve months later, when the movie emerged, it was a very different picture. Ratings for the third series, which launched on April 7, 1999, were almost 40 percent down on the previous year, and *Entertainment Weekly* was mourning that *South Park* simply wasn't "the pop-culture behemoth it was last year."

Parker shrugged. "Suddenly we suck and we're not cool anymore. The funny thing is, last year we were saying the same things and we were hip, fresh, and cute. Now they're telling us we're pushing thirty, we're failures, and we're sellouts."

The perfect time, then, to release a movie.

Seriously, it was. As Stone reflected in its aftermath, "I think one of my career highs was after the *South Park* movie came out, because before that the trajectory was *South Park* had hit really big, and then we were kind of on the down. We didn't feel that way, but all the press and the outside world was saying, 'Well that was nice but now it's kind of on its way out.' And then the movie came out and it defied expectations and bought us years of legitimacy.

"A lower point was probably just two months before that when we were doing the *South Park* movie and the whole world was like ... The summer movie previews would come out and it was the first *Star Wars*, *Austin Powers 2* and all this great stuff and then it would be the little short ones like documentaries and movies from Iran, and then 'the *South Park* movie. Uggh.' It was hard making a movie under those circumstances."

So what exactly is *South Park: Bigger, Longer & Uncut* about?

No, a word, first, about what it isn't about. It isn't about beauties, beasts, lions, and mermaids, although anybody sitting through the output of the Disney studios of the late 1990s might well have felt a glimmer of recognition.

It is not a Broadway musical, although much of the pacing and several of the songs certainly glance in that direction as well.

It is not, as *Entertainment Weekly* pointed out, even remotely related to "the conventions of Broadway show tunes and, especially, the Disney-formula ditties of Alan Menken." Although it did "brilliantly parody" them.

And it is not a statement on the modern way of life, in America or elsewhere, although in picking up on Sheila Broflovski's opposition to the original *Terrance and Phillip Show*, as seen in the first-season episode, "Death," it does do much to blur the line between reality and the artistic fantasies that society likes to blame for its own private ills.

As Parker explained, "Paramount already wanted to make a *South Park* movie, and we sort of thought [that] episode would make the best model just because we liked the sort of pointing at ourselves kind of thing."

That the movie itself received an R rating (for "pervasive vulgar language and crude sexual humor, and for some violent images") from the Motion Picture Association of America (MPAA) should not be a surprise. The fact that the certificate was not delivered until just two weeks before the movie's June 30, 1999, release, however, perhaps indicates the MPLA's own uncertainty as to the movie's actual purpose.

Was it, as some critics complained, simply an excuse to fire off all the nasty little notions that even cable television is unwilling to air? Was it a brutal indictment of the modern media? Or was it, as Stone told *Entertainment Weekly*, all just a way of really pissing off the MPAA?

"We aren't trying to make a film that offends anybody, except we're trying to offend the MPAA.

"We mention them in sentences like 'You mean the MPAA is ineffective?' We're spending tons of Paramount's money to do a big middle finger to the MPAA."

Not that he wholly disagreed with the organization itself. When anti-smoking crusader Rob Reiner suggested that any movie that features smoking should automatically be rated R, the MPAA promptly shot it down. "Luckily," said Stone.

But still the MPAA provided the *South Park* team with an irresistible target, at the same time as they were dependent on its good will for the sake of the movie. For Parker and Stone, the R certificate was vital, a means of maintaining the movie's links with the television series and its audience.

The MPAA, however, was pushing for a more restricted NC-17 rating, with private memos circulating between the organization and Paramount detailing specific concerns with the movie's content. None of which, for anyone who has seen it, should appear that surprising.

Five times the MPAA went back to Paramount arguing that they had no alternative but to opt for the higher rating; five times Paramount pleaded their case and asked the MPAA to rescreen the movie, and the sixth time proved to be the charm.

Talking to the *New York Times*, Parker pointed out that "The ratings board only cared about the dirty words. They're so confused and arbitrary; they didn't blink twice because of violence. They had a problem with words, not bullets."

They also appeared to have overlooked the extraordinarily obscene connotations of the movie's title—porn slang for an uncircumcised penis.

Entertainment Weekly discussed one of the memos that flew as the release date grew closer. "The transcript, dated March 24, reveals a smudged line separating R from NC-17. [The phrase] 'God f---ing me up the a—' is grounds for an NC-17, but 'God's the biggest bitch of them all' is perfectly R-rated. Say the word 'fisting,' and it's an R; define that word on screen and nobody under 17 is admitted."

Another bone of contention was the scene in which a cartoon Winona Ryder performs her "famous ping pong trick" to the delight of the USO audience.

"'The Ping-Pong balls are supposed to look like they're coming from her vagina,' the exec says after concerns are raised about Ryder's talented private parts, 'but she stands up and you know that it's not. She's holding a paddle.' The board seems satisfied. 'That helps,' one representative says."

The *New York Times* also carried stories about the strife, remarking on one board member who "listed words describing oral and anal intercourse and bestiality, which were considered objectionable, as well as disrespectful references to God."

Of course, Stone and Parker's stance against the MPAA drew some heavyweight support, as well. The *Washington Post's* Rita Kempley described the movie as "outrageously profane" and "wildly funny," and pointed out that "censorship is the filmmakers' main target," with the MPAA, "self-appointed guardians of the nation's chastity," elected the movie's "favorite monster . . . . It's all in good dirty fun and in service of [Parker and Stone's] pro-tolerance theme."

If the MPAA were upset over the movie's graphic content, however, that is nothing compared to Paramount Pictures' response. From the outset of the project, Paramount had been pushing for an even lighter PG-13 branding, fearful of losing the more juvenile elements of the television series' following. But Comedy Central spokesman Tony Fox told *TV Guide*, "[Parker and Stone] really wanted to be able to go beyond the *South Park* television show. They really fought hard for and won the right to make an R-rated movie."

Not even Paramount's projections of how much more money might be made by a PG-13 movie could sway the pair. Nor, once the movie was released, could reports of armies of schoolchildren being turned away, disappointed, from movie houses across the land. Executive producer Scott Rudin certainly wasn't concerned. He told *Entertainment Weekly*, "I think kids will either force their parents to take them, or they'll figure out a way to get in under the radar." And, ultimately, Paramount accepted the moviemakers' own intentions.

Talking to the *New York Times*, Robert G. Friedman, vice chairman of the Paramount Motion Picture Group, said: "This is a difficult process between filmmakers and the ratings board. It is also extremely difficult to discuss in the context of an article of this nature the level of discussion between all the concerned parties. But suffice it to say we are satisfied with the rating that we achieved."

Still it was a hard-fought victory, as Stone detailed to *Playboy*. "We burned so many bridges, especially with their marketing department. The production people at Paramount were great to us, and our producer Scott Rudin was a big reason why the movie turned out as good as it did. But then you had marketing battles, legal battles, all these battles. It was such a perfect lesson in why so many bands come out and their first album is really great, and then their sophomore effort sucks. Even with the clout of having this huge franchise that had earned Viacom hundreds of millions of dollars, the studio did everything they could to beat us down and beat the spirit out of the movie."

Even the trailer for the movie was the cause of unrest, as Paramount demanded a Disney-style teaser, emphasizing the movie's humor and describing it as "the laughiest movie of the summer."

Parker and Stone demanded the trailer be redesigned, but Paramount's second attempt was scarcely any different from the first. In frustration, the pair snatched the videocassette from the player, broke it in half, and mailed it back to Paramount in its original envelope. "It was war," Stone reflected. "They were saying, 'Are you telling us how to do our job?' And I was going, 'Yes, because you're fucking stupid and you don't know what you're doing.'"

From left to right, Wendy, Kenny, Cartman, Kyle, and Stan. Another day in a quiet little redneck podunk, white-trash mountain town.

The internecine battle moved to a second front. Anxious to promote the movie through MTV, but cautious of the need to remain in compliance with broadcasting standards, Paramount created what Parker later called a "horrible little medley" of songs that, in excising any moments of R-certificate language, also managed to delete much of the humor.

Again, Parker and Stone responded with what might be called childish spite. Paramount were on a deadline. They needed to have the duo's approval of the video by the following Monday, so that it could enter the MTV schedules on Wednesday. Stone put the tape in his trunk and forgot about it. At one point in the conflict, there was even talk of Paramount suing Parker and Stone,

That issue, too, was eventually calmed. But controversy continued to rage. *South Park* had swiftly established itself as a strong performer in the merchandising stakes, with T-shirts and toys already appearing. They were sold, however, for the most part in specialty stores and comic book outlets. Moving into the major chains had never felt like an option. But careful management of the nature of the products, most notably the removal of any rude or offensive language from T-shirts and other items, would see *South Park* break into this highly lucrative market ... only to break out again when JC Penney responded to customer complaints and announced it would no longer be carrying *South Park* merchandise ... just two months before the movie was set to open.

Further damage was wrought in the aftermath of the Columbine school massacre, when it was reported that a friend of the shooters had been seen wearing a black *South Park* T-shirt. The linkage was tenuous at best, and was further weakened by Parker and Stone's own roots to Colorado. But again, once the media gets its teeth into a topic, logic is often the first thing to be spat out.

What was the outcome of all this? That's for the viewer to decide—and, suffice to say, there was a lot of them. Produced on a $21 million budget, the movie earned almost four times that in the theaters, with one of the songs, "Blame Canada," earning its creators an Academy Award nomination for Best Original Song.

And why should we blame Canada?

Because it's there. And because it spawned Terrance and Phillip.

The dastardly duo have a movie out, their big-screen debut after years of botty-burp related hijinks on the small screen, and, like *South Park* itself, they luxuriate in the comparative freedom from censorship that the world of movies offers.

The opening moments of *Asses on Fire* set the stage. Kyle, Stan, Kenny, Cartman, and little egg-shaped Ike had already been forced to resort to subterfuge in order to gain entrance to the movie house—the "R" rating dictated that they could only watch the film if accompanied by an adult. So they bribed a homeless guy to negotiate their way past the ticket seller, and in a darkened movie house, where they were clearly surrounded by mature and responsible adults, they settled down to enjoy the show.

Within five minutes, they were the only people left in the theater.

The duo opened with a new joke. "What did the Spanish priest say to the Iranian gynecologist?" And an inevitable punch line: "Fart." Then Terrance called Phillip a pigfucker; Phillip retaliated with "you shit faced cockmeister"; Terrance hit back with "donkey-raping shit eater" and suddenly we were into the first, and greatest, musical number, "Uncle Fucka." A song, in case the title does not make it clear, about fucking your uncle, and one that was taken out onto the streets of Any Town, Canada, where the entire populace, it seemed, wanted to join in the chorus.

Three hours later . . . .

Leaving the movie house, the five boys possessed an entire new vocabulary. Which, naturally, spread around their classmates as they, too, piled in to see the film. Inevitably, their newfound coarseness reached the ears of sundry adults— first in school, and then at home. But neither admonition nor punishment, nor even intensive rehab, could dull the school's delight in the coarser elements of our mother tongue's Anglo-Saxon heritage.

It took the tragic death of Kenny, hospitalized after igniting one of his own farts (in emulation of a scene in the movie, of course), but killed when doctors replaced his heart with a baked potato, to bring home the magnitude of the problem.

The boys were grounded, the parents declared that they were boycotting Canada, and Kenny found himself in Hell, where Satan and Saddam Hussein were gay lovers.

At first, the earthly controversy only fueled the popularity of the movie. A spin-off single of "Uncle Fucka" topped the charts. The movie dominated the box office. As a midget in a bikini reported on the evening news, "It appears that the effects of the Canadian comedy are far-reaching, indeed. All over America, children seem to be influenced.

"At a Washington spelling bee, the leading competitor eschewed the opportunity to spell out "forensics," in favor of "suck my ass." And when Canada's own Minister of Movies was asked to comment on the plague, he was utterly unrepentant over the movie's effect on American children. His government, he explained, had already apologized for Bryan Adams on several occasions. But that was different. "We can't believe that a movie with some foul language would piss you off so much."

Back in South Park, however, Sheila Broflovski was more than pissed off. As the self-appointed head of a new organization, Mothers Against Canada, she condemned the Canadian entertainers as corruptors of American youth, and arranged for them to be publicly arrested during an appearance on the *Conan O'Brien Show*. O'Brien, horrified by his own complicity in the coup, committed suicide; Canada retaliated for the unlawful incarceration of two of its citizens by bombing the Baldwin brothers, then following up with an attack on the Arquette residence.

War was now inevitable, with the president joining Mrs. Broflovski on television to spell out the country's intentions. To have Terrance and Phillip executed live at a USO show.

Which was exactly what Satan has been waiting for, the fulfillment of the so-called Final Prophecy. The moment a drop of the Canadians' blood touched American soil, he would rise from the pit and conquer the planet. Saddam, of course, would accompany him.

Kenny to the rescue. His ghost appeared to Cartman and warned him of the dastardly duo's plans. But how could a bunch of schoolboys convince their parents to listen to reason? The war fever had gripped them all now; common sense, or anything even vaguely approaching rational thought, had gone completely out the window. Gung ho patriotism is an ugly beast at the best of times, but when it is fired by an unshakable belief in the right of one's cause, no argument on earth can dislodge it.

The boys went underground. A new secret movement, La Resistance, was founded, built around the calm maturity of Wendy Testaburger's new boyfriend Gregory and a mysterious French mercenary known only as the Mole. Together, they planned to infiltrate the USO show and rescue Terrance and Phillip before the executions could be carried out.

There would be casualties—the Mole himself would fall. But the rescue was eventually effected, and it might even have been successful had the Canadian military not arrived with its own rescue attempt. A full-scale battle broke out, at the bloody height of which Sheila Broflovski herself gunned down Terrance and Phillip. The cue, to the boys' horror and the adults' absolute bewilderment, for Satan and Saddam to rise from the ground—and themselves fall to fighting as Hussein declared that he would be ruler of this new world, and Satan his underling.

The two lovers battled; Saddam was killed; and Satan, remembering the little boy in the outsized parka who had warned him of his lover's infidelity long before, offered Kenny any reward he should choose. Selflessly, Kenny asked that everything return to how it was before the war broke out . . . a request that did not restore him to life, but did bring Terrance and Phillip back into being, together with everybody else killed during this most terrible conflict. And Kenny went to Heaven. In fact, the only loser would seem to have been Ike, the Broflovskis' youngest son, an adopted Canadian.

Hidden away in an attic by his parents for fear that he might be swept up in the merciless anti-Canadian witch hunt that Mrs. Broflovski herself had ignited, we last see him alone and scared . . . and hungry. The movie ends with him eating a rat.

Ike was cute in those days. A far cry from the abusive pubescent monster he would be transformed into after a Canadian computer malfunction switched his laxatives for Tom Brady's hormone tablets, he talked cute, he

Saddam and Satan spend some quality time together.

looked cute, he even ate his ratty cute. It's hard not to shed a soft tear as the final credits roll.

The critics adored it.

The *New York Times*'s Stephen Holden spoke of the movie's "self-justifying moral"; the *Washington Post*'s Michael O'Sullivan described the lampooning as "more broad than incisive," but celebrated that, "under the bludgeoning of this blunt instrument very few sacred cows are left standing."

Richard Corliss of *Time* even cautioned, "You may laugh yourself sick—as sick as this ruthlessly funny movie is." And Roger Ebert wrote of a "vicious social satire" that stood proud as "the year's most slashing political commentary. It serves as a signpost for our troubled times. Just for the information it contains about the way we live now, thoughtful and concerned people should see it. After all, everyone else will."

Unfortunately, he continued, it was also "too long" and ran "out of steam" long before its conclusion. Mr. Ebert would later become the subject of a *South Park* episode in his own right. And you remember the thing about kids not being able to get in to see the movie? According to *USA Today* on July 15, 1999, it didn't prove that great a problem.

"A movie-industry crackdown meant to make it tougher for minors to sneak into R-rated films isn't keeping kids out of *South Park*—their parents are taking them. Despite warnings from theater employees, parents are giving in to the pleadings of young fans of TV's *South Park* and taking kids as young as nine to see the R-rated, in-your-face film, starring potty-mouthed cartoon characters in a satire that has critics applauding."

Across the pond in Britain, the *Guardian* newspaper even published a helpful guide to the "Tell-tale signs that your child has sneaked in to see the *South Park* film . . . : "[an] increasing use of foul language . . . and the tendency to break into song about the sexual proclivities of a nameless uncle."

Proclivities that live on in the continued success of Terrance and Phillip.

With Satan having magically returned life in America to where it stood immediately before war broke out, and having erased all memory of the war itself, Terrance and Phillip's career continued unabashed and unabated.

A second movie, *Asses of Fire 2*, was released to grand acclaim, and while the pair would briefly break up their partnership, it was only a temporary glitch. Today, as for the past however many decades, Terrance and Phillip stand supreme at the very apex of Canadian . . . nay, international . . . comedy.

And fart jokes remain the height of comedic invention and sophistication.

Cast

- Trey Parker—Stan Marsh / Eric Cartman / Gregory / Satan / Mr. Garrison / Phillip Niles Argyle / Randy Marsh / Tom—News Reporter / Midget in a Bikini / Canadian Ambassador / Bombardiers / Mr. Mackey / Army General / Ned Gerblansky / Christophe—Le Mole / Big Gay Al / Additional Voices
- Matt Stone—Kyle Broflovski / Kenny McCormick / Saddam Hussein / Terrance Henry Stoot / Ticket Taker / Jimbo Kearn / Gerald Broflovski / Bill Gates / Butters Stotch (one line) / Additional Voices
- Mary Kay Bergman—Liane Cartman / Sheila Broflovski / Sharon Marsh / Carol McCormick / Wendy Testaburger / Clitoris / Additional Voices

- Isaac Hayes—Chef Jerome McElroy
- Jesse Howell, Anthony Cross-Thomas, Franc[h]esca Clifford—Ike Broflovski
- Bruce Howell—Man in Theatre
- Deb Adair—Woman in Theatre
- Jennifer Howell—Bebe Stevens
- George Clooney—Dr. Gouache
- Brent Spiner—Conan O'Brien
- Minnie Driver—Brooke Shields
- Dave Foley—The Baldwin Brothers
- Eric Idle—Dr. Vosknocker
- Nick Rhodes—Canadian Fighter Pilot
- Toddy E. Walters—Winona Ryder
- Stewart Copeland—American Soldier #1
- Stanley G. Sawicki—American Soldier #2
- Mike Judge—Kenny's Goodbye
- Howard McGillin—Gregory (singing voice) (uncredited)
- Brian Dennehy—Himself (uncredited)

Awards

- American Film Foundation: Nominated for the E Pluribus Unum Award for Feature Film
- Nominated for three Annie Awards
- Outstanding Achievement in an Animated Theatrical Feature
- Outstanding Individual Achievement for Voice Acting in an Animated Feature Production for Mary Kay Bergman as "Sheila Broflovski"
- Outstanding Individual Achievement for Writing in an Animated Feature Production
- MTV Movie Award—Best Musical Performance for "Uncle Fucka."
- Chicago Film Critics Association: Best Original Score (Marc Shaiman and David Newman)
- New York Film Critics Circle Awards: Best Animated Feature
- Las Vegas Film Critics Society Awards: Nominated for Best Animated Film
- Los Angeles Film Critics Association Awards: Best Music
- Motion Picture Sound Editors: Best Sound Editing—Music—Animation, Nominated for Best Sound Editing—Animated Feature
- Online Film Critics Society Awards: Best Original Score

- Satellite Awards: Nominated for Best Motion Picture, Animated or Mixed Media and Best Original Song for "Quiet Mountain Town"
- AFI's Greatest Movie Musicals—Nominated

19

South Park and the Struggle for Civil Rights

Seven Episodes That Changed the World (or Not)

Big Gay Al's Big Gay Boat Ride

When Stan's dog, Sparky, realizes he is homosexual, around the same time as he overhears his master remark that he wishes he had a butch hound, the poor pooch feels he has no alternative but to run away. Now, of course, Stan is distraught, even skipping practice for a vital game against the Middle Park Cows so that he might search for the missing animal.

Instead he finds Big Gay Al, to whose Big Gay Animal Sanctuary Sparky has turned for shelter and understanding.

There, he is sat down and calmly listens as Big Gay Al explains to him about homosexuality; and with a wider understanding of the subject, Stan receives a second reward. Sparky agrees to return home with him.

A simple tale, but sometimes the most important lessons are the easiest.

Cartman's Silly Hate Crime 2000

Of all the kids at South Park Elementary who would be well served by a little "sensitivity training" (as it is called this week; next week, they'll probably have come up with an even more irritating name), Eric Cartman stands head, shoulders, and belly above the remainder of his classmates.

Not that the others are absolutely immune to prejudice. No matter how many great strides have been taken in the past half century, from race relations (unless you're looking for a really good bass player) to not taking advantage of the homeless (unless you want to get into an R-rated movie); from gay rights (unless you're worried that your dog isn't butch enough) to sexual equality (unless . . . but you get the picture), still there are subtleties that might never truly translate away from their stereotypical origins—a point proven when Stan Marsh's father Randy blurted out the "N-word" on *Wheel of Fortune*.

No matter how hard his son tried to comprehend the rage that consumed his friend Token Black, it was only when he acknowledged that he couldn't comprehend it that he truly understood the other boy's anger.

Eric Cartman, on the other hand, would not acknowledge such a failing; would not even consider the need to do so. And while psychologists and the like will point to his mother Liane's own innate hostility toward minorities as the root cause of Cartman's insensitivity, there is no doubt that her son has taken what might be acknowledged as a character flaw and built an entire ballroom from it.

Across which he dances with ever greater abandon.

Kyle, the sole Jew in the school community, is the most frequent target for Cartman's scorn; little people, as Snow White certainly didn't call her erstwhile companions, offer him another. And then there is Token . . . like Kyle, the sole representative of a specific minority group at the school, but one whom Cartman regards with just enough respect (bluntly, Token could kick the crap out of him) that he either chooses his battles very carefully, or he doesn't choose them at all. They just happen.

Such as the time he threw a rock that hit Token on the head, and set in motion a chain of events that saw Cartman charged with, and convicted of, committing a hate crime. He was sent to Alamosa Maximum Security Juvenile Hall, where he was reduced to smuggling contraband into his cell via his rectum. For prisoner 24601 (a number he shared with Jean Valjean in *Les Miserables*), producing that Tic-Tac-Throw game from the place where the sun doesn't shine was the only way to win the respect of his cellmate, Romper Stomper.

Cartman was eventually pardoned. While few people back in South Park would ever have claimed they missed him or even regarded him as a friend, still he was a vital component in their downhill sledding team. Something to do with his weight and the force of gravity, you see. A Free Eric Cartman Now committee formed and petitioned the governor for the boy's release, which was effected just in time for the race.

Down Phil Collins Hill the teams plummeted, and victory was South Park's. Which meant it was time to celebrate.

Cartman: "Do British people count as an ethnicity for hate crimes?"

The others: "Naah."

Cartman: "Sweet."

Pip was promptly flattened by a flying rock.

Fun with Veal

Of all mankind's most contradictory traits, his relationship with the animal world is possibly the most glaring. A society that loves animals sufficiently to maintain them as de facto members of the family, to treat them with as much love and respect as a child or a grandparent, at the same time thinks nothing (or, more accurately, doesn't think at all) about the inhumane conditions in which other animals live and die as they ride the conveyor belt toward our meal table. "It's a million miles," as English songwriter TV Smith once sang, "from a slaughterhouse to a hamburger."

This lesson is brought home with ruthless precision when the kids of South Park Elementary are taken on a field trip to a cattle ranch, where they discover that veal, a meat that they all enjoy, is made from calves. Cute barely born calves, with big calf eyes and little calf bodies, many of whom spend their entire eighteen- to twenty-week lives chained inside two-feet-wide wooden stalls, so narrow that the animal cannot even turn around, lie down, or clean itself, let alone walk, run, or play. They never breathe fresh air, they never feel sunlight. They are tortured prisoners from birth until death.

But, as Cartman somewhat insensitively points out, they do taste scrumptious. So that's alright then.

Or is it? Outraged by what they witness, and led by the now wholly committed and vegetarian Stan, Kyle, Kenny, Cartman, and Butters kidnap the calves and stash them in the only place they can think of where they'll be safe. Stan's bedroom.

Unfortunately, what they—and, indeed, many other people—considered a humane act of animal welfare has taken on new coloring in the eyes of the government. Animal Liberation is now considered a terrorist act, and is punishable as such. The FBI swoop in, and the house is surrounded, not only by law enforcement but also by hippies, keen to add their voices to the rising tide of support that the action has encouraged.

Television is less interested. Although the networks are all in attendance, so little is actually happening (at least in terms of the only reason why networks ever attend these events, in the hope of hearing gunfire, seeing explosions, and maybe asking a neighbor "how does it feel to see your street reduced to a war zone, your family choked by teargas and your home destroyed by heavy artillery?") that live coverage of the event is preempted by *Puppies from Around the World*, a tender, touching documentary . . . enough!

Back in South Park, a tense standoff develops, with Cartman electing himself the putative terrorists' spokesman. Miraculously, he is good at it as well, not only negotiating the boys' safe passage out of the country, but also winning another, equally vital concession. The cattle truck that will take boys and beasts to the airport will be driven by Michael Dorn, star of *Star Trek: The Next Generation*.

There is, however, a reason why the authorities were so willing to negotiate with the boys. Because they had no intention of upholding their side of the deal. Far from being whizzed away to a safe haven in Mexico, the terrorist gang has not even reached Denver airport before it is arrested.

But the boys' actions were not in vain. Though the calves were returned to the ranch, they were no longer to be kept in those inhumane pens. Rather, they would be freed to live with the other cows, and live as long and full a life as any other walking, mooing side of beef. And while veal will still be served in restaurants across the country, the FDA has instituted one final, necessary provision. It will henceforth be named "Little Tortured Baby Cow."

Veal sales plummet.

I'm A Little Bit Country

War fever had been building for months.

In the red corner, President George Bush, British Prime Minister Tony Blair, and, clutched tightly in their sweaty little paws, a host of damning dossiers, sobering statistics, and horrifying headlines that revealed, among many other things, that:

Iraq was forty-five minutes away from launching a nuclear strike.

Iraq had a massive stockpile of weapons of mass destruction.

Iraq was a leading supporter and financier of the terrorist organization Al-Qaeda.

Iraq was a key player in organizing the 9/11 attacks on the American homeland.

And Iraq tried to kill George's daddy.

One of these, the latter, turned out to be true. Possibly. The remainder, almost gleefully discredited by analysts, researchers, and observers from both sides of the political divide, and both sides of the Atlantic, were rampant bull-cookies, dreamed up by a pair of allegedly responsible world leaders for reasons that we probably really don't want to understand.

Neither did much of this come as a surprise to many folk. Long before the war began, great swathes of the American and British people, not to mention the majority of the rest of the world, looked at the two leaders' "evidence" with ever more distrustful eyes. When CNN organized a massive poll of their fellow Americans in January 2003, 64 percent of people said they would approve military action against Iraq. But 63 percent cautioned that diplomacy should be exhausted first, and when the first antiwar protests were staged on February 15, an estimated 36 million people worldwide marched against the impending conflict.

They were ignored. On March 19, the invasion began. And on April 9, the protests—both for and against the war—arrived in South Park.

What better reason could there be to take a day off school?

Stereotypes exist because, somewhere deep within, they represent a certain truth. The British really do walk around in bowler hats, apologizing to everyone and drinking tea. The French really do wear stripy shirts and berets, and say "'allo 'allo" a lot.

The Finnish language really is comprised of just two letters, "k" and "a," distinguished from one another by a plethora of accent symbols. And the Germans really aren't funny.

It is stereotyping that allows us to instinctively recognize the different characters in *South Park*, whether or not we personally want to acknowledge the accuracy of the portrayal.

Mr. Mackey looks like a school counselor, regardless of how many school counselors we have met who do not look like Mr. Mackey.

We knew Ike Broflovski was a Canadian long before we discovered that fact.

And if Big Gay Al had been named Small Straight Simon, we would have laughed and assumed he was being ironic.

So, when the fourth graders arrived at the antiwar rally and discovered it peopled on one side by hippies and on the other by country music fans, they did not need to read the flags and banners to know which side was which. Neither did they need to be told that, if it came to a fight, only one side had guns. The others probably had flowers, which they would try to insert into the barrels of those guns.

Conflict was ultimately averted, but via perhaps the two most unlikely sources imaginable—a class project instigated by Mr. Garrison to discover what the Founding Fathers would have thought of the standoff; and its successful commission by Cartman, who taped fifty hours of History Channel documentaries before hurling himself, the tapes, and the recording system into a bathtub full of water.

The ensuing electric shock blasted him back to 1776, where he discovered a truth that, perhaps, could be spread with equal merit across many of the other concerns and ideologies that divide us today.

"This country was founded by some of the smartest thinkers the world has ever seen. And they knew one thing: that a truly great country can go to war, and at the same time, act like it doesn't want to."

The people who were in favor of the war, he learned, needed the antiwar contingent because they ensured "the country look[s] like it's made of sane, caring individuals." And the people who opposed the war needed the prowar lobby just as badly, "because, if our whole country was made up of nothing but soft pussy protesters, we'd get taken down in a second. That's why the founding fathers decided we should have both. It's called 'having your cake and eating it too.'"

Mission accomplished.

Krazy Kripples

Race, religion, sexuality, and another man's sporting allegiances notwithstanding, there is one topic on which we all agree that jokes should not be made: physical and mental handicap.

The English language is littered with derogatory terms for these disabilities, all of which appear to have been designed exclusively in order that we might congratulate ourselves daily for never having actually used them. Perhaps that is why the handful of terms that were once considered appropriate to use have themselves been consigned to the dustbins of iniquity, to be replaced by an entire vocabulary of new, sympathetic terms.

"Differently abled."

"Handi-capable."

"Uniflippered mongy-spaz burger." Oops, who let Cartman into the room?

In fact, when the first differently abled youth arrived at South Park Elementary, in the form of the very differently (and often contentiously) abled Timmy Burch, even Cartman confined his scorn to brainstorming fresh purposes to which the trisyllablic youth's wheelchair could be put. And when the second turned up a short time later, Jimmy Valmer's own willingness to include references to his disabilities in his stand-up comedy routines was sufficient to render redundant any external attempts to mock or belittle him.

Being marginalized, on the other hand . . . well, that's something that society seems unable to help itself from doing, and Jimmy could not help but feel brushed off when his comedy act was utterly sidelined by the much-ballyhooed visit of Christopher Reeve, the former Superman actor rendered quadriplegic after being thrown from a horse in 1995.

Confined to a wheelchair and reliant on a breathing apparatus for the remainder of his life (he died in 2004, a year after this episode aired), Reeve was visiting South Park to publicize and popularize a whole new cure for his disabilities.

Sucking the juices from recently aborted fetuses.

He also did so at a time when American society was rancorously divided over the benefits of stem-cell research . . . or at least at a time when a handful of loudmouths on one side of the divide were dominating current affairs programming by arguing with a handful of loudmouths on the other side. All of which only added piquancy to his plight.

The so bitterly contested research, after all, represented a potentially enormous step forward for many disabled people, with attempts to limit or even outlaw the research widely regarded as a form of prejudice as pernicious as any of those others that a so-called polite society had already taken steps against. Especially when it was revealed that the funding that President Bush had so benevolently approved purposefully limited fresh research to an existing stockpile of human embryonic stem cell lines that had been contaminated with mouse cells.

But—and, as Cartman's detractors would say, it's a big butt—what if Reeve's dreams went beyond merely curing the disabled?

What if he was simultaneously scheming an organization committed to world domination, never-ending evil, and an equally ceaseless conveyor belt of fresh fetuses?

That was the hideous truth behind Reeve's lust for embryos, and it became apparent, too, that it was not only future generations of unborn babies whose (lack of) life was endangered by Reeve's wicked ambition.

Those handicapped people whose lives would not be changed by the research, too, found themselves at risk of being utterly overlooked by the celebrity drive against sickness.

Jimmy thought he had the answer. He founded an organization dedicated, and open exclusively, to people who had been disabled since birth. No Born Again Cripples, no one-legged bandwagon jumpers (hoppers?), no scientifically developed half-man, half-dolphin hybrids. The Crips were the real thing.

Imagine his surprise and delight, therefore, when he discovered that another organization of the same name already existed, and that it had a chapter located in nearby Denver! And imagine his shock if he had learned that it was actually the local branch of one of the most notorious street gangs in all of America!

Thankfully, he never did, just as he never comprehended, when he and his own Crips applied for membership, that "popping some punk-ass Bloods" did not mean buying soda and treats for another gang.

What he could imagine was a day when Crips and Bloods were united in song, and while he set those wheels into merry motion, a rough 'n' ragged representation of Gene Hackman was busy taking care of Christopher Reeve. Imprisoned within another dimension and then blasted into space, Reeve would never again terrorize the earth with his bloody desires.

At the time, the episode merely surprised viewers. Watched in reruns in the years since Reeve's real-life death, however, it possibly takes on another timbre altogether. Indeed, if there were a *South Park* Disgust-o-meter, on which we could register just how offended normally loyal and understanding viewers were by the show's treatment of the victim du jour, "Krazy Kripples" would now be right up there near the top. But it would not be alone, as viewers of "Hell on Earth 2006" will testify.

On September 4, 2006, Australian wildlife expert Steve Irwin died after an encounter with a stingray, whose spine punctured his lung. On October 25, 2006, he was among the guests at a South Park Halloween costume party, walking around in full wildlife expert drag, with a stingray barb protruding from his chest. He was promptly kicked out of the party for not wearing a costume.

A friend of the Irwin family later issued a statement saying the episode "goes too far too soon."

Butt Out

Smoking.

(Pause for the gasps of horror to die down.)

Cigarettes.

(Quick puff break while society in general regains its equilibrium.)

Death sticks, cancer canes, cough cookies, lung removers . . . .

It is hard to think of any legal, so-called entertainment that is quite so evil, dangerous, and inconsiderate as smoking.

Prescription medicine abuse? So long as the user doesn't fall asleep at the wheel and pile into a bunch of people (and let's face it, you don't need to be on drugs for that to happen), it's harmless.

Alcohol? Naah. Leave the drinker alone with enough bottles of the stuff and he'll soon be happily comatose.

Nuclear proliferation (remember, it wouldn't be called an "arms race" if there were not an element of jocular competition involved)? Duck and cover, my child. Duck and cover.

Firearms? Now you're just being stupid. Bullets don't kill people. Smoking kills people.

Smoking slays. Smoking damages. Smoking bankrupts society. But most of all, smoking gathers in so much revenue from taxes that, were it to be outlawed tomorrow, we'd have so many new things to worry about that all of those other ills would be mere bug bites by comparison.

Nevertheless, let's hear it for Butt Out, a band of concerned non-smoking musicians who have taken it on themselves to travel the nation's schools and educate kids against cigarettes in terms they will understand. With pop music!

"Butt out!" they sing. "Yeah yeah! Kids, that cigarette butt is gross.

"Butt out! Uh huh! Smokin's got to go!"

And such an uplifting message to end on as well. "If you don't smoke, you can grow up to be Just Like Us."

By which time, Kenny had already eaten his own hands, Cartman was contemplating suicide, and Kyle and Stan appeared comatose. They awakened, however, in time to consider those last awful words. "If you don't smoke, you can grow up to be Just Like Us."

What happens if you don't want to be Just Like Them, though? You take up smoking. And if you take up smoking, you will set the school on fire. And if you set the school on fire, your parents will be called to the principal's office. And if your parents are called to the principal's office, you will be grounded for three weeks . . . for smoking.

But we should also remember that, after all is said and done, there is only one thing that is worse than smoking. It's called fascism. And you can ask a badly drawn and poorly impersonated cartoon of antismoking campaigner Rob Reiner about that.

Or Matt Stone. As he told *Hollywood Interrupted*, "PC Hollywood feels the need to pass laws because the rest of us can't take care of ourselves. The smoking ban is a perfect example. It's bad to smoke, but that's irrelevant. If people want to do it to themselves, then that's fine. If you don't want to go in that bar with the smoke, don't go in that bar. Rob Reiner is . . . one of the most evil people on the earth. That guy's completely evil in his intentions if you look at the way he's passed the cigarette taxes, which are the most aggressive taxes in the world. Let's punish the poor people.

"He always sells it on the back of some children's program, which is fucking bullshit. He just hates smoke. Somebody blew smoke in his face one time, and he fucking hates it, and he has to start using his celebrity power. When Rob Reiner needs to take a break, he can go to some fucking spa in Arizona for five days, but your average Joe may only have his cigarette. He's probably got a fucking hard job that's shitty and thankless, and at the end of the day, he wants to hang out with his friends and have cigarettes. And Rob Reiner is saying, 'I hate that.'"

Butt Out, in support of happy smokers everywhere, simply reminded him that the feeling is mutual.

Ginger Kids

Racial purity means different things to different people.

To the Nazis of Hitler's Germany, it spoke of an unsullied race of blonde, blue-eyed supermen, which made it seem odd that their leader was a short, dark-haired dude with one testicle (or so the song said), but no matter.

To the Daleks of television's *Doctor Who*, it means being a vaguely squid-like one-eyed blob riding around in a bad-tempered pepperpot.

To a specific kind of beetle, it means being a specific kind of beetle.

And to Eric Cartman, it means not being ginger.

Gingers. We've all seen then, we have all cowered away from them. The Vikings were gingers, or a lot of them were. So was Lucille Ball. So was (and presumably still is) the actress in that early 2000s sitcom who, at the height of the Elian Gonzalez kerfuffle (or "Quintuplets 2000," as *South Park* preferred) made a PSA insisting the boy stay in America because being raised by strangers in a strange land was a lot better than being a Communist.

A red. A . . . ginger?

Gingers. It has been estimated that between 1 percent and 2 percent, or 70 to 140 million people, around the world have red hair. And in August 2013, some 200 people took part in the UK's first Ginger Pride march. The following month, the world record for the largest gathering of natural redheads was shattered when 1,600 attended the Redhead Day Festival in the Dutch town of Breda.

But where do they all come from?

According to Cartman, giving a class presentation one day, gingers are the victims of a condition known as gingervitus, itself caused by being born without a soul. Sufferers of gingervitus are instantly identifiable by their red hair, pale skin, and freckles. In addition, they are creepy. They are also akin to vampires because their pale skin means they cannot go out in the sun.

It's a damning presentation, rendered all the more damaging by the discovery that, while most of Cartman's facts are utterly wrong, even the non-ginger parents of ginger kids do wonder what went awry.

Kyle, whose lack of any ginger traits beyond pale skin does not deter Cartman from considering him to be numbered among the damned, fights fire with science. He proves conclusively that ginger coloring is a perfectly normal matter of genetic coding, and has nothing to do with soullessness.

Cartman, however, cannot be halted. Spewing his gingerist venom every place he goes, the fat kid is not simply gearing up for a racial war, he is creating it in an area that no past fanatic had ever even imagined there being scope for one.

There is just one option left; just one audacious scheme that might rein in Cartman's bile. He, too, needs to contract gingervitus.

Which is easy enough to arrange. Just break into his house while he is sleeping, dye his hair a vivid carrot, bleach his skin, and add some henna freckles. Voila! Cartman is ginger.

He is also furious. Laughed at for his skin coloring, teased about his hair, mocked for his freckles, condemned for his soullessness, Cartman does not see the prejudice that he engendered in the first place is coming back to bite him. He sees only that he is now a member of an unjustly persecuted minority.

Predicting the fury that will consume him years later, when he perceives the injustice of people not being permitted to eat themselves into rampant obesity and then ride around on mobility scooters complaining that bathrooms aren't large enough, Cartman rallies other sufferers to his cause.

Gingers have been prejudiced against for too long, he declares. He launches the Ginger Separatist Movement, proclaims actor Ron Howard its spiritual leader, and campaigns not merely for equal rights but for more than equal rights.

Hatred must be fought with hatred. When he hears reports of a non-ginger actress being recruited to play the role of Annie in the stage show of the same name, Cartman arranges for her to be beaten up. "The bitch isn't ginger!" he roars in justification. "She's just using makeup to look ginger!

"And pretending to be ginger with makeup is the worst thing anybody can do."

He declares gingers to be the chosen people, selected by God to rid the world of the lowlife, dark-skinned rats that inhabit the rest of the planet. He unveils the slogan Red Power, and outlines his dream . . . a world in which the very concept of hatred has been eradicated, because so have all the non-gingers who ever walked the Earth.

Cages are discussed, in which to imprison the deviants. Tortures are devised to punish them for their crimes. And pits of lava will be constructed, into which their broken bodies will be hurled. Even his erstwhile friends are captured, dragged to the gingers' headquarters at the Airport Hilton, and readied for execution.

There is just one fatal flaw in Cartman's master plan, and it is up to Kenny to tell him what it was. The fact that he is not really a ginger after all. That his hair is dyed, his skin is bleached, his freckles are fake . . . Oops.

Maybe we can all live together in harmony after all, announces Cartman, and the Scourge of Ginger Supremacy ends right there.

20

School's Out ...

"The idea was, let's do the Joseph Smith story as a musical. We pretty quickly realized that wouldn't make a very good one; there would be covered wagons, and while it's all really fascinating, none of those characters were that great of people. And so we decided, let's do a story that talked about Mormonism and let's set it in today's world. And then we realized the vessel that most people hear about this stuff is through missionaries, so we could use missionaries as our way to tell the audience what we know about Mormons."

—Matt Stone

While Trey Parker and Matt Stone will undoubtedly remain best known as the creators of *South Park*, they have also stepped several times outside of the town, for a clutch of projects that ... well, generally, they get written off because they're not as "good" (or at least the "same") as *South Park*. But they still do them.

Within a year of the show's 1997 debut, the pair had completed a live-action feature called *Orgazmo*; scripted a prequel to *Dumb & Dumber*; costarred in another feature, *BASEketball*; and launched their own band, DVDA. And why? Well, their philosophy, the duo admitted, was simple. Nobody knew how long *South Park* was going to last, and everybody knows that for every ten (or so) deals an artist is offered, only one is actually likely to take wing. So they accepted everything that was thrown at them. Yep, that simple.

Ideas flew. There was talk of an animated series for Fox telling the stories of various historical characters.

There was *That's My Bush!*, a live-action sitcom parody based around the fictional life of the newly elected President George W., a conflation of contemporary current affairs with the blundering life of an accident-prone Dubya.

And there was a projected series of thirty-nine episodes in a new series, *Princess*.

Intended for release via Macromedia's shockwave.com website, these three- to five-minute shorts would revolve around the flash-animation adventures of an adorable Lhasa apso dog, a beast prone, according to the opening credit, to riding around in hot air balloons, admiring rainbows, and wearing a darling little bow on her tousled little head.

Sadly, just two episodes were produced.

In the first, "Princess Hears a Strange Noise," the titular pooch is awakened by the sound of her master being loudly masturbated by his wife, whose lack of enthusiasm for such an intimate moment is echoed only by her husband's apparent inability to reach an orgasm. He has, it transpires, just taken something approaching an overdose of Viagra, and nothing can bring him to his peak. Not fellatio, not cable porn ... but a home decorating show? That's the ticket.

He ejaculates and—boom! Off flies his wife's head in a messy mass of blood, bone, and bodily secretions ... and that's it. End of episode.

"Princess Meets Officer Friendly" was next, picking up where the pilot left off, with the police investigating the death scene, while a necrophiliac who claims to be the coroner is upstairs having sex with the corpse, and dad is trying to explain to his son precisely how mommy met her end. And episode three, "Princess Finds a Red Balloon," was already in the planning stages when the series' sponsors announced they would not be pursuing the venture any further. Apparently, it was too extreme.

Princess was never heard of again.

That's My Bush! was more successful, at least inasmuch as a full season was aired. One full season, eight episodes. Would that the real thing had been just as brief.

In 2004 came the duo's next movie, *Team America: World Police*, an action comedy cowritten with Pam Brady as a satire of both conventional action movies and American politics' growing insistence that the nation's duty was to police the world. Eschewing both cartoon and live action, the movie was shot with marionettes, in a similar fashion to the 1960s UK cult adventures *Stingray* and *Thunderbirds*; and, like them, focusing on a crack band of adventurers—paramilitary antiterrorist operatives—based out of a secret location ... Mount Rushmore.

The team's original scheme was, in fact, to acquire the rights to *Thunderbirds* itself and make a movie of their own; a plan that was scuppered when they discovered that director Jonathan Frakes's live-action version of the same show was about to go into production.

That's My Bush! episode guide

1. "An Aborted Dinner Date"—George tries to combine a big-ticket publicity dinner with a romantic meal for two with wife Laura.
2. "A Poorly Executed Plan"—George attempts to impress his old frat buddies by arranging an execution.
3. "Eenie Meenie Miney MURDER"—a telephone psychic warns George that somebody in the White House is planning to kill him.
4. "SDI Aye Aye!"—trying to set up an illegal cable hookup, George accidentally blasts Austria with a laser beam.
5. "The First Lady's Persqueeter"—when Laura mishears George arranging to have the family cat put to sleep, she sets to work beautifying her lower body area.
6. "Mom 'E' DEA Arrest"—George takes ecstasy during a War on Drugs Arrest ceremony.
7. "Trapped in a Small Environment"—George and Laura set Karl up with a blind date, unaware that he is already married.
8. "Fare Thee Welfare"—Dick Cheney has George removed from office and cast out into the cruel world alone.

Next up was a puppet-driven parody of the disaster movie *The Day After Tomorrow*, only for the lawyers to scupper that one by pointing out that *The Day After the Day After Tomorrow* would probably be more trouble than it was worth, at least in terms of legalities and copyrights.

They returned, then, to the *Thunderbirds* concept, by taking it as far from the *Thunderbirds* prototype as they could. *Thunderbirds* revolved around an independently run organization's efforts to prevent disaster. The government-sponsored Team America, despite being armed with a supercomputer named INTELLIGENCE, was more likely to be the cause of carnage. One operation saw them destroy several of Paris's best-loved landmarks; another leveled Cairo; another, the Panama Canal.

Neither were Team America's problems confined to overseas. At home, their methods brought them up against the superliberal Film Actors Guild (FAG), a protest body led by representations of Alec Baldwin, and also featuring Helen Hunt, Ethan Hawke, Tim Robbins, Susan Sarandon, George Clooney, Liv Tyler, Janeane Garofalo, Samuel L. Jackson, Sean Penn, and Danny Glover, all real-life opponents of America's international belligerence, and all hell-bent on making their feelings known.

Stone and Parker, on the court for *BASEketball.*

It was a standoff that saw filmmaker Michael Moore suicide bomb the team's headquarters, before a violent finale in which most of the FAG supporters were killed during a world peace ceremony being staged by North Korean leader Kim Jong-il.

Add plenty of sex, bad language, and the revelation that one of the Team America team, Chris, has hated actors ever since he was raped by the cast of *Cats*, and it was clear that the MPAA, Parker and Stone's adversary from the days of *Bigger, Longer & Uncut*, was going to have its work cut out for it And so it did, as *Team America: World Police* followed its predecessor into a long and grueling war. Nine times that august body returned the movie with an NC-17 rating, before finally accepting sufficient cuts (a matter of a few seconds) that enabled them to give it an R.

The movie was not a flop. True, Stone later revealed that "The biggest backlash we've ever had from anybody, from any religious organization, Mormons, from anybody, is liberals who saw *Team America* and were pissed off at us."

But reviews were generally good, and a worldwide gross of almost $51 million was not bad considering Paramount had so loudly insisted that you couldn't make money with an R-rated puppet show. Parker and Stone merely reminded them that they'd said much the same thing about an R-rated musical cartoon.

Other people probably said the same thing about the pair's next major venture—a musical about Mormons.

Having grown up and lived, as they said, in a part of the country where Mormons numbered heavily among their friends and neighbors, Parker and Stone both viewed the faith with considerably more affection than they apparently regarded some of the other belief systems out there.

Not that that stopped them from having fun with it. Mormons were featured in the 1997 *Orgazmo* movie, while the 2003 *South Park* episode "All About Mormons" took the fascination even further. Joseph Smith, the Church's founder, had been among the characters being considered for the aforementioned Fox network show; now his story was told in at least some of its glory, and the pair later admitted that, while the show's younger viewers were generally nonplussed by the episode, their Mormon friends loved it.

It was during that same year, 2003, that Parker and Stone found themselves in New York City, discussing the then-gestating script of *Team America: World Police* with their long-time ally, producer Scott Rudin. During the course of the meetings, Rudin suggested they spend a night on

Parker and Stone toying with Team America.

Broadway, at the musical *Avenue Q*—itself an adventurous effort that employed puppets. There they were recognized in the audience by the musical's creators, Robert Lopez and Jeff Marx, who themselves had been inspired to create *Avenue Q* by the *South Park* movie.

Later, over drinks and discussing future plans and dreams, both teams of writers revealed that they really wanted to write something about Joseph Smith and the Mormons—which, if you think about it, is a pretty obscure ambition for two sets of total strangers to bond over. Nevertheless they did, and soon a story line was taking shape.

Trey Parker ... O is for *Orgazmo*!

It was not all drinks and typing. At one point the four traveled to Salt Lake City to meet with Mormon missionaries and ex-missionaries alike, gathering different takes not only on the Church's history, but also its peculiarities.

For many people, the all-singing, all-dancing Osmond family were the Mormon faith's best-known export, with the sometimes soap-operatic saga of their post-seventies pop star career playing out in the glare of both fascinated and baffled spotlights.

They were followed into the spotlight by erstwhile presidential candidate Mitt Romney, and again there was as much confusion as acceptance in the media's acknowledgment of his beliefs. That there was a lot more to the faith than the soundbite deliveries with which the mainstream media is happiest was obvious. But as for what it actually entailed . . . well, that, in part, was one of the fascinating elements of the unfolding story line.

Research trips to Palmyra, New York, the childhood home of Church founder Joseph Smith; to the Mormon festival in Rochester, New York; to all the hubs of the Mormon religion, piled up. "We're not on the inside," Stone explained, "but we are white Americans from the western part of the United States, and we know that culture a little bit.

"We had a Mormon story line in *Orgazmo*. . . . We've been on the Mormon thing for a long time, since before Mitt Romney showed up on the scene and people started getting interested in it. We grew up in Colorado, and we grew up with Mormons. Mormons lived on my street." Parker's first girlfriend was a Mormon. "So, we have some personal experience, not just book experience with them."

With both Parker and Stone's *South Park* commitments and Lopez and Marx's *Avenue Q* involvement necessarily devouring a lot of their time, it was 2006 before work on the slowly unfolding production could continue.

"We have our day job, which is *South Park*," Stone told the *Boston Globe*, "and Bobby [Lopez] was really busy doing things. . . . We would work whenever we had time, and we would put it down for six months. It certainly wasn't rushed, and maybe that's why it got to marinate a little longer. Whereas I think if you said, 'You guys have to write a musical in two years and launch it,' that would be pretty tough. It was just nice that we weren't under the gun, until we made ourselves go under the gun, and then it started to suck and was work, but that was only the last year and a half or so."

Still, the 2006 encounter saw Stone, Parker, Marx, and Lopez meet up in London, where *Avenue Q* was about to make its West End stage debut, and the first songs began to form. Parker recalled, "We wrote four or five songs and came up with the basic germ of the idea there. That they would go somewhere not Salt Lake City-like."

There was another pause after Marx and Parker had a falling-out over creative control issues (resulting in Marx removing himself from the project), but slowly what they were calling *The Book of Mormon: The Musical of the Church of Jesus Christ of Latter-day Saints* took shape.

Lopez explained the trio's goals. "We didn't want to take down Mormonism, or any other religion. We realized that we shared this world view about how religions are created and the function that religion serves in society. It's very similar to the function of musicals. At their best, they are both shared experiences that can bring people together, and provide hope and uplift them."

He told the *New York Times* that he had studied the Bible as literature while at Yale and was fascinated with the original *Book of Mormon* as a work of "Bible fan fiction. But people believe in it so strongly, and their lives are demonstrably changed for the good by it."

The plot, the *Wall Street Journal* would later explain, was "exiguous." *The Book of Mormon* was, or would become, the story of two young Mormon missionaries, Elders Kevin Price and Arnold Cunningham, who find themselves dispatched to take the word to a remote village in northern Uganda, unaware that they will be competing for the locals' attention not only with a murderous local warlord, General Butt-Fucking Naked, but also with the problems of AIDS, famine, war, grinding poverty, and maggot-infested scrotums.

It also doesn't aid their cause to discover that only Price has actually read the *Book of Mormon* itself, and that Cunningham is an overweight, compulsive liar. Or that the locals' favorite song, sung whenever they are feeling down, is not the sweet, soporific ditty that the missionaries imagined, but something far darker and deeper. The words "hasa diga eebowai," with which the missionaries have so often joined in, translate into English as "fuck you, God."

There were some ... shall we say ... exaggerations and misinterpretations, of course. The song "I Believe," in which Elder Price effectively lays out the tenets of his faith, starts out on safe enough ground, with its insistence that "ancient Jews built boats and sailed to America." The opening pages of the *Book of Mormon* include God leading a party of Jews out of Babylon on the eve of its destruction in 587 BC, commanding them to

The Songs of *The Book of Mormon*

Act I

"Hello," performed by Price, Cunningham, and Mormon Boys

"Two by Two," performed by Price, Cunningham, and Mormon Boys

"You and Me (But Mostly Me)," performed by Price and Cunningham

"Hasa Diga Eebowai," performed by Mafala, Price, Cunningham, and Ugandans

"Turn It Off," performed by McKinley and Missionaries

"I Am Here for You," performed by Price and Cunningham

"All American Prophet," performed by Price, Cunningham, Joseph Smith, Angel
    Moroni, and Company

"Sal Tlay Ka Siti," performed by Nabulungi

"I Am Here for You" (Reprise), performed by Cunningham

"Man Up," performed by Cunningham, Nabulungi, Price, and Company

Act II

"Making Things Up Again" performed by Cunningham, Cunningham's Dad, Joseph
    Smith, Mormon, Moroni, Uhura, Hobbits, and Ugandans

"Spooky Mormon Hell Dream," performed by Price and Company

"I Believe," performed by Price

"Baptize Me," performed by Cunningham and Nabulungi

"I Am Africa," performed by McKinley, Cunningham, and Missionaries

"Orlando," performed by Price

"Joseph Smith American Moses," performed by Nabulungi, Mafala, and Ugandans

"Hasa Diga Eebowai" (Reprise), performed by Nabulungi

"Tomorrow Is a Latter Day," performed by Price, Cunningham, McKinley, Nabulungi,
    and Company

"Hello" (Reprise), performed by Company

"Finale," performed by Company

---

build a boat, and sending them across a great ocean to an unnamed Promised Land. Which could have been America.

A lyric insisting that the Garden of Eden is in Missouri, too, is taken from founder Joseph Smith's own pronouncements. But the business about God having his own planet, Kolob, misreads one of Smith's later pronouncements (in the Book of Abraham) in which Kolob was a star close to God's throne, and when the song continues on to claim that Jesus, too, has his own planet, that's just plain wrong.

What is carried off with devastating aplomb is the sheer sense of dislocation that awaits the missionaries when they arrive in Uganda. "We wanted it to be that place where you always read about ... where you go 'Can this place get a break? They have earthquakes and then cholera and then a warlord and then a famine and then no water?,'" Stone explained. "It was just supposed to be that place. And we settled on Uganda because they speak English there ... and it borders Congo and Sudan. It's supposed to be just [a] generic, war-torn worst place on Earth. If you're in Utah, nothing you've learned in Utah when you're eighteen or nineteen years old makes any sense when you get there."

They steered clear, however, of perhaps the most controversial aspect of the religion, which is therefore the one element that everybody seems to know about. "The only thing [we avoided]," Parker explained, "was the polygamy aspect. We wanted to do your everyday Salt Lake City Mormon ... That was a misconception among a lot of people — that Mormons are polygamist. No, they're not. I mean they obviously have that in their history and there are some fundamentalists." But in general, Mormons take no more wives than anybody else.

Other aspects, some of which were actually already scripted, were removed because they required too much in-depth knowledge of the faith itself from the audience. And some, again already written, were excised because they no longer worked. The song "All American Prophet," for example, started life as "The Bible Is a Trilogy."

According to Parker, "it used to go 'The Bible is a trilogy ...' and it made movie references. It was all a joke about how the third part of a trilogy is always the best movie and how the third *Matrix* is actually the best—which is a great joke. So it started with the African guy stepping forward saying 'Can you imagine if *The Matrix* had ended after the first one ...' and then the other African guy says, 'I actually thought the third *Matrix* was the worst one.' It was this thing we had [in the script] for the longest time and we finally decided 'The Bible Is a Trilogy' doesn't make sense with the story anymore. So we changed it to this other thing and we lost that great [line] but we thought what else could he come forward and say ..."

He said, "I have maggots in my scrotum."

Uncertainty as to what form the production would ultimately take ... was it a movie, was it a cartoon, was it an album, was it whatever ... was resolved by Lopez. Parker told the *Collider*, "When we first started working on it ... we toyed with the idea of it being a Broadway show or being a movie. Obviously since Matt and I know how to make a movie, we were like 'let's make a movie.' Because we can do that pretty quick. I was always visualizing it as a movie because that's what I do, so I don't think it would be a really difficult thing."

Lopez, however, had consistently visualized it as a stage musical, and when Parker and Stone agreed, it was Lopez who introduced them to the concept of developmental workshops through which rough spots could be ironed out, fresh ideas could be introduced, and the entire creation could stretch out to its natural shape and size.

It was a whole new world for the *South Park* pair. "Hollywood people would be like, 'Why the hell would you do that?,'" Stone recalled. "And we'd be like, 'Because it's fucking funny!'"

And very hard work. "In animation, we would simply have people do an 'animatic,' something we could look at on an Avid," Stone continued. "But for Broadway, you need twenty actors and auditions—and that means dealing with Equity, the actors union. They have a pay scale just for workshops."

Ultimately some half a dozen workshops, directed by Jason Moore and starring the likes of Cheyenne Jackson, Daniel Reichard, and Benjamin Walker, would be staged over the next four years, ranging in length from half an hour on up. Finally, February 2008 brought the first fully staged rendition with Walker and Josh Gad in the lead roles of Elders Price and Cunningham. Then, pausing only for director Casey Nicholaw to replace Moore in June 2010, a final five-week workshop was launched in August 2010.

Stone recalled, "Trey's and my instincts have served us pretty well, and those instincts are usually [to] 'forget the normal way. We're a little two-man unit that does things our way.' But the 2008 reading had this magic, to hear live actors speaking and singing, and then a live audience respond with laughter."

Initial plans hatched by producer Rudin were for *The Book of Mormon* to debut off-Broadway, at the New York Theater Workshop. But realizing that Parker and Stone "work best when the stakes are highest," he instead decided to go the whole hog and book the Eugene O'Neill Theatre, 230 West 49th Street.

He told the *New York Times*, "In most of the things that I've been involved with that have turned out to be good, there is a moment when you have to face your maker. You either sink or swim. And this was the moment."

Team America stand by for action.

A twenty-eight-strong cast of players, an $11 million budget, a frantic burst of rewrites and rehearsals, and on February 24, 2011, *The Book of Mormon* played its first preview performance, a mere six days after its creators heard the full thing for the first time themselves. A month later, on March 24, *The Book of Mormon* opened for business; and what business it was.

"The filthiest, most offensive, and—surprise—sweetest thing you'll see on Broadway this year," declared *Vogue*, electing *The Book of Mormon* "quite possibly the funniest musical ever."

The *New York Times* went even further. Having already compared *The Book of Mormon* to such past Broadway sensations as *The Sound of Music* and *The King and I*, the review went on, "[it] achieves something like a miracle. It both makes fun of and ardently embraces the all-American art form of the inspirational book musical. No Broadway show has so successfully had it both ways since Mel Brooks adapted his film *The Producers* for the stage . . . ."

Not all the reviews were positive. The *Wall Street Journal* continued, "Making fun of Mormons in front of a Broadway crowd is like shooting trout in a demitasse cup. And while we're on the subject of imitation courage, let it be duly noted that if the title of this show were *The Quran*, it wouldn't have opened." Referring back to past controversies, the paper sniffed, "The boys have learned their lesson well: Never shoot at anybody who shoots back."

According to an approving *Entertainment Weekly*, however, "Jon Stewart is somewhere probably still raving about *The Book of Mormon*." "There is a song in this," Stewart said, "that I think . . . when the aliens come thousands of years from now, it may exist as the only memory of Earth, and I gotta say, I'm happy to go down with it."

Throughout its first year onstage, *The Book of Mormon* ranked consistently among the top five best-selling Broadway shows, in the process of setting no less than twenty-two new weekly ticket sales records for the Eugene O'Neill Theater. It gathered up nine Tony Awards (including Best Musical), and when the original Broadway cast recording was released on CD in May 2011, its chart high of number three established it as the highest-charting Broadway cast album since *Hair* in 1969. It also grabbed a Grammy for Best Musical Theater Album.

August 2012 saw the play commence its first North American tour at the Denver Center for the Performing Arts; December saw it open in Chicago; February 2013 brought its UK debut; October 2013 saw a second North American tour get underway. According to *Mercury News*, "The profane parody sold out in less than two hours for its long-awaited five-week run at San Francisco's Curran Theatre [in 2011] and prime seats are now going for as much as $1,500 a pop on StubHub. The same thing also happened at the launch of the national tour in Denver."

As for the Mormons themselves, they generally saw the play for what it was, even taking out advertising in the musical's Playbill as it toured the United States. The Church's official statement explained, "The production may attempt to entertain audiences for an evening, but *The Book of Mormon* as a volume of scripture will change people's lives forever by bringing them closer to Christ." To which Parker and Stone issued their own statement, coming out in full agreement.

"The Mormon church's response to this musical is almost like our QED at the end of it. That's a cool, American response to a ribbing—a big musical that's done in their name. Before the church responded, a lot of people would ask us, 'Are you afraid of what the church would say?' And Trey and I were like, 'They're going to be cool.' And they were like, 'No, they're not. There are going to be protests.' And we were like, 'Nope, they're going to be cool.' We weren't that surprised by the church's response. We had faith in them."

"I don't think anybody would want to see a two-hour-long Mormon-bashing, and we wouldn't want to see that either," Parker told *Fresh Air*'s Terry Gross. "We love the goofiness of Mormon stories. Some of them are incredulous, and we loved almost all the Mormons that we had ever met. So this was sort of this conundrum that we like to talk about—we think what they believe is really, really ridiculous, and yet they seem like pretty happy people."

That faith was apparently rewarded. *USA Today* quoted two LDS Church members who attended the play in New York, and seemed as surprised as they were by the musical's treatment. "I was expecting to be offended," said one, twenty-two-year-old Anne Christensen, "but was pleasantly surprised by how incredibly sweet it was"; while her mother, Janet, continued, "it's not G-rated, but they treated us with affection. And they did their homework."

Two years later, in May 2013, the Church's official publication, the *Deseret News*, reported on a Boston theatergoer who spent the entire show laughing delightedly at the musical itself, but was nevertheless sufficiently intrigued that she began investigating the truth about Mormonism for herself. A process that ended in her conversion, and the cheerful revelation, "My mom will sometimes say, 'I can't believe I brought you to that show. None of this would have happened.' I tell her that it still would have, just in a different way."

But head of Public Relations Michael Otterson was also at pains to explain, "parody isn't reality, and it's the very distortion that makes it appealing and often funny. The danger is not when people laugh, but when they take it seriously—if they leave a theater believing that Mormons really do live in some kind of a surreal world of self-deception and illusion." To combat this, he went on to outline the real-life Mormon Church's contributions to improving life in Africa, beneath a headline that insisted, "Why I won't be seeing . . . the musical."

"Four million in 17 countries have gained access to clean water.

"More than 34,000 physically handicapped children have received wheelchairs.

"Millions of children in 22 countries have been vaccinated against measles and other killer diseases.

"More than 126,000 individuals have had their sight restored or improved.

"Some 52,000 trained in neonatal resuscitation to help struggling newborns breathe."

But ultimately, he insisted, *The Book of Mormon* was no cause for alarm. "In the great sweep of history, parodies and TV dramas are blips on the radar screen that come and go. Sure, the Church of Jesus Christ of Latter-day Saints pushes back when the record needs correcting or when legal rights need defending, but the world of popular entertainment is more likely to be met with a collective shrug than by placard-waving Mormon protesters."

21

Who's Who (Concluded)

A Q–Z of *South Park* Celebrities, Nonentities, and Random Stuff That Fits the Difficult Letters

Q

Q is for Queen Spider, because when . . . after a lot of other stuff has happened, of course, including the transformation of a badly drawn Barbra Streisand into the ravenous, town-destroying Mecha-Streisand, there is only one thing left to do. Chef is instructed to contact Robert Smith, front man with the Cure across a decade of the genre-defying and, simultaneously, defining albums that lie at the heart of Gothic rock. Only he can slay the beast.

Voicing his own animated character, Smith promptly transformed himself into a massive moth-like creature that . . . after even more other stuff has happened, of course . . . successfully launched Mecha-Streisand into outer space, where she exploded. He then departed the town with the applause of the grateful populace ringing in his ears, and a word of extra thanks from Kyle. *Disintegration*, the Cure's eighth album, the little boy declares, "is the best album ever!"

Which may be true. But equally significantly, it is also the only international chart-topping album to include a song, the misleadingly titled "Lullaby," about being eaten alive at night by spiders. "I want people to like the Cure for the right reasons," Smith sniffed, "because it's different to everything else, and not really accessible. It's a bit of a crass generalization, but people whose favorite Cure albums are *Pornography* and *Disintegration* are generally more alert, and have thought about things."

Things like spider diners?

That same generalization might also explain the Cure's record company's reaction the first time the assembled bigwigs heard *Disintegration*. They professed it akin to commercial suicide. "I thought it was our masterpiece," Smith mourned. "They thought it was shit."

Around the distractions and disasters (as though it were an episode of *South Park* itself, the studio caught fire during the recording), *Disintegration* took on a life of its own. Many nights, the band stayed up until dawn simply playing, something they hadn't done since they were making *Pornography*.

In the studio itself, Smith deliberately made life difficult for himself, just to force himself to breach new frontiers. "Things got very intense. We put songs like "Disintegration" into a key I can't sing, so it hurt me. It sounds really good from a physical point of view."

The result was an album that spun off three hit singles, provoking an outbreak of Cure mania that saw the band's faces adorn seemingly every even vaguely music-oriented magazine throughout the summer of 1989. And it filled MTV nights with a horror that scuttled straight out of Smith's personal fear of spiders. But not the cute, cuddly (albeit vastly outsized) spiders like the politely spoken Queen Spider who presides over the Vatican and is, therefore, even more powerful than the Pope. He was scared of the really nasty ones.

"Fat spiders," he said, "with long thin legs that look like they're going to burst make me go really weird. When I was young, I was really scared of spiders and they always used to be in my bed. They weren't actually there at all, but I imagined they were. I'd try to get over the phobia the way you get over any phobia. I'd approach them and force myself to pick them up. I can hold spiders now, even the big hairy ones. But I wouldn't let them near my face."

He must have loved making the "Lullaby" video.

R

R is for Really? Another show about social media? Oh good.

This may come as something of a shock, but the animated Baldwins were not all wiped out when the Canadian Air Force so ruthlessly blasted them into oblivion at the outset of the great North American War.

Not all of them, anyway. Drawings of Daniel, William (Billy), and Stephen may indeed have perished as the bombs rained down on their luxurious Hollywood abode. But the oldest of the brothers, Alec . . . he was made of sterner stuff. He didn't simply survive the onslaught. He survived and prospered, and in 2013, he returned to South Park via a new television commercial, extolling the virtues of the latest and greatest development in social networking, Shitter. And was it fate? Or mere coincidence that dictated that six days after that advertisement began airing, Edward Snowden, the fugitive American former intelligence worker, was confirmed as one of three nominees for the Sakharov prize, Europe's top human rights award?

For without Snowden and his bone-chilling revelation that government spies actually spy on people for a living, Cartman would never have felt the need to infiltrate the NSA. And without Shitter, the thumbs-free network that allows subscribers to upload their very thoughts to the Internet without any tiresome typing, touch pads, or even computers and phones, Cartman's revelations would never have been broadcast live to the nation on Alec Baldwin's new cable show.

It's such a shame that nobody else was listening.

Shitter is, perhaps, the ultimate frontier for social networking as we know and use it today. Yet it is also just the latest in a long line of technological developments that have effectively freed us forever (or at least until the power goes out) from the dictatorship of pen and paper; has allowed us, too, to tap the hitherto unimagined potential of that most humble of household commodities, the telephone.

There are people alive and functioning today who could never dream that once, a phone was for speaking into, and who would never dream of using it for such a mundane purpose. It's a notebook, it's a music player, it's a secretary, it's a keyboard, it's a camera (perfect for those occasions when Cartman needs to send a picture of his balls to Stan), it's a portable pornography collection.

Shitter changed that forever. Once it was sufficient simply to say "telephone, dude? What century are you living in?" Now computers themselves were outmoded. The power of thought, that's all Shitter requires. Well, that and the brain implant that will broadcast your thoughts to your followers. All of your thoughts. Even, sadly, the ones that probably shouldn't be broadcast. And people think Sookie Stackhouse has it tough.

The sheer magnificent power of the Internet, social media and all, arrived in South Park early, and did so with a bang. Although it wasn't quite as big a bang as it could have been. When the Queen of England secretly planted a nuclear device inside the former First Lady's vagina, it was via social media that Stan and Kyle were unable to unravel the multitudinous strands of seemingly unconnected detail that linked the divergent elements of the plot.

From shady Russian hit men to Cartman's mistaken suspicions of a local Muslim family, and all the way up to Buckingham Palace, a Google search for "Hilary Clinton Campaign Rally" led to a link to YouTube, "where this Russian guy had a bunch of videos . . . . [then] I cross-referenced his YouTube profile with MySpace, and according to his blog, he's an old-school Communist. [Then] I got a text of the Russian guy's podcast. It's all a bunch of links to eBay . . . ."

Cross-reference that with JDate . . . double-check it on eHarmony . . . "According to PayPal, the Russian guys are just hired mercenaries who had ads up on Craig's List and got paid through eBay so that Boston could be attacked by . . . the British."

Of course, there are those people, those who arrived tragically late to the cyber revolution, who continue to pooh-pooh all this as merely a forum where the word "fun" is used as an adjective, "asap" is a two-syllable word, and "LOL" is a catchall roar of approval that too many people use inappropriately.

A mind-numbing panacea that allows the most friendless, soulless social retard to maintain the facade of a happy and fulfilling life whose only price is feigning deafness to the echoing blackness of their own relentless solitude and misery.

But to a generation raised to LMAO whenever they see a photo of somebody's breakfast . . . and that presumably includes most of the governments of the world, given the amount of time they allegedly spend trawling through all their citizens' updates and comments . . . the Internet is more than a means of communication, it is a tool. Like a screwdriver or a bradawl. And one day, we will discover what it's actually for. Beyond giving everyone an inflated sense of self-worth, that is.

Everyone, that is, aside from Kip Drordy, an outcast third grader who signed up to Facebook in a fit of futile optimism and who, six months later, had still to register a single friend.

It was so sad to watch. Every day, the boy sank deeper and deeper into a slough of despair; every day, he did nothing but stare disconsolately into his computer screen, hoping and praying that one day, someone would add him as a friend.

And then a miracle!

Kyle Broflovski barely knew the boy, but word of his predicament had spread, and being a pleasant, well-brought-up kid, Kyle does the decent thing. He befriended Kip—and immediately his entire world turned upside down. Suddenly, both in real life and the cyber environment, Kip was the only friend Kyle had. All of his other friends deserted him.

Peer pressure is a terrible thing. While Kyle watched in horror as his tally of Facebook friends plunged inexorably toward zero (or one; Kip would never abandon him), Stan was equally mortified to discover that his newly opened account was overflowing with friends and acquaintances, most of whom he didn't even know. And how strange is that, to be sharing the most intimate details of your pet cat's grooming habits with a bunch of people you've never met in your life?

A world in which sad sack semiacquaintances post updates specifically designed to wring sympathy and support from their "friends," and who will then threaten to "unfriend" those who aren't supportive enough.

A world in which the death of a celebrity will uncork a tsunami of grief that is pornographic in its need to seem deeper and more sincere than anyone else's.

A world in which . . . did you know the term "Facebook" is phonetically identical to the French words for "goat's ass"?

Classy!

Stan had not wanted to sign up to Facebook; was cajoled into doing so by precisely the same social mechanism that was simultaneously destroying Kyle's life. Stan was an outcast because he hadn't pledged his soul to the vampire squid; Kyle was cast out because he chose the wrong friend from amongst the manifold tasty lures being dangled by that same vampire squid.

Now, neither was content. Stan discovered that the most unexpected people were now angry that he has not yet added them as friends. His father, for example. Stan didn't know his father even had a Facebook page . . . .

Or Wendy, who noticed that Stan's relationship status said "single," when clearly he should have acknowledged his long-standing attachment to her.

Small wonder that the antipathy he initially felt toward a Facebook membership was now barreling uncontrollably toward full-fledged hatred; nor that, having acquired 845,000 friends without even trying, he now desired nothing more than to delete his account.

But like the small print in the Apple terms and conditions that nobody in the world has ever read, despite the fact that they allegedly contain some remarkably alarming subclauses . . . including the late Steve Jobs's right to graft your mouth to someone else's anus . . . Facebook is not an easy place from which to escape.

Indeed, it swiftly appeared that the more Stan struggled, the deeper into the system he was sucked, until his entire being was consumed by the Internet, and all human interactivity was predicated on either befriending or being befriended by others . . . none of whom you know, few of whom you will ever speak to or hear from again.

But all of whom will bombard you on an hourly basis with pictures of cats, photos of meals, and invitations to join them playing games that aren't really games. Not really.

S

S is for Scientology, and to outsiders, it is hard to know what to make of the entire shebang. Its detractors paint it as a cult, offering veiled and hopefully exaggerated comparisons to such apocalyptic doom-mongers as David Koresh's Branch Davidians, Jim Jones's People's Temple, and David Blaine's . . . oops, that one was made up, wasn't it; and damning it with the attentions of bodies as disparate as the IRS and the Cult Awareness network.

Its supporters, however, argue just as convincingly in its favor, pointing not only to personal growth but to personal success, as evidence that Scientology, the Science of the Mind, does work. And nowhere is this doctrine more pronounced than in the membership of the Celebrity Center.

The Celebrity Center began taking shape in 1955, around a year after the Church itself developed out of founder L. Ron Hubbard's self-help blockbuster *Dianetics: The Modern Science of Mental Health.* Project Celebrity was Hubbard's personal brainchild, a manifesto that called on Scientologists to introduce the Church to the rich and famous, to "forward the expansion and popularization of Scientology through the Arts."

Attached to the memo was a list of sixty-three names that Hubbard personally hoped to recruit to the cause, among them Walt Disney, Pablo Picasso, Ernest Hemingway, and Liberace.

In the event, not one of that original list joined. Indeed, many of them were dead before the Celebrity Center finally got off the ground and started operating out of a rented building at 1809 West Eighth Street, in 1969. Neither were its earliest recruits what one would call prima facie examples of the caliber of entertainer Hubbard was so anxious to attract.

One early convert, Bobby Lipton, for instance, was merely the brother of *Mod Squad* star Peggy Lipton.

Slowly, however, the numbers, and the attendant cachet, swelled. Actress Karen Black became involved in the early 1970s, with screenwriter/director Ernest Lehmann after he worked with Black on the movie *Portnoy's Complaint*, and saw how totally unflappable she was, during even the greatest crisis. She ascribed her calm to Scientology.

"It was nice being around a lot of people who felt it was bad form to be gloomy and self-absorbed," Lehmann explained to *Premiere* magazine. "They were very cheerful, upbeat, which is not something you see much of in the film community." He went on to describe the Celebrity Center itself as "more of a social thing than anything else, with cocktail parties and art exhibits. If you had nothing to do, you'd drop in."

Among the myriad celebs who have since "dropped in" can be numbered actor Tom Cruise, singer Isaac Hayes, and singing actor John Travolta, who arrived in January 1975, introduced to Scientology by actress Joan Prather, whom he met on the set of the movie *Devil's Rain*.

This was pre-*Saturday Night Fever*, pre-*Grease*, pre-any of the things for which we revere Travolta today. But he was the star of *Welcome Back, Kotter*, and when he turned up on set with a cold one day and Prather offered to perform "an assist," a healing method developed by Scientology, he was both curious and, afterwards, convinced.

"I'd get very depressed for no reason. Psychoanalysis wasn't for me, but Scientology made sense right away, because it seemed like a means of self-help. A meter shows you when you're responding to a bad experience in your past; you find the source of pain, acknowledge it, deal with it. That seemed to me very logical, and I was right. I get answers that way."

This meter, the E (for Engram)-Meter as it is known, lies at the heart of Scientology. Engrams, according to Hubbard's teachings, are essentially the points of negativity that affect one's mood. It is these Engrams that are addressed during what Scientologists call the Auditing process—a form of therapy in which traumatic past experiences are relived, until one learns to accept them.

Controversy and cynicism have, of course, been attached, in varying degrees, to the efficacy of this system, but the fact remains, coming to terms with a painful experience is often tantamount to beating it. Travolta describe the Auditing process to journalist Barbara Grizzuti Harrison.

"Basically you sit opposite [the Auditor] with . . . an E-meter, a little oval-shaped machine that has a motor and a needle that registers when you hold it. You just go through what you haven't said to people that you should have, what you did to people, what upsets I have with people that bother me.

"There are three . . . 'rods'—rods means basics. Okay: things get out of whack when you flaunt your rods—upsets with people that involve a breaking of affection with them, a breaking of communication with them, a breaking of your point of view versus my point of view, your reality versus my reality. That's really the basics, what Scientologists call ARC—Affinity, Reality, Communication. So you discuss it."

Ah yes, discussion. Debate. The conducting of an informed argument during which both sides of a divide are allowed equal time in which to state their case and make their claims.

A lot of the people watching *South Park* on the night of . . . let's say November 16, 2005; and even more of those who lashed out against "Trapped in the Closet" afterwards, could have done with some of that.

T

T is for Time Travel, and while that is often regarded as a modern concept, a staple of twentieth-century science fiction that arose from author H. G. Wells's legendary novel *The Time Machine*, the notion that man might journey not only through space but also through the centuries is almost as ancient as man himself.

Celtic myth, Hindu spiritualism, and Japanese legend all feature tales in which a character is projected forward in time, usually as the result of some form of supernatural intervention, and what is Washington Irving's Rip Van Winkle if not an admittedly very relaxed and time-consuming kind of time traveler?

Ebenezer Scrooge, in Charles Dickens's *A Christmas Carol*, is a time traveler, as he drifts between Christmases Past and Future, and so is Mark Twain's *Connecticut Yankee in King Arthur's Court*. But it was indeed Wells who first popularized the notion from which modern concepts of time travel have developed, that a machine could be constructed that allowed its operator to journey at will through the years.

Fifty years young, television's *Doctor Who* is the longest-running and most successful time-traveling adventure, although shows such as the British *Timeslip*, the American *Time Tunnel*, and the animated Mr.

Peabody's WABAC machine have all challenged its supremacy at different points in time, while recent fiction has seen author Connie Willis weave some fascinating tales of time travel through the novels *The Doomsday Book* and *Blackout / All Clear*.

There, a starting point is fixed some years into Earth's future, acknowledging that no matter how profound time travel's theorists might be, mankind is still some distance away from actually perfecting it. A truth that South Park, too, discovered when a new mature student, claiming to be named Bill Cosby, arrived at the Elementary and began showing what seemed a quite disproportionate interest in Cartman's new Trapper Keeper. Well, we say "disproportionate," but it was a *Dawson's Creek* Trapper Keeper. And it was certainly far more advanced than the basic model that Kyle had just acquired.

Too advanced! In just three years, Bill Cosby explains, "the Dawson's Creek Trapper Keeper that belongs to an Eric Cartman in South Park [will] manifest . . . itself into an omnipotent super being, and destroy . . . all of humanity."

First it will connect to a satellite uplink computer; from there it will seize control of every computer in the world. Then it would grow more and more powerful until, in the year 2018, it shattered the last vestiges of loyalty to, or dependence on, mankind, "and there was nothing the humans could do."

The Mighty Trapper Keeper turned on it former overlords, destroying everything and everyone in its path. "Finally, the humans decided to send one of their robots into the past to destroy the Trapper Keeper before it even got started."

Cartman, unwillingly of course, allows his pride and joy to be destroyed—and then cajoles his mother into buying him a new one. Which, of course, turns out to be the one that will destroy the world. It takes the bravery of the boys, and the inadvertent self-sacrifice of an exaggerated rendition of TV hostess Rosie O'Donnell, to destroy the machine just as it is poised to devour the military nerve center at Cheyenne Mountain, and Bill Cosby fades away. The world has been saved; he never existed. You could say he was terminated.

But the future was not yet finished with South Park. Just a few short years later, a portal in time opened up, connecting the twenty-first century with the twenty-ninth (the year 3045, to be precise) and facilitating a ceaseless flood of time immigrants. Whose quest for jobs and willingness to accept low rates of pay (Stan's own family took on an immigrant servant for ten cents an hour) blatantly echoes the war cries of all those who have opposed more conventional forms of immigration in our own time.

The solution to the problem was simple. To prevent the future from ever taking place. Not through "getting gay," as advocated by the most vociferous anti-Gooback protestors, but by ensuring that the horrendous conditions of the future never come to pass, by planting trees, recycling waste, caring for the poor, and singing environmental songs.

Which seemed to be working really well until Stan suddenly stopped; looked around at the happy, smiling, tree-planting, jingle-singing masses; and declared "this is gay." Even gayer, agreed Cartman, than when all the men in town were gathered in a big pile of sweaty, writhing male flesh together.

All work stopped, the men piled back on top of one another. The future would have to look after itself.

Conservation and ecology would not be left on the backseat, of course. The emergence of the first hybrid cars sent many of South Park's more concerned citizens to the auto showrooms to do their own little bit for the planet. Unfortunately, the ensuing deluge of smugness emanating from such vehicles' owners itself became a major health hazard. Particularly after it collided with a similar mass that had developed over San Francisco.

For the first time in history, meteorologists found themselves forced to issue a Smug Alert, one that could be rescinded only after all hybrids had been destroyed.

So yeah, the future can look after itself. It always has in the past.

U

U is for "Uncle Fucka," and it has to be admitted that, at this very late stage in human development, it is highly unlikely that anybody—and here we include such giants of classic songsmithery as the surviving Beatles, the still-rolling Stones, Bono, Sting, and even Steamy Ray Vaughan—will ever write a song as succinct and all-powerful as "Uncle Fucka."

True, some may come within spitting distance. Others, unknowingly plagiarizing either lyric, melody, form, or content, might consider themselves in roughly the same ballpark.

But if Fishsticks is (and who are we to disagree) the funniest joke ever told, and the Aristocrat joke is the filthiest (ditto), then "Uncle Fucka" is the most uniquely singable, hummable, tap-your-foot-along-to-able song written across any of the millennia that have elapsed since the first man banged the first bone on the first rock. Because even then, there was probably some dude in the next cave down who accused the composer of ripping him off.

Performed in their classic and inimitable style by Canadian popular entertainers Terrance and Phillip, "Uncle Fucka" rips nobody off. "Uncle Fucka" is un-rip-offable. When "Blame Canada," from the motion picture *South Park: Bigger, Longer & Uncut*, was nominated for an Academy Award for Best Original Song in 1999, around the world voices rose in protest, insisting that "Uncle Fucka" should have been nominated instead. And it should.

Preparation for that ceremony was fraught. According to CNN, the first obstacle arose when ABC (broadcasting the ceremony on television) demanded "Blame Canada" be given new, television-friendly lyrics for the occasion.

Its composers refused, not because they felt the word "fuck" should be aired on national network television . . . that was a bridge they were happy to leave uncrossed. But because ABC were objecting to "fart" as well! And we all know what happens if you hold back your farts. You burst into flame.

Tricky, too, was securing a name performer to sing the song. Canadian singer Anne Murray was Parker and Stone's first choice, all the more so since she is referred to as "that bitch" in the song itself. She declined, but Robin Williams accepted. "We thought he could pull it off and he would get it, and not cheese it up too much," Parker said. "It was either that or go the other route and have, like, Jewel do it acoustically."

In the event, the song did not win. It was beaten out by Phil Collins, an award that was to unleash a world of hurt on the hapless percussionist. Nevertheless, Parker and Stone could at least take solace from the fact that *South Park: Bigger, Longer & Uncut* was only the second R-Rated movie ever to receive an Academy nomination, and they celebrated in fitting style. By attending the ceremony in drag, clad in replicas of dresses previously worn at the Oscars by Jennifer Lopez and Gwyneth Paltrow. And, they claimed, by dropping acid beforehand.

"We were fully expecting to lose," admitted Parker, later. "Just not to Phil Collins"

Other awards tumbled into their grasp, however. "Uncle Fucka" received an MTV Movie Award for Best Musical Performance, while the 2001 *Guinness Book of World Records* credited *South Park: Bigger, Longer & Uncut* for boasting the "Most Swearing in an Animated Film," reckoning up a total of 399 profane words (on top of 128 offensive gestures), among them 144 uses of fuck. Close to 25 percent of these are included in "Uncle Fucka."

Yet "Uncle Fucka" (and "Blame Canada") is just one (are just two) of the multitude of songs with which *South Park* has soundtracked the past almost-two decades; and just one (two) of the reason(s) why an iPod stuffed with *South Park* songs would have very little space left over for anything else. Appendix 2 will prove that.

V

V is for Queen Victoria. The great-grandmother of the Queen of England; the progenitor of a bloodline that has, over the past century or so, included such alleged cultural heroes as Jack the Ripper, the Monster of Glamis, and a man who wanted to be a tampon, Queen Victoria is generally regarded amongst history's greatest prudes.

In 1837, one of her first acts upon acceding to the British throne was to issue a "Proclamation for the Encouragement of Piety and Virtue, and for the Preventing and Punishing of Vice, Profaneness and Immorality." Her famous, if apocryphal, declaration that "we are not amused" remains a vital part of the British comedian's cultural arsenal; and apocrypha continues to insist that she refused to criminalize lesbianism because she refused to accept that it even existed.

Her private life, too, is shrouded in a wrap of similar disapproval. Although she lived to the age of eighty-two, popular history describes Victoria enjoying just two personal relationships throughout her entire life, with her husband Prince Albert and, toward the end of her life, with the groom John Brown.

Yet she was clearly a woman of intense passions. Victoria married Albert when she was twenty-one. By the time of his death, in 1861, the couple had had nine children, each of whom would carry the Queen's blood to the farthest corners of nineteenth-century Europe.

Indeed, their prolificacy was legendary; even in an age when large families were the societal norm, the couple's otherwise loyal staff unhesitatingly nicknamed them "the Royal Rabbits," while in satirical circles, Albert's proud military bearing was frequently employed as a euphemism for other parts of his anatomy. Here was a man, the city wags remarked, who seemed always to stand to attention.

Neither was Victoria averse to a certain amount of ribaldry. When Victor Emmanuel, the King of Sardinia, visited London in 1855, Victoria's court awaited their meeting in mortal terror, convinced that Victor's notoriously salacious tongue would send the Queen into paroxysms of horror. Instead, Victoria emerged from their meeting remarking simply that the Sardinian's conversation was "startling in the extreme," and that she would be decorating him with the Order of the Garter.

Indeed, far from the bitter, pleasureless curmudgeon she is customarily portrayed as, Victoria very much packed a lighter side.

In 1848, during a visit to a distillery, she mortified the country's growing teetotal lobby by gaily swilling down several glasses of whiskey.

She supported the notion that a woman's clothing should generally disguise the wearer's figure, but she acknowledged, and approved, the one prevalent exception—that evening dress could and should "exploit the top half of the [wearer's] breasts."

In private, she would snort merrily at the assumption, cast forth by the socialite Mary Philadelphia Merrifield, that men were disgusted by overt displays of breast and cleavage. Victoria herself was heartily endowed, and once sent her chambermaid squealing delighted to bed by informing her that Prince Albert, at least, had never complained.

How she might have snorted then, had she sat and watched "The Snuke," an episode of *South Park* in which the current occupant of the British throne commits suicide with a handgun, her dreams of finally bringing an end to the American Revolution shattered by the destruction of her fleet by a bigoted fat boy. Oh, and the unraveling of her frankly foolproof plan to detonate a nuclear bomb hidden inside Hilary Clinton's vagina.

Victoria would simply have spanked another bare behind.

W

W is for Whore. An Old Anorexic Whore who, according to Kenny, "wore out her welcome years ago, and . . . she now suddenly speaks with a British accent and she thinks she can play guitar and she should go fuck herself."

Which is no way to speak of anybody, but Kenny was about to die and, for the first time, it looked as though his death might this time be fatal.

As we have already seen, it is misleading to say, as some folk do, that Kenny died in every episode of *South Park*. He didn't. But he did die in a lot of them and, elsewhere in this book, we list every passing, near-passing, and postpassing mutilation the poor lad has ever suffered.

Why, then, did the episode titled "Kenny Dies" seem so final?

Because it very nearly was. Week after week, Kenny died, and every time it needed to be a new, fresh, and dynamic death. After a while, it just grew wearying, for Kenny, for his parents, for his friends, and, most of all, for Parker and Stone, who had simply had enough of having to freshen up the boy's demise.

So this time, when Kenny died, he died. He even had a funeral, his first since his spontaneous combustion two years previous, and so moving was the ceremony that even Mr. and Mrs. McCormick, who had surely run out of tears long before, were drawn to fresh heights of grief and despair.

Thank goodness, then, for Chef, able as always to give such an apparently random tragedy some very real meaning.

"Sometimes God takes those closest to us, because it makes him feel better about himself. He is a very vengeful God. He's all pissed off about something we did thousands of years ago. He just can't get over it, so he doesn't care who he takes. Children, puppies, it don't matter to him, so long as it makes us sad. Do you understand?"

X

X is for Xmas, and Xmas in South Park is very special indeed. For of all the characters that have established South Park as their home, few have the panache of Mr. Hankey.

Nor do they have the history. According to Trey Parker, he had been drawing Mr. Hankey since childhood, inspired by the dire warnings delivered by his parents, Randy and Sharon, of what would befall him if he didn't flush the toilet after use.

Parents do say the most horrific things to their children. The little girl who was warned never to enter her father's garden shed, for fear of the squirrels who would tie her up with fishing line. The little boy who, years later, recalled for BBC America's *Graham Norton Show*, being warned against touching his private parts because the Penis Fairy would come out and eat them. And Trey Parker who . . . well, let's allow him to tell the tale.

"My dad is a really fucked-up guy," Parker declared. "And he would just . . . mess with me all the time. And one day, I think I was three or four, and my mother — I guess I had a problem with flushing the toilet. Like I would go poo and then wouldn't flush it. And my mother would yell at me and yell at me. And finally she said, 'Randy, you've got to have a talk with Trey about flushing the toilet.' And my dad said, 'Well, Trey, you uh, you need to flush the toilet because uh, if you don't, Mr. Hankey is going to come out and kill you.' And I was like — you know, I'm three years old, and I'm like, 'what do you mean?' And he goes, 'Well, it just sits there, and you flush it. But if you don't, he'll come to life and he sings a little song and he kills you.' And I was just like — so I fuckin' flushed the toilet, man, seven, eight times."

Toilets are a dangerous place. Musical poo is certainly a menace of which we should all be aware. But even after the lavatory has been flushed, there are certain niceties to attend to. Such as closing the lid. Clyde, one of the students at South Park Elementary, neglected to do so, and his mother paid the ultimate price, falling into the open toilet and, having activated the flush mechanism during her struggles to escape, being sucked into the very bowels of the mechanism. Sadly, the rescue crew had no option. They had to disconnect the toilet at the mains and risk the change in pressure causing the trapped woman to explode. Which she did.

The tragedy brought the TSA—the Toilet Safety Administration—into South Park, placing the town under an all but intolerable reign of lavatorial discipline and propriety.

No more peeing on the seat. No more refusing to use the safety belt. No more sitting facing the wall, to use the cistern as a shelf for snacks and

The talking turd, the prattling poo, the garrulous guano, the multiloquent meadow-muffin. It's Mr. Hankey!

toys. One cannot help but wonder how Mr. Hankey might have handled the affair.

Mr. Hankey was among the stories that Parker intended to tell when *South Park* was in development stage, and he got as far as the Fox network before realizing that, perhaps, "a little piece of poo that sings" was just one small step too far. Mr. Hankey returned to the depths of the toilet bowl, and South Park found new suitors.

But he hadn't been forgotten. Far from it.

Parker was adamant. Mr. Hankey was never intended to be "talking poo just for the sake of talking poo. It had a point. It's about Kyle feeling like an outcast, feeling like he can't relate to Christmas in the way other kids can, and it sucks."

We the viewers met Mr. Hankey for the first time during a time of great stress and conflict. South Park Elementary was preparing its annual Christmas play, but the school was riven by dissent. No matter what aspect of the festive season the staff and pupils chose to represent, notions of political correctness rose up from their consciousness to point out that someone, somewhere, might be religiously offended by it.

It is a battle, of course, that plays out across America every December, a multifaith society attempting to place a single-faith holiday into a context that everybody can enjoy. Similar battles could have, and have been, played out over the wording on our coins and paper money, but they are rarely so newsworthy—the government tends not to rise to the bait, and just keeps on making the money the same as always. Christmas controversies, however, can draw an opinion, and a reaction, out of almost everybody.

In South Park, where the religious divide would appear to be heavily weighted in favor of an overwhelmingly Christian majority, it was the town's one Jewish family, the Broflovskis, that ignited the debate. Their eldest son Kyle had been cast as Joseph, the father of the newborn savior, and if one really wanted to interpret the Bible accurately, the fact that Jesus's parents were Jewish is one element that can never be argued with.

Unless, of course, you happened to be Kyle's mother Sheila.

As so often with her complaints, matters swiftly flamed out of control. Not to the extent of war breaking out, as would happen when she decided to take on those icons of Canadian entertainment, Terrance and Phillip. But South Park was enflamed, and swiftly, all conceivably offensive references were removed from the town's Christmas celebrations.

No nativity scene, no manger, no shepherds. No lights, no tree, no Santa. No wreaths, no candy canes. Where would it end? And, more importantly, what could replace them?

Kyle, seemingly drawing on the deepest realms of his imagination, suggested they employ Mr. Hankey, the Christmas Poo. He even sang a little song about him. Nobody could be offended by that. Or, equally plausibly, everybody could be offended by it. An equal opportunities insult.

He was laughed away. Not only by his friends and the school (Mr. Garrison went so far as to accuse the Broflovskis of raising their son as a pagan), but by his own parents. He was forbidden ever again to speak of this puerile invention.

Except Mr. Hankey was not an invention. And he was not especially puerile, either.

Has there ever been a more cheerful, good-natured, and generally happy piece of festively clad human excrement than Mr. Hankey? With his wide smiling eyes, his joy-filled smile, his crazy voice overloaded with goodwill and delight, Mr. Hankey is the ultimate feel-good fece, and he lives in the Broflovskis' toilet. From whence he will pop out to shoot the shit with Kyle. The fact that he also smears it around the bathroom as he leaps happily from surface to surface is merely an unfortunate by-product of his glee.

He also delivers presents to all the good little boys and girls. That goodness being defined by the amount of fiber in their diets. (Hence his disgust when an outbreak of trendy so-called healthy eating followed the arrival in South Park of Robert Redford's Sundance Film Festival. All that couscous, falafel, and tofu was destroying the sewer's ecosystem.)

Kyle had an idea. It was not a particularly good one, and hindsight is adamant that it will end in chaos. Which it did. But he decided that the only way to convince people that Mr. Hankey was not a figment of his imagination would be to take him to school with him. In a little cardboard shoebox, of course.

The set for the school play was being demolished that day, and Mr. Garrison was still trying to come up with something, anything, that could carry the spirit of Christmas throughout the town without actually offending anybody. "Anybody," rather pointedly, meaning Mrs. Broflovski—a subliminal message that Cartman immediately seized on as he suggested a festive song of his own. It was called "Kyle's Mom Is a Stupid Bitch" (in D Minor) and, unbidden, he launched into a very long rendition of it.

Which so offended Mr. Hankey that he muscled his way out of the box and hurled himself at Cartman.

Everything that could go wrong now proceeded to do so. Kyle was sent to the counselor's office, to explain to Mr. Mackey why he thought it was a good idea to throw excrement at one of his classmates. And while he was utterly failing to succeed in this endeavor, Mr. Hankey decided he needs a bath. In Mr. Mackey's coffee. The boy was promptly committed to the South Park Mental Institution; Mr. Hankey retired to his shoebox.

Back at the school, the South Park Elementary Holiday Experience was underway. No fresh ideas had been hatched, no suitable songs had been unearthed. The organizers had no alternative but to invite experimental minimalist Philip Glass to soundtrack their play, a decision that not only pacified nobody whatsoever, it also caused a full-scale riot.

In the midst of this, Chef asked what happened to Kyle.

His friends explained the sad story of the boy's delusions, only for Chef to regard them in absolute astonishment.

"We committed him," explained Stan, "because he kept seeing this little brown piece of Christmas poo everywhere that he went."

"Christmas poo?," replied an incredulous Chef. "You . . . you mean Mr. Hankey!"

Mr. Hankey exists! Mr. Hankey appears! Christmas is saved, Kyle is released, Kenny doesn't die, and in the words of the talking turd, we all learned a lesson that Christmastime.

We learned that sometimes people focus so hard on the things they consider to be wrong about Christmas that they completely forget all the things that are right about it.

"Don't you see? This is the one time of year we're s'posed to forget all the bad stuff, to stop worrying and being sad about the state of the world, and for just one day say, 'Aw, the heck with it! Let's sing and dance and bake cookies.'"

And so we do.

Mr. Hankey swiftly became an integral part of the South Park Christmas, one year even hosting his own broadcast of the most timeless holiday songs, as performed by some of his own closest friends, from home and abroad. Satan's rendition of "Christmastime in Hell" and Adolf Hitler's spirited rendition of "O Tannenbaum" will live long in the memory of all who have heard them, while even Jesus and Santa, age-old festive enemies, were briefly reconciled for the occasion.

But something had changed in South Park. Just a year later, with the holidays again upon us, even the ever-insensitive Cartman felt as though the season had lost its luster somehow. Boldly, the boys descended into a sewer to consult Mr. Hankey, there to meet his lovely wife Autumn and his three children, Simon, Amber, and Cornwallis—collectively, the nuggets.

A sympathetic Mr. Hankey promptly sent the nuggets to the surface to do their bit to raise some Christmas cheer, but they reported back in dejected defeat. Failure, too, awaited *The Spirit of Christmas*, an animated holiday special the boys created under Mr. Hankey's auspices, and which they premiered at the old deserted drive-in on the outskirts of town. Nothing, it seemed, could arouse South Park from its torpor.

But Mr. Hankey would not be beaten down, not by the sourpusses of South Park, not by anybody. This was the jobbie, after all, who brought Christmas to the people of Iraq; this was the clinker who one day hid Santa Claus inside a bear costume.

People simply needed to be reminded what Christmas is really all about, and for that message he (and *South Park*'s creators) returned to the words that concluded the very first *South Park* Christmas story, back when Parker and Stone were still at college, and their animation made even Terrance and Phillip look like da Vincis.

Christmas is about presents.

Hurrah.

Y

Y is for You've got cooties and other dread diseases.

It's true! You do!

We live in diseased times, after all.

Throughout history, disease and the world's end have traveled hand in hand. From the typhus that brought the Roman Empire to its knees in the first century, to the yellow fever outbreak that decimated Philadelphia, then this nation's capital, in 1793, and on to the modern AIDS epidemic and the "Judgment of God" hypotheses that still turn up in the extremist media but were once much commoner currency, plague, the biblical Fourth Horseman, continues to strike paralyzing fear wherever he rides, long after his three companions have been dulled by commonplace repetition.

Science long ago stripped away the mysteries of the microbiological world, to prove without doubt how the plagues and pestilence that once haunted superstition are actually transmitted by virus and bacteria.

But still man quakes before the unknown; and, as the second decade of the twenty-first century unfolds, the unknown yawns wider with every passing day.

From the herpes scare of the early 1980s, an early warning for the promiscuous West of the arrival of the killer AIDS; through to the massive revival of green monkey fever in mid-'90s Africa; from the horrific outbreaks of "flesh-eating disease" to the latest deadly strains of MRSA and flu, it sometimes feels as though the entire planet is in the grip of a terrifying pandemic, the likes of which have not been witnessed since the potpourri of diseases that swept medieval Europe and post-Columbian America.

The news gets worse every day. Drugs that should kill the diseases have in some cases been shown to feed and nourish them. Textbook studies of early cases become comedy routines for later ones, and the only genuine triumph has been purely etymological: green monkey fever sounds a lot more frightening (or at least a lot less like a Halloween costume) when its name is changed to Ebola.

Even more terrifying than that, however, is the growing conviction, spawned on the outer limits of human imagination but growing ever more credible with each passing outbreak, that although the diseases themselves work alone, they are acting in concert as well, a guerrilla army of highly trained killers.

It already sounds like a slice of quaint antique mythology, but it is less than two decades since great swathes of the conspiratorial underground were swept by the fear of a vast biological coalition, timed to coincide with the approach of the millennium and feeding greedily on the apocalyptic fears that had already seen cult fever unleashed tragically through the subways of Japan, the suburbs of Canada, the forests of France, and the compounds of America.

It was established two centuries ago that pestilence and living conditions are inextricably linked, and that health and hygiene are better bug-killers than all the penicillin in the world. The question more recent fringe scientists have started to ask is, what if the bacillus changed the battlefield? What if it is no longer our physical state that encourages their awful rise, but our mental state as well?

What better cure for a sick society than a sickness that wipes out that society?

Nestled in the mountains high above South Park Hospital, in the picturesque (if somewhat inhospitable) passage for which it is named, Hell's Pass Hospital would be on the forefront of such a cataclysm, because Hell's Pass has seen almost everything that the mad microbe can throw at it.

It has seen it, and, at least occasionally, it has sent it back to its room without supper, to ensure that whatever other fate might befall the tiny town that the hospital overlooks, no matter whether *South Park* ends with a bang or a whimper, it will not first fall victim to a pantechnicon of pains and pustules, deformed, devoured, and excreting its own innards onto the clean white sheets of time.

The first major epidemic to visit the hospital and its staff of dedicated medics struck, indeed, on the cusp of the millennium, scant weeks after the town's veterinarians were themselves perplexed by the wave of cattle mutilations that presaged an alien invasion. South Park had fallen prey to an outbreak of pinkeye, but one that left conventional medical science baffled.

No simple irritation of the eye characterized this strain of the once-familiar and relatively harmless condition. Instead, it transformed its sufferers into zombies. Rotting, stinking, roaring, shambling zombies.

What is the fascination with zombies? Okay, they have a grisly appetite and they hunt in packs, and if they bite you hard enough, you'll turn into one as well. But seriously, stacked up alongside all the other supernatural horrors that could be pursuing you, from ghosties and ghoulies to long-legged beasties, succubi, vampires, and any one of the myriad radiation-fed fiends that haunted B-movie Americana, a bunch of slow-moving dead folk in search of fresh brains are a pretty lame foe.

Then again, words like that are easy to write if you're sitting in an impregnable zombie-proof shelter with an unending supply of ammunition, food, and water, and you also happen to be a champion marksman. Zombies on the streets of South Park, on the other hand, were less of a walk in the park, primarily because you'd have to be very stupid indeed to even consider a walk in the park. Because the zombies would get you before you arrived there.

It's a good thing there was a cure, then. It's a good thing there was a hospital handy. And it's a good thing the entire business was sorted out relatively swiftly, because where zombiedom had passed, other plagues waited to take its place.

Perhaps the greatest challenge ever faced by the hospital ... by the town ... by the entire planet ... arrived with the 2008 outbreak of la muerte peluda, "the furry death."

As is so often the case with new and emergent diseases, the origins of the furry death were shrouded in obscurity. There was no easy fix for television news anchors, sounding off about different forms of bird-borne influenzas; there was no fail-safe panacea for concerned citizens to resort to; or "well, it worked for a friend of mine" quack cures to be marketed by smartly suited, grinning imbeciles buying up ad space on network TV because they know we're all suckers if we think it'll save our lives.

The furry death was exactly like it sounded. Death. In a furry fashion.

Research was the key.

Experts had already established that Peru was the source of the plague, but it was the decidedly inexpert inquiries of a group of young boys from South Park, Colorado, who made the startling breakthrough discovery.

The local populace discovered the savage truth about guinea pigs long, long ago. Discovered that, far from being adorable bundles of squeaky fuzz that are welcome in every child's home, they are actually ferocious predators, bent on killing, maiming, and devouring anything in their path. Only one thing can hold back their nightmarish advance—the sound of the Peruvian flute. And, for centuries, it worked. Bands of roaming flautists were dispersed across the globe to perform their merry airs, supporting themselves on the largesse of tourists and passersby who, without even knowing why, felt instinctively drawn to throw money to the performers.

Then came the awful day when, seemingly unaware of the purpose served by these street musicians, the US government declared the Peruvian flute to be weapon of mass distraction and condemned all of its practitioners either to exile or imprisonment at the notorious Guantanamo Bay. The guinea pigs were freed from the sonic prison that had restrained them for so many centuries, and they descended on America in droves.

A terrifying scenario in its own right, yet there was worse to come. For it transpired that one person in authority did know of the efficacy of the Peruvian flute, Michael Chertoff, head of Homeland Security. And how did he know? Because he was a guinea pig himself.

Sometimes, the most dread diseases have the simplest remedies.

Z

Z is for Sleeping Through Independent Films. Z is for "Zzzzzzzzzzzzzz."

The Bijou movie house is one of the centerpieces of South Park, a Main Street staple that has withstood every one of the manifold trials and tribulations wrought on the town by pernicious fate. Even when it was destroyed by the rampaging Mel Gibson, it was quickly rebuilt, a far cry from so many similar establishments elsewhere in America, where out-of-town multiplexes and avaricious property developers have apparently conspired to rid every community of its trusty old movie house.

The Bijou specializes in first-run box-office sensations. Gibson's so beautifully realized *The Passion of the Christ* was shown here; so was the gripping adventure of *Indiana Jones and the Kingdom of the Crystal Skull*. *The Longest Yard*, *Avatar*, *X-Men First Class*, *Jack and Jill*, and *Big Wars* Movie (whatever that might be). Terrance and Phillip's *Asses of Fire* was a major draw during its cinematic heyday.

Yet *South Park* does not simply consume movies. It often finds itself reliving them too, a strange distortion of the old "life imitates art" canard that does not simply echo events that first played out on the silver screen, it twists and torments them too. If South Park were a fictional town, one could almost say it parodied them.

Who, after all, could fail to compare Eric Cartman's rise to power in the world of black-market fried chicken with that enjoyed by Tony Montana in *Scarface*?

Who didn't sit through the seemingly interminable *Avatar* without at least once comparing it to an extraordinarily overwrought edition of *The Smurfs*? And then agreeing with Matt Stone when he lamented, "I thought [the *South Park* episode] 'Dances with Smurfs' was better, actually. Obviously, we hadn't seen [*Avatar*] when we did that. We just had to guess what the movie was about, based on the trailer. But I am surprised how close we got. I thought the movie was going to be a better version of itself."

Who did not come away from that strange episode in *South Park* history that we now recall as "D-Yikes" without grimly recollecting *300*—and without, on another subject entirely, a new appreciation for the word "scissoring"?

We have seen the 1981 smash hit movie *Heavy Metal* reinvented around one young man's quest for the latest kind of high, cat urine; and George Romero's *Night of the Living Dead* gloriously reanimated around an equally chilling *Night of the Living Homeless*, and playing out many of the same parallels, as well, as a sudden influx of people sleeping rough around the town revealed the heartless disregard that lurks in the soul of so many small communities.

While Cartman employed one sleeping unfortunate as a skateboard jump, and doubtless schemed encasing them all in concrete for the joy of future generations, other suggestions include distributing free sleeping bags, so that at least the occupants would look more attractive; or recycling them to be used as car tires. Solutions that probably wouldn't have worked in Romero's original movie, but will probably be revisited by *The Walking Dead* if it drags on for too many more seasons.

The nightmarish scenarios laid bare by *Cloverfield* were revisited when South Park was overrun by a devastating plague of its own, Peruvian flute bands. Mayoral cyborg and potential presidential mechanoid Arnold Schwarzenegger's *The Terminator* was reborn when a *Dawson's Creek* Trapper Keeper turned out to be the greatest threat to life on Earth ever known. Yes, it feels strange today to recall a day when the Trapper Keeper was considered the very apex in organizational chic. But even a passing glimpse at a *Dawson's Creek* rerun serves to remind us of how close we came to oblivion.

Movie-born science went awry, too, when the brains who bought us the Apple empire unveiled their latest technological marvel, the HUMANCENTiPAD, a multiuser mouth-to-anus device that could have revolutionized the way we communicate (not to mention regulated our diets) had the movie *The Human Centipede* not already cautioned us to the possible, horrible consequences . . .

. . . of not reading the user's agreement that accompanies every online service or device for which we sign up.

Perhaps the Bijou's most prominent role in modern community life was when it hosted the first, and thankfully only, South Park Independent Film Festival.

Wendy Testaburger said it best. "Sometimes," she mused, "I forget that even though a few independent films are great, most of them suck ass."

Since the dawn of moving pictures, "independent films" have been the underground lifeblood of the industry, a hatchery from which some of Hollywood's most talented filmmakers arose, having first proven their worth by making, and financing, their own movies without any assistance from the major studios.

At least, that's the theory. The reality is that most people who start out as independent filmmakers will end as independent filmmakers too. Not necessarily through any fault of their own, or any fault of their films. Simply that they don't get the breaks that others might snag; their films are not seen by the right people at the right time to be regarded as the zeitgeist-zapping zenzation for which Hollywood is currently on the prowl.

It is for their world that an alternative industry of independent film festivals has sprung up, and it is the plaudits of those events that provide the oxygen by which the filmmakers exist. And of these, the granddaddy is the Sundance Film Festival.

Sundance launched in 1978 under the somewhat less tactile title of the Utah/US Film Festival. It was the brainchild of Sterling Van Wagenen, head of Robert Redford's Wildwood company, and it was initially dedicated to encouraging more filmmakers to work in Utah. An emphasis on American movies, and preferably indie ones, followed onto that goal, and, while the Utah/US Film Festival was by no means the first annual celebration of independent filmmaking, it swiftly rose to become the most visible.

Van Wagenen left the organization after a year to head up the similarly intentioned but as yet fledgling Sundance Institute. Six years later, in 1984, the Utah/US Festival came under the Institute's banner and changed its name accordingly. A decade later, Sundance had become so integral to the movie industry as a whole that it virtually represented an alternate Hollywood in its own right.

Which is why, according to the official history of South Park, Colorado, the organizers chose to abandon their long-time home of Park City, Utah in 1998, and seek out new horizons. "This used to be a quaint little mountain town," Robert Redford mourned. "Now look at it. Sushi restaurants, upscale clothes stores, $25 parking, Liam Neeson . . . ."

He sought someplace new where his festival could begin afresh. Someplace new that they could "drain . . . and morph . . . into a new Los Angeles."

It was an ill-starred move, and one that would have unbelievably messy consequences for all who descended on South Park in its wake.

Hindsight demonstrates to us the unimagined havoc that can be wrought on a community when the spotlight of fame falls on it. Otherwise gainfully employed citizens abandon past vocations and pursue, instead, dreams that offer short-term gains but can irredeemably damage their long-term futures. Shysters and con men take to the streets, taking vile advantage of new visitors and old neighbors alike.

Not everybody is enamored of the film festival's fare, of course. But even the naysayers are often caught up in the gold rush. As South Park's own mayor marveled as she gazed out over her town, "Traffic jams at every intersection, hoards of people pushing their way through the crowd. It's almost like we're a real city."

The library was demolished, to be replaced by a branch of the trendy eatery Hollywood Planet. The Bijou cinema, once a beacon for mass-consumption Hollywood fodder, was now creaking beneath its polar opposite, its single screen and plush red seats groaning beneath the existentialist weight of such moody epics as *Witness to Denial . . . The Body Decayeth . . . A Bunch of Gay Cowboys Eating Pudding . . .* and, coming soon, *Bow Down to Hollywood, South Park.*

The world was unrecognizable.

We saw Chef, hitherto the shimmering epitome of decency and respectability, establish himself as nothing more than a cheap entrepreneur, specializing in a confectionary product called Chef's Chocolate Salty Balls.

We saw Eric Cartman abandon his education and become a common street trader.

And we saw the very ecosystem of South Park shudder and die as new language, new practices, and, most damagingly of all, a new diet took control. Steamed celery. Couscous. Raw vegetables. Tofu. The trendiest people consume the trendiest food—that is how it has always been. But in the past, trendy food tended to be stuff that was actually good for you. Good for your system, good for your digestion, good for your bowels. This new diet . . . well, Mr. Hankey explained it best.

"The sewer is a fragile ecosystem." The new diet "[is] destroying my environment." And destroying Mr. Hankey.

Something must be done. And so it was. Mr. Hankey, so close to death as he battled the myriad infections that his changing environment had unleashed on his fragile frame, was miraculously revitalized by a suck on Chef's chocolate salty balls. And, though he had never previously appeared on the surface at any time but Christmas, now he was enraged.

Taking a leaf from Mickey Mouse's *Fantasia* masterpiece, Hankey donned a sorcerer's hat and clapped his hands. The skies darkened above the town . . . the manhole covers leapt in concert from the street, and a tsunami of shit, a veritable poo-nami of plops, roared from the sewers, plowing down man and woman, director and starlet, auteur and actor.

None were spared. The beautiful were bathed as black as the ugly, the rich stank as terribly as the poor. Bathrooms overflowed, porta-potties exploded. South Park was drowning beneath a waterfall of whoopsies.

The festival organizers fled, never to return, and South Park—once it had been thoroughly cleaned and disinfected—was allowed to return to normal. A quiet, quaint little mountain town where nothing whatsoever ever happens.

Beyond the entire place being destroyed every once in a while.

Appendix 1
South Park Episode Guide

Season One

"Cartman Gets an Anal Probe"   August 13, 1997
Cartman has a nightmare in which alien visitors abduct him from his bed. Stan, Kyle, Kenny, and Chef quickly discover that it was not a dream.

"Weight Gain 4000"   August 20, 1997
Cartman goes on a weight-gain program, at the same time as Mr. Garrison attempts to assassinate Kathie Lee Gifford.

"Volcano"   August 27, 1997
A hunting trip into the mountains turns lethal when a nearby volcano erupts. Thankfully Scuzzlebutt is on the scene to save the day.

"Big Gay Al's Big Gay Boat Ride"   September 3, 1997
Stan's dog is gay, and Stan turns out to be okay about that.

"An Elephant Makes Love to a Pig"   September 10, 1997
A genetic engineering experiment sees the boys trying to breed an elephant with a pig. You know Dr. Mephesto is going to be somehow involved.

"Death"   September 17, 1997 106
In which a pair of two botty-burping Canadian entertainers find themselves blamed for the attempted murder of a helpless, harmless old man.

"Pinkeye"   October 29, 1997 107
Halloween is just days away when the town is overrun by a plague of zombies. Worcestershire sauce, of course, was to blame.

"Starvin' Marvin"   November 19, 1997 109
Sally Struthers accidentally sends the boys a boy from Ethiopia. And there's mutant turkeys on the loose.

"Mr. Hankey, the Christmas Poo" December 17, 1997
When every other manifestation of the festive season is considered offensive, there is only one thing left to celebrate.

"Damien" February 4, 1998
The Devil had a son and he enrolled him in the third grade.

"Tom's Rhinoplasty" February 11, 1998
Mr. Garrison gets a nose job. And Wendy gets jealous.

"Mecha-Streisand" February 18, 1998
Barbra Streisand battles Robert Smith. First prize—a small Colorado mountain town.

"Cartman's Mom Is a Dirty Slut" February 25, 1998
Eric Cartman tries to discover the identity of his father. It turns out there's a lot of people to choose from.

Season Two

"Terrance and Phillip in Not Without My Anus" April 1, 1998
Terrance and Phillip save Canada from Saddam Hussein.

"Cartman's Mom Is Still a Dirty Slut" April 22, 1998
Cartman finally discovers who his father is, while the *America's Most Wanted* team turn up to investigate the shooting of Dr. Mephesto.

"Chickenlover" May 20, 1998
There is only one way to apprehend the evil Chickenlover. Officer Barbrady must learn how to read.

"Ike's Wee Wee" May 27, 1998
The boys are horrified to discover what circumcision actually entails.

"Conjoined Fetus Lady" June 3, 1998
The boys travel to China to compete in a dodgeball championship.

"The Mexican Staring Frog of Southern Sri Lanka" June 10, 1998
There can only be one winner when Uncle Jimbo and Jesus go head to head on cable access.

"City on the Edge of Forever " June 17, 1998
The boys' lives flashback while the school bus rocks on the edge of a vertiginous cliff.

"Summer Sucks" June 24, 1998

Fireworks are banned and Mr. Hat is missing. Will Cartman learn to swim?

"Chef's Chocolate Salty Balls" August 19, 1998

When Sundance comes to town, Mr. Hankey fights to expel the trendies.

"Chickenpox" August 26, 1998

Why do parents think it's appropriate to rub their healthy children with the skin of their diseased colleagues? How'd they like it if it was done back to them?

"Roger Ebert Should Lay Off the Fatty Foods" September 2, 1998

Cartman auditions to become poster child of the Cheesy Poofs empire.

"Clubhouses" September 23, 1998

The boys build a clubhouse. Divorce cannot be far away.

"Cow Days" September 30, 1998

The annual South Park rodeo and carnival is here.

"Chef Aid" October 7, 1998

When Chef is nailed by Johnny Cochran, the boys organize a festival to pay his legal costs.

"Spookyfish" October 28, 1998

Broadcast in SPOOKYVISION, a demonic fish from an evil parallel universe blights Stan's nights, but there is one consolation. The same dimension's Cartman is actually very pleasant.

"Merry Christmas Charlie Manson!" December 9, 1998

Who would want to spend Christmas Day with Cartman's relatives? Stan, apparently.

"Gnomes" December 16, 1998

Nobody believes Tweek when he claims gnomes are stealing his underpants. Nobody believes Harbucks when they claim to sell decent coffee. A lot of people are about to learn a lot of things.

"Prehistoric Ice Man" January 20, 1999

Kyle and Stan are astonished to discover a man who has been frozen since 1996. What strange tales of the past will he be able to tell them?

Season Three

"Rainforest Shmainforest"   April 7, 1999
The boys join a choir to help save the rainforest.

"Spontaneous Combustion"   April 14, 1999
Randy Marsh discovers the cause of—and cure for—spontaneous human combustion.

"The Succubus "   April 21, 1999
Chef gets engaged and becomes another person.

"Jakovasaurs"   June 16, 1999
The town rallies to preserve a species on the brink of extinction.

"Tweek vs. Craig"   June 23, 1999
It's the bout of the decade!

"Sexual Harassment Panda"   July 7, 1999
Who better to warn against the dangers of sexual harassment than a cute and cuddly panda bear?

"Cat Orgy"   July 14, 1999
Cartman blackmails his babysitter.

"Two Guys Naked in a Hot Tub"   July 21, 1999
Randy and Gerald sitting in a bath, one jerks off and the other one . . . watches?

"Jewbilee"   July 28, 1999
Kenny joins Kyle and Ike at a Jewish scout camp.

"Korn's Groovy Pirate Ghost Mystery"   October 27, 1999
A truly scooby dooby adventure. With added necrophilia.

"Chinpokomon"   November 3, 1999
Warning! Japanese game shows can damage your health.

"Hooked on Monkey Phonics"   November 10, 1999
Can Phonics Monkey defeat the homeschooled kids in the spelling bee?

"Starvin' Marvin in Space"   November 17, 1999
Crashed alien spacecraft, rampant Christian missionary groups, and everyone's favorite hungry Ethiopian.

"The Red Badge of Gayness"   November 24, 1999
South Park's annual Civil War reenactment goes mildly awry.

"Mr. Hankey's Christmas Classics"   December 1, 1999
Mr. Hankey hosts a special festive musical.

"Are You There God? It's Me, Jesus"   December 29, 1999
Puberty strikes. Or does it?

"World Wide Recorder Concert"   January 12, 2000
The brown note and how to play it.

Season Four

"The Tooth Fairy Tats 2000"   April 5, 2000
Who would believe that anyone would try and get rich from the tooth
fairy's munificence?

"Cartman's Silly Hate Crime 2000"   April 12, 2000
Being that Cartman hates absolutely everyone and everything, and has no
compunction about demonstrating that, is it right that he should be jailed
for just one specific instance?

"Timmy 2000"   April 19, 2000
Attention deficit disorder is no laughing matter. But it might be a great
way for the medical profession to make money from completely normal
behavior.

"Quintuplets 2000"   April 26, 2000
The arrival of quintuplets attracts the media's attention. Well, it's news,
isn't it?

"Cartman Joins NAMBLA"   June 21, 2000
A lonely boy seeks out mature friends.

"Cherokee Hair Tampons"   June 28, 2000
Cartman donates a kidney to a Jew.

"Chef Goes Nanners"   July 5, 2000
We all agree that tradition must be respected. But what happens when that
tradition is ever-so-slightly offensive?

"Something You Can Do with Your Finger"   July 12, 2000
The boys form a boy band.

"Do the Handicapped Go to Hell?"   July 19, 2000
It's an interesting question. And the answer is . . .

"Probably"   July 26, 2000
Cartman and the boys start their own church

"Fourth Grade"   November 8, 2000
After three years in third grade, the boys are finally advanced. They have
been there ever since.

"Trapper Keeper"   November 15, 2000
One day, Cartman's trapper keeper will destroy all life as we know it.
Unless . . . .

"Helen Keller! The Musical"   November 22, 2000
Timmy needs a turkey.

"Pip"   November 29, 2000
Charles Dickens's *Great Expectations.* Starring Pip.

"Fat Camp"   December 6, 2000
Cartman goes to weight loss camp.

"The Wacky Molestation Adventure "   December 13, 2000
Sometimes if your parents really piss you off, you can make up stories
about them and have them sent to jail.

"A Very Crappy Christmas"   December 20, 2000
Mr. Hankey lets the side down.

Season Five

"It Hits the Fan"   June 20, 2001
In which we learn the ill effects of constantly repeating the "S" word. No,
not that one. The other one.

"Cripple Fight "   June 27, 2001
Jimmy vs. Timmy. May the best man win.

"Super Best Friends"   July 4, 2001
Stan and Jesus go up against a bunch of cults.

"Scott Tenorman Must Die"   July 11, 2001
Yum yum. Chili!

"Terrance and Phillip: Behind the Blow"   July 18, 2001
A bad-tempered feud divides Terrance and Phillip on the eve of an Earth Day assembly.

"Cartmanland "   July 25, 2001
Cartman buys an amusement park, and Kyle develops a lethal hemorrhoid.

"Proper Condom Use "   August 1, 2001
Cartman discovers a new way of playing with dogs.

"Towelie"   August 8, 2001
Starring a talking towel.

"Osama bin Laden Has Farty Pants"   November 7, 2001
The boys must go to Afghanistan to give them back a goat.

"How to Eat with Your Butt"   November 14, 2001
Kenny's picture on a milk carton brings him a whole new family.

"The Entity"   November 21, 2001
When Kyle's cousin Kyle comes to visit, Cartman unleashes one of his foulest anti-Semitic quips ever. The boy can't concentrate in class. Maybe they should send him to a concentration camp.

"Here Comes the Neighborhood"   November 28, 2001
Token tires of being scion of South Park's only wealthy family.

"Kenny Dies"   December 5, 2001
Kenny dies.

"Butters' Very Own Episode"   December 12, 2001
Kenny remains dead, so Butters sets out to discover what his father bought his mother for their anniversary.

Season Six

"Jared Has Aides"   March 6, 2002
Butters becomes the official weight-loss spokesman for City Wok.

"Asspen"   March 13, 2002
Terror on the slopes.

"Freak Strike"   March 20, 2002
Butters goes on Maury Povich.

"Fun with Veal"   March 27, 2002
The boys become animal rights activists.

"The New Terrance and Phillip Movie Trailer"   April 3, 2002
Stan's TV breaks down at a most inopportune moment.

"Professor Chaos"   April 10, 2002
Distraught at being dropped as a friend by the boys, Butters discovers his
secret identity.

"The Simpsons Already Did It"   June 26, 2002
Butters's plan for world domination runs into an insurmountable
difficulty.

"Red Hot Catholic Love"   July 3, 2002
Priest Maxi goes to the Vatican to solve one of the Church's darkest
dilemmas.

"Free Hat"   July 10, 2002
Steven Spielberg and George Lucas have some questions to answer.

"Bebe's Boobs Destroy Society"   July 17, 2002
Bebe develops boobs—and a lot of male admirers.

"Child Abduction Is Not Funny"   July 24, 2002
Panic in South Park as child abduction hits the headlines.

"A Ladder to Heaven"   November 6, 2002
Bad enough that Kenny's dead. But he took the candy shopping spree
raffle ticket with him.

"The Return of the Fellowship of the Ring to the Two Towers"
                                                        November 13, 2002
The hottest porno movie ever made meets *Lord of the Rings*.

"The Death Camp of Tolerance"   November 20, 2002
Just because Mr. Garrison is acting really weird, apparently that's no reason
for his pupils to feel disgusted.

"The Biggest Douche in the Universe"   November 27, 2002
Cartman needs to have Kenny's soul exorcised . . . although he shouldn't
have drunk it in the first place.

"My Future Self 'n' Me"   December 4, 2002
Stan meets his alcoholic future self.

"Red Sleigh Down"   December 11, 2002
Christmas (and Cartman) comes to Iraq.

Season Seven

"Cancelled"   March 19, 2003
The ultimate reality show faces the end.

"Krazy Kripples"   March 26, 2003
Christopher Reeve sucks fetuses dry.

"Toilet Paper"   April 2, 2003
The art teacher's house gets TPed.

"I'm a Little Bit Country"   April 9, 2003
Antiwar protests come to South Park.

"Fat Butt and Pancake Head"   April 16, 2003
What happens when a Jennifer Lopez hand puppet becomes more popular
than the real thing?

"Lil' Crime Stoppers"   April 23, 2003
The boys pretend to be police detectives.

"Red Man's Greed"   April 30, 2003
Casino-owning Native Americans take over the town.

"South Park Is Gay!"   October 22, 2003
Metrosexuality embraces the men and boys of South Park.

"Christian Rock Hard"   October 29, 2003
Cartman forms a Christian rock band.

"Grey Dawn"   November 5, 2003
The AARP respond when the elderly have their driver's licenses taken
away.

"Casa Bonita"   November 12, 2003
Cartman wants an invite to Kyle's birthday party.

"All About Mormons "   November 19, 2003
Yes, all.

"Butt Out"   December 3, 2003
Rob Reiner leads a drive against smoking.

"Raisins"   December 10, 2003
Devastated when Wendy dumps him, Stan needs a boost.

"It's Christmas in Canada"   December 17, 2003
Ike's biological parents return to claim their son.

Season Eight

"Good Times with Weapons"   March 17, 2004
The boys attend a weapons fair, and the world turns anime.

"Up the Down Steroid"   March 24, 2004
Jimmy takes steroids prior to competing in the Special Olympics.

"The Passion of the Jew"   March 31, 2004
Mel Gibson's latest movie sucks so bad that Stan and Kenny want their
money back.

"You Got F'd in the A"   April 7, 2004
Stan forms a dance group.

"AWESOM-O"   April 14, 2004
Anxious to discover Butters's deepest secrets, Cartman pretends to be a
robot.

"The Jeffersons"   April 21, 2004
A new neighbor arouses everyone's admiration. Except for the police's.

"Goobacks"   April 28, 2004
Future immigrants are taking all our jobs!

"Douche and Turd"   October 27, 2004
The school votes for a new mascot.

"Something Wall-Mart This Way Comes"   November 3, 2004
Wall-Mart opens a branch in South Park, and the rest of the town falls
apart.

"Pre-School"   November 10, 2004
The past returns to haunt the boys.

"Quest for Ratings"   November 17, 2004
The boys' school news show meets stiff competition from Craig's rival
broadcast.

"Stupid Spoiled Whore Video Playset"   December 1, 2004
Paris Hilton mania takes over the school.

"Cartman's Incredible Gift"   December 8, 2004
Cartman becomes a psychic detective.

"Woodland Critter Christmas"   December 15, 2004
The darling denizens of the local woods ask Stan to help out at the birth of their savior.

Season Nine

"Mr. Garrison's Fancy New Vagina"   March 9, 2005
Mr. Garrison gets a sex change.

"Die Hippie, Die"   March 16, 2005
Cartman sets to work eradicating South Park's burgeoning hippy population.

"Wing"   March 23, 2005
The boys launch their own talent agency, planning to make money from Token.

"Best Friends Forever"   March 30, 2005
Kenny, killed by Heaven, is on a life support machine. Should it be turned off?

"The Losing Edge"   April 6, 2005
Facing a summer spent playing baseball, the boys try to lose their games on purpose.

"The Death of Eric Cartman "   April 13, 2005
When all the kids agree to ignore him, Cartman thinks he's dead.

"Erection Day"   April 20, 2005
Jimmy starts getting erections at awkward moments.

"Two Days Before the Day After Tomorrow"   October 19, 2005
Global warming is coming. Global warming is here.

"Marjorine"   October 26, 2005
Butters fakes his own death.

"Follow That Egg!"   November 2, 2005
Mrs. Garrison combats same-sex marriage.

"Ginger Kids"   November 9, 2005
Cartman contracts gingervitus.

"Trapped in the Closet"   November 16, 2005
With his closet full of Scientologists, Stan investigates a new religion.

"Free Willzyx"   November 30, 2005
The boys meet a talking whale. From the Moon.

"Bloody Mary"   December 7, 2005
When Randy descends into alcoholism, a miraculous statue of the Virgin
Mary might hold the answers.

Season Ten

"The Return of Chef"   March 22, 2006
Chef returns from the Super Adventure Club . . . but there is something
very wrong with him.

"Smug Alert!"   March 29, 2006
A plague of hybrid cars sees South Park threatened by a killer smug.

"Cartoon Wars Part I"   April 5, 2006
When *Family Guy* threatens to air an image of Muhammad, South Park
panics.

"Cartoon Wars Part II"   April 12, 2006
The Muhammad controversy explodes.

"A Million Little Fibers"   April 19, 2006
Towelie (a talking towel) attempts to blot out his miserable life with drugs.

"ManBearPig"   April 26, 2006
On a mission to slay the ManBearPig, Al Gore causes the boys to become
trapped in the Cave of the Winds.

"Tsst"   May 3, 2006
Liane Cartman finally accepts that Eric is out of control.

"Make Love, Not Warcraft"   October 4, 2006
A mad gamer threatens to destroy the World of Warcraft.

"Mystery of the Urinal Deuce"   October 11, 2006
Cartman cuts through all the conspiracies to unearth the true architect
of the 9/11 attacks.

"Miss Teacher Bangs a Boy"   October 18, 2006
A South Park Elementary School teacher is found to be having an affair with one of her students.

"Hell on Earth 2006"   October 25, 2006
Satan throws a party!

"Go God Go"   November 1, 2006
Cartman freezes himself until the release of the new Nintendo Wii. But something goes wrong.

"Go God Go XII"   November 8, 2006
Trapped in the future, Cartman effects his escape.

"Stanley's Cup "   November 15, 2006
Stan takes up coaching a peewee hockey team.

Season Eleven

"With Apologies to Jesse Jackson"   March 7, 2007
Randy is a contestant on *Wheel of Fortune*.

"Cartman Sucks"   March 14, 2007
Butters is sent to a special camp where they pray the gay away.

"Lice Capades"   March 21, 2007
Hair lice infest South Park Elementary.

"The Snuke"   March 28, 2007
Who put the nuke in Mrs. Clinton's snook?

"Fantastic Easter Special"   April 4, 2007
Stan contemplates the linkage between Easter eggs and the crucifixion.

"D-Yikes!"   April 11, 2007
Ms. Garrison gets dumped again.

"Night of the Living Homeless"   April 18, 2007
The boys battle to rid South Park of a plague of homeless people.

"Le Petit Tourette"   October 3, 2007
A delighted Cartman discovers Tourette's syndrome.

"More Crap"   October 10, 2007
Randy battles Bono for the honor of producing the world's biggest big job.

"Imaginationland Episode I"   October 17, 2007
The boys find themselves trapped in a mysterious land full of imaginary creatures.

"Imaginationland, Episode II"   October 24, 2007
The evil creatures shatter the barrier between their world and ours.

"Imaginationland, Episode III"   October 31, 2007
Who will save the world? Stan and Butters, of course.

"Guitar Queer-O"   November 7, 2007
Stan becomes a Guitar Hero hero . . . and casualty.

"The List"   November 14, 2007
The girls make a list rating the boys in terms of attractiveness.

Season Twelve

"Tonsil Trouble"   March 12, 2008
Cartman undergoes a routine tonsillectomy and catches HIV.

"Britney's New Look"   March 19, 2008
The boys join Britney Spears on a trip to the North Pole.

"Major Boobage"   March 26, 2008
Kenny becomes addicted to the latest drug craze.

"Canada on Strike"   April 2, 2008
The World Canadian Bureau leads the country into industrial action.

"Eek, a Penis!"   April 9, 2008
Mrs. Garrison looks to reverse her sex change.

"Over Logging"   April 16, 2008
The Internet crashes and Randy can't live without it.

"Super Fun Time"   April 23, 2008
A field trip becomes lethal when everyone is taken hostage.

"The China Probrem"   October 8, 2008
Cartman fights to rid the world of the latest scourge.

"Breast Cancer Show Ever"   October 15, 2008
Wendy is into trouble after she threatens to beat up Cartman.

"Pandemic"   October 22, 2008
Another epidemic . . . another opportunity to make money.

"Pandemic 2: The Startling"   October 29, 2008
Randy documents the destruction while battling to save his family.

About Last Night . . .   November 5, 2008
Presidential election time . . . .

"Elementary School Musical"   November 12, 2008
It's a bit like *High School Musical*, without the edge of desperation.

"The Ungroundable"   November 19, 2008
Butters sees a vampire at school, but it might just be a Goth.

Season Thirteen

"The Ring"   March 11, 2009
Kenny and his girlfriend receive purity rings from the Jonas brothers.

"The Coon"   March 18, 2009
A new vigilante arises from the trash.

"Margaritaville"   March 25, 2009
Randy solves the economic slowdown.

"Eat, Pray, Queef"   April 1, 2009
The boys are bewildered by a new television series featuring the Queef
Sisters.

"Fishsticks"   April 8, 2009
Jimmy (mostly) and Cartman (not at all) create the best joke in the world.

"Pinewood Derby"   April 15, 2009
Randy works to ensure Stan wins the Pinewood Derby.

"Fatbeard"   April 22, 2009
Cartman leads a band of would-be pirates to Skull Island. Which they
believe is near Somalia.

"Dead Celebrities"   October 7, 2009
TV's Ghost Hunters descend on South Park to save Ike from some very
famous psychic entities.

"Butters' Bottom Bitch"   October 14, 2009
Butters buys his first kiss, then sets out selling more.

"W.T.F."   October 21, 2009
The boys take up wrestling.

"Whale Whores"   October 28, 2009
Stan joins Greenpeace in a bid to prevent the Japanese from killing dolphins and whales.

"The F Word"   November 4, 2009
The boys come up with a new insult for Harley riders.

"Dances with Smurfs"   November 11, 2009
Cartman goes on the offensive against Wendy.

"Pee"   November 18, 2009
The Pi Pi Waterland is at the center of a major urine catastrophe.

Season Fourteen

"Sexual Healing"   March 17, 2010
Sexual addiction comes to South Park Elementary.

"The Tale of Scrotie McBoogerballs"   March 24, 2010
The boys write a potential best seller.

"Medicinal Fried Chicken"   March 31, 2010
Randy needs medical marijuana, and he needs it bad.

"You Have 0 Friends"   April 7, 2010
Facebook Mania strikes South Park Elementary

"200"   April 14, 2010
An army of two hundred celebrities declare their intention to sue the town of South Park in a major class-action lawsuit.

"201"   April 21, 2010
Is this the end of South Park? And who is Eric Cartman's father?

"Crippled Summer"   April 28, 2010
Jimmy goes surfing and Towelie goes into therapy.

"Poor and Stupid"   October 6, 2010
Cartman competes in the NASCAR championships.

"It's a Jersey Thing" October 13, 2010

New Jersey is taking over the country, and only Randy and the boys stand in its way.

"Insheeption" October 20, 2010

Mr. Mackey was once a fourth grader . . . . This is his story.

"Coon 2: Hindsight" October 27, 2010

Coon leads the struggle to help the victims of DP's latest catastrophic drilling accident in the Gulf.

"Mysterion Rises" November 3, 2010

Mysterion and the dark lord Cthulhu as well!

Coon vs. Coon & Friends November 10, 2010

The conclusion of the battle of the century.

Crème Fraiche November 17, 2010

Randy discovers the Food Network, and his home life goes to hell.

Season Fifteen

"HUMANCENTiPAD" April 27, 2011

Steve Jobs and Apple prepare to launch their most amazing product yet.

"Funnybot" May 4, 2011

When Jimmy describes Germans as the least funny people in the world, Germany promises violent reprisals.

"Royal Pudding" May 11, 2011

Canada is about to celebrate the Royal Wedding—when somebody abducts the Princess!

"T.M.I." May 18, 2011

Penis size becomes a bone[r] of contention in South Park Elementary.

"Crack Baby Athletic Association" May 25, 2011

Cartman launches his latest business venture.

"City Sushi" June 1, 2011

While Butters combats multiple personality disorder, City Wok guy finds himself in a battle to the death with a rival restaurant.

"You're Getting Old" June 8, 2011

Stan's tenth birthday sees him develop a very different worldview.

"Ass Burgers"   October 5, 2011
Cartman develops Asperger's syndrome and then makes a profit from selling it.

"The Last of the Meheecans"   October 12, 2011
Cartman joins the Border Patrol.

"Bass to Mouth"   October 19, 2011
Phone hacking strikes South Park Elementary, and the students' most secret thoughts are suddenly available on a new gossip website.

"Broadway Bro Down"   October 26, 2011
Randy discovers a passion for Broadway musicals.

"1 percent"   November 2, 2011
Cartman fails physical education, and the entire school suffers.

"A History Channel Thanksgiving"   November 9, 2011
Revolutionary new theories on the origins of Thanksgiving suggest aliens were somehow involved.

"The Poor Kid"   November 16, 2011
Cartman discovers that he is the second poorest kid in South Park.

Season Sixteen

"Reverse Cowgirl"   March 14, 2012
Or the perils of not putting the toilet seat down after use.

"Cash for Gold"   March 21, 2012
Cartman launches his own gemstones TV show.

"Faith Hilling"   March 28, 2012
Evolution accelerates, but not only for mankind.

"Jewpacabra"   April 4, 2012
A mysterious monster jeopardizes the annual Easter egg hunt.

"Butterballs"   April 11, 2012
Stan decides to confront the dangers of bullying head-on.

"I Should Have Never Gone Ziplining"   April 18, 2012
A day of sport in the mountains takes a turn for the deadly.

"Cartman Finds Love"   April 25, 2012
There's a new girl in school, and Cartman's in love.

"Sarcastaball"   September 26, 2012
Randy develops a new national pastime.

"Raising the Bar"   October 3, 2012
Fatty Poo Poo battles Honey Boo Boo for the right to be America's unhealthiest sweetheart.

"Insecurity"   October 10, 2012
The UPS man becomes public enemy number one.

"Going Native"   October 17, 2012
Butters and Kenny find themselves at the heart of the Hawaiian Revolution.

"A Nightmare on Face Time"   October 24, 2012
Randy opens a new video store.

"A Scause for Applause"   October 31, 2012
A beloved sporting icon is revealed to have been a cheating drug abuser.

"Obama Wins!"   November 7, 2012
Cartman holds the future of American politics in his bedroom.

Season Seventeen

"Let Go, Let Gov"   September 25, 2013
Cartman infiltrates the NSA and broadcasts his discoveries via the latest social media network.

"Informative Murder Porn"   October 2, 2013
The boys fight to keep their parents safe from televised spouse slayings.

"World War Zimmerman"   October 9, 2013
Patient Zero must be destroyed.

"Goth Kids 3: Dawn of the Posers"   October 23, 2013
The ghost of Edgar Allan Poe joins the Goth kids and the vamp kids in their final struggle against the Emos.

"Taming Strange"   October 30, 2013
Ike goes through early puberty while the school wrestles with a new computer system.

"Ginger Cow"   November 6, 2013
A miraculous cow appears to fulfill a biblical prophecy and brings to an
end centuries of warring between Jews, Christians, and Moslems. Trust
Kyle to mess it all up.

"Black Friday "   November 13, 2103
The biggest shopping day of the year is coming, and *Game of Thrones* alone
can determine the biggest bargain winners of them all.

"A Song of Ass and Fire"   November 20, 2013
Black Friday moves closer, and wheels within wheels are grinding louder.

"Titties and Dragons"   December 4, 2013
Black Friday is here.

"The Hobbit"   December 11, 2013
Kanye West sets out to assure the world that Kim Kardashian is not a
hobbit.

Other Episodes

Unaired Pilot (revised to become "Cartman Gets an Anal Probe")   1997

"Jay Leno Comes to South Park "   November 20, 1997
And kills Kenny.

"Chef Aid: Behind the Menu "   October 7, 1998
Behind the scenes at the greatest concert on Earth.

"The Dead Friend Sketch "   October 9, 1999
A bit like the Dead Parrot Sketch. Only with a dead friend.

"Great Destinations "   June 19, 2002
aka The Most Notorious Episode

"South Park 5th Anniversary Special "   September 3, 2002
Five years of poorly drawn, badly impersonated etc.

"The Aristocrats Sketch "   2005
Included in the movie *The Aristocrats*.

"Six Days to Air: The Making of 'South Park' "   October 9, 2011
An hour-long special describing life behind the scenes.

Appendix 2
South Park Songs

The following list, included specifically to piss off people who hate it when they buy a book and find it full of lists, is a list of every significant song included throughout the first seventeen seasons of *South Park*.

You can probably sing along with every one. (Episode titles are in bold)

"Cartman Gets an Anal Probe"

"I Love to Singa"	Eric Cartman
"I'm Gonna Make Love to You Woman"	Jerome "Chef" McElroy
"School Days"	The Boys

"Weight Gain 4000"

"If My Friends Could See Me Now"	Kathie Lee Gifford
"Oh Kathie Lee"	Jerome "Chef" McElroy

"Volcano"

"Hot Lava"	Jerome "Chef" McElroy
"Kumbaya"	Ned Gerblansky

"Big Gay Al's Big Gay Boat Ride"

"Loving the Football"	Jerome "Chef" McElroy
"It's Okay to Be Gay"	Big Gay Al
"Loving You"	Richard Stamos

"An Elephant Makes Love to a Pig"

"Love Gravy"	Jerome "Chef" McElroy
"Pig and Elephant DNA Just Won't Splice"	Jerome "Chef" McElroy

"Pinkeye"

"It's the Most Wonderful Time of the Year"	Liane Cartman
"Make Love Even When I'm Dead"	Jerome "Chef" McElroy as a zombie

"Mr. Hankey, the Christmas Poo"

"Christmas Lovin'"	Jerome "Chef" McElroy
"Dreidel, Dreidel, Dreidel"	Kyle Broflovski
"Happy, Happy, Happy"	Parody of Philip Glass
"Howdy-ho"	Mr. Hankey
"Kyle's Mom's a Bitch"	Eric Cartman
"Mr. Hankey, the Christmas Poo" (song)	Mr. Hankey
"The Lonely Jew on Christmas"	Kyle Broflovski

"Tom's Rhinoplasty"

"No Substitute"	Jerome "Chef" McElroy

"Damien"

"Ave Satani"	Damien Thorn
"We're All Special"	Jerome "Chef" McElroy

"Mecha-Streisand"

"Bar-bura, Bar-bura"	Japanese singer
"Rabartu Smitu, Rabartu Smitu"	Japanese singer

"Cartman's Mom Is a Dirty Slut"

"There You Are!"	Celine Dion
"Waitin' on a Woman"	Jerome "Chef" McElroy

"Terrance and Phillip in Not Without My Anus"

"O Canada"	Terrance and Phillip

"Cartman's Mom Is Still a Dirty Slut"

"Come Sail Away"	Eric Cartman

"Conjoined Fetus Lady"

"Dodgeball Song"	Jerome "Chef" McElroy

"City on the Edge of Forever (Flashbacks)"

"Runaway, Come Home"	Randy Marsh and Gerald Broflovski

"Chef's Chocolate Salty Balls"

"Chocolate Salty Balls"	Jerome "Chef" McElroy

"Roger Ebert Should Lay Off the Fatty Foods"
"Cheesy Poofs Theme Song"   Eric Cartman
"She Works Hard for the Money"   Eric Cartman

"Clubhouses"
"Piece of Meat"   Dr. Know

"Chef Aid"
"Cheddar Cheese Girl"   Elton John
"German Dance"   Eric Cartman
"Stinky Britches"   Alanis Morissette

"Spookyfish"
"Jimmie Cracked Corn"   Officer Barbrady
"My Best Friends"   Eric Cartman

"Merry Christmas Charlie Manson!"
"Happy Holiday"   Charlie Manson
"Over the River and Through the Liane Cartman
    Woods"

"Gnomes"
"Underpants Gnomes Work Song"   Underpants Gnomes

"Rainforest Shmainforest"
"Getting Gay with Kids" (song)   Getting Gay with Kids

"Spontaneous Combustion"
"You and Me, Girl"   Randy Marsh

"The Succubus"
"Love Bug"   Jerome "Chef" McElroy
"The Morning After"   Veronica and Chef duet

"Jakovasaurs"
"I Hate You Guys"   Eric Cartman

"Sexual Harassment Panda"
"Sexual Harassment Panda" (song) Sexual Harassment Panda

"Cat Orgy"

"Shelly, Shelly"	The Lords of the Underworld
"Turds!"	Shelly Marsh and the Lords of the Underworld
"Wild Wild West Rap"	Eric Cartman

"Korn's Groovy Pirate Ghost Mystery"

"Silver Bells"	Eric Cartman
"Sleigh Ride"	Eric Cartman

"Chinpokomon"

"Got to Buy Chinpokomon"	Chinpokomon theme.
"Help Me Buy Chinpokomon"	Eric Cartman

"Hooked on Monkey Phonics"

"Home School Miracle"	Eric Cartman
"Rebecca's Song"	Kyle Broflovski

"Starvin' Marvin in Space"

"Soaring So High"	Flying the Marklar spaceship

"Mr. Hankey's Christmas Classics"

"Carol of the Bells"	Mr. Mackey
"Christmas Medley"	Jesus Christ and Santa Claus
"Christmas Time in Hell"	Satan
"Dreidel, Dreidel, Dreidel"	The Broflovski Family
"Have Yourself a Merry Little Christmas"	Mr. Hankey
"I Saw Three Ships"	Shelly Marsh
"Merry Fucking Christmas"	Herbert Garrison
"Mr. Hankey, the Christmas Poo (song)"	Mailman Timmy and children.
"O Holy Night"	Eric Cartman
"O Tannenbaum"	Adolf Hitler
"What the Hell Child Is This?"	Jerome "Chef" McElroy

"Are You There God? It's Me, Jesus"

"The Menstrual Cycle Song"	Jerome "Chef" McElroy

"World Wide Recorder Concert"

"The Brown Note"	A very messy note

"The Tooth Fairy Tats 2000"
"I Can't Wait Until I Grow Up"   Jerome "Chef" McElroy

"Timmy 2000"
"Bu Bu Budio"   Phil Collins
"Spilled Blood on the Footsteps of   Sisters of Mercy Hold No Pain
    My Mind (Revisited)"   Against the Dark Lord
"Timmy and the Lords of the   The Lords of the Underworld
    Underworld" (song)

"Quintuplets 2000"
"Con te Partiro"   Kenny McCormick
"Der Hölle Rache"   Kenny McCormick
"La Donna e Mobile"   Kenny McCormick

"Cherokee Hair Tampons"
"Get Well, Kyle"   Butters Stotch

"Something You Can Do with Your Finger"
"Fingerbang" (song)   Fingerbang
"Itsy Bitsy Spider"   Ike Broflovski
"Little Bunny Foo Foo"   Butters Stotch
"Wendy's Audition Song"   Wendy Testaburger
"You Got It, Girl"   Ghetto Avenue Boys

"Do the Handicapped Go to Hell?"
"Hukilau"   Satan
"Do the Handicapped Go to Hell?" The townsfolk

"Fourth Grade"
"Third Grade Memories"   Eric Cartman

"Trapper Keeper"
"I Don't Want to Wait"   Eric Cartman

"Helen Keller! The Musical"
"The Miracle Worker"   The fourth-grade class.

"Fat Camp"
"The Prostitute Song"   James Taylor and Jerome "Chef"
                                            McElroy

"The Wacky Molestation Adventure"
"Democracy in Cuba"   Kyle Broflovski

"A Very Crappy Christmas"
"The Circle of Poo"   Mr. Hankey

"It Hits the Fan"
"Shitty Shitty Fag Fag"   Herbert Garrison

"Cripple Fight"
"Too Fat Polka"   Marc Shaiman

"Here Comes the Neighborhood"
"Why Can't I Be Like All the Other Token Black
    Kids"

"Kenny Dies"
"Heat of the Moment"   Eric Cartman

"Butters' Very Own Episode"
"Happy Anniversary from Everyone Butters Stotch
    at Bennigan's"
"It's Butters!"   Butter's Show theme.

"Jared Has Aides"
"Jared's Theme"   Commercial

"Freak Strike"
"True Freaks Union"   The True Freaks Union

"The Simpsons Already Did It"
"Sea People and Me"   Eric Cartman
"Sometimes You Kill Your Teacher" Jerome "Chef" McElroy

"Red Hot Catholic Love"
"The Catholic Boat"   Randy Marsh daydream

"A Ladder to Heaven"
"A Ladder to Heaven" (song)   Parody of Alan Jackson
                                            Sung while the boys build a
                                            ladder to Heaven
"The Death Camp of Tolerance"   "The Ballad of Lemmiwinks"

"The Biggest Douche in the Universe"
"The Biggest Douche in the   Biggest Douche in the Universe
 Universe (song)"   Committee

"My Future Self 'n' Me"
"My Future Self 'n' Me (song)"   Stan Marsh and Future Stan
                                  montage

"Red Sleigh Down"
"Poo-Choo Train"   Eric Cartman and Mr. Hankey
"The Twelve Days of Christmas"   Jimmy Valmer

"Krazy Kripples"
"Crips and Bloods"   Parody of TV theme Fat Albert

"I'm a Little Bit Country"
"Bleeding Heart Rock Protest Song   Randy Marsh and Skeeter
 vs. Pro War Country Song"

"Fat Butt and Pancake Head"
"Taco Flavored Kisses"   Eric Cartman as Hennifer Lopez
"Taco Flavored Kisses for My Ben"   Eric Cartman as Hennifer Lopez

"Casa Bonita"
"Casa Bonita" (song)   Eric Cartman

"If You Leave Me Now"
Butters Stotch   In the bomb shelter

"All About Mormons"
"Joseph Smith Was Called a   Mormon history story
 Prophet"

"Butt Out"
"Cigarettes All Hidey Lidey Day"   Factory Workers

"Raisins"
"YMCA"   The Raisins Girls

"It's Christmas in Canada"

"Ding Dong They Caught Saddam"	Canadians
"Follow the Only Road"	Canadians
"French Canada"	Canadians

"You Got F'd in the A"

"I've Got Something in My Front Pocket"	Butters's tap-dancing song

"AWESOM-O"

"I Like to Brush My Teeth"	Butters Stotch
"My Robot Friend"	Butters Stotch
"Touch My Body"	Eric Cartman

"The Jeffersons"

"Let's Ride the Train"	In the style of Michael Jackson
"The Power to Change"	In the style of Michael Jackson
"My Wishing Tree"	In the style of Michael Jackson

"Goobacks"

"The Future Begins With You and Me"	Narrator

"Quest for Ratings"

"Animals Close-Up with a Wide-Angle Lens" (song)	In the style of Boots Randolph's "Yakety Sax"

"Stupid Spoiled Whore Video Playset"

"Ballad of Paris Hilton"	While Paris Hilton is trapped inside Mr. Slave
"I've Got Some Apples"	Butters Stotch
"Stupid Spoiled Whore Video Playset" (song)	Wendy Testaburger, Jessie, Kal

"Cartman's Incredible Gift"

"Seasons Change"	Eric Cartman

"Woodland Critter Christmas"

"Christmas Time Is Once a Year"	Woodland Critters
"Woodland Critter Christmas" (song)	Woodland Critters

"Mr. Garrison's Fancy New Vagina"
"Swim with the Dolphins"   Gerald Broflovski

"Die Hippie, Die"
"Signs"   Stan Marsh
"This World O' Mine"   Cartman's captive hippies.

"Wing"
"Dancing Queen"   Wing Han Tsang
"Fernando"   Wing Han Tsang
"Sing"   Wing Han Tsang
"You'll Never Find Another Love   Token Black
    Like Mine"

"The Losing Edge"
"I See a Lady Bug"   Butters Stotch

"The Death of Eric Cartman"
"Make It Right"   Eric Cartman

"Erection Day"
"Talent Shows Are for Fags"   Goth Kids
"The Yankee Doodle Boy"   Ike Broflovski

"Follow That Egg!"
"Love Lost Long Ago"   Herbert Garrison

"Ginger Kids"
"We Can Live Together"   Eric Cartman

"Smug Alert!"
"Hey People, You Gotta Drive   Stan Marsh
    Hybrids Already"
"Smuggy San Francisco Town"   Lounge singer narrator

"Tsst"
"Don't Stop Believin'"   Eric Cartman
"Who's Got the Greatest Mom in theEric Cartman
    World?"

"Hell on Earth 2006"
"I'm Goin' Back to Cali"   Butters Stotch

"Miss Teacher Bangs a Boy"
"Dawg's Crew Theme Song"   Eric Cartman

"Cartman Sucks"
"Help Me"   Butters Stotch

"Fantastic Easter Special"
"Easter Parade"   Randy Marsh
"Here Comes Peter Cottontail"   Hare Club for Men members

"Night of the Living Homeless"
"California Loves the Homeless"   Eric Cartman

"Le Petit Tourette"
"(I've Got a) Golden Ticket"   Eric Cartman

"Imaginationland"
"Imagination Song"   Mayor of Imaginationland

"Tonsil Trouble"
"AIDSburger in Paradise"   Parody of Jimmy Buffett

"Canada on Strike"
"Chocolate Rain"   Parody of Tay Zonday
"What, What in the Butt"   Butters Stotch imitating Samwell

"Eek, a Penis!"
"Someone, Somewhere"   Mouse and penis duet

"Over Logging"
"My Internet Done Up and Went   Randy Marsh
   Away"

"Super Fun Time"
"Super Fun Time" (song)   Eric Cartman

"Pandemic 2: The Startling"
"Cars"   Peruvian pan flute cover

"About Last Night . . ."
"Celebrate Good Obama"   Randy Marsh

"Elementary School Musical"
"East Side, West Side"   Wendy Testaburger and the fourth-grade class

"Everyone Is Special"   Wendy Testaburger and the rest of the students

"Stan's Song"   Stan Marsh

"The Ungroundable"
"Burn Down Hot Topic"   DVDA

"Eat, Pray, Queef"
"Queef Free"   The Men of South Park

"Fatbeard"
"Somalian Pirates We"   Eric Cartman

"Dead Celebrities"
"Just a Little Girl"   Parody of Michael Jackson

"Whale Whores"
"Japanese Prison Blues"   Eric Cartman

"Pee"
"Minorities at My Water Park"   Eric Cartman
"We're Going to the Water Park"   Eric Cartman

"Crippled Summer"
"Lake Tardicaca Hula Gal"   Jimmy Valmer

"Mysterion Rises"
"You and Cthulhu"   The Coon and Cthulhu montage

"Coon vs. Coon & Friends"
"Faith"   Eric Cartman

"Crack Baby Athletic Association"
"Boom Boom Pow"   Butters Stotch

"You're Getting Old"
"Rattlesnake"   Steamy Ray Vaughn

"Ass Burgers"
"Turn on Your Heartlight"   Eric Cartman
"The Last of the Meheecans"
"Work Mexican Work"   Butters Stotch
"Bass to Mouth"
"Lemmiwinks vs. Wikileaks"   Lemmiwinks vs. Wikileaks fight
                                                 montage

"Broadway Bro Down"
"Put That Heart to Work"   Randy Marsh
"The Woman in White"   Randy Marsh

"Faith Hilling"
"The Only Memeing I'll Ever Do"   Eric Cartman's parody of Faith Hill

"Jewpacabra"
"Our Love Grows"   Eric Cartman

"Butterballs"
"Jackin' It in San Diego"   Stan Marsh
"Make Bullying Kill Itself"   Stan Marsh

"I Should Have Never Gone Ziplining"
"Little Green Frog"   Zipline tourists

"Raising the Bar"
"Here Comes Fatty Doo Doo"   Randy Newman

"Songs of Ass and Fire"
"A Chorus of Weiners"   George R. R. Martin and choir

"South Park: Bigger, Longer & Uncut"
"Blame Canada"   Sheila Broflovski
"I Can Change"   Saddam Hussein
"I'm Super"   Big Gay Al
"It's Easy, Mmm'kay"   Mr. Mackey
"Kyle's Mom's a Bitch"   Eric Cartman
"La Resistance"   La Resistance (Organization)
"Mountain Town"   The Boys
"The Mole's Reprise"   The Mole
"Uncle Fucka"   Terrance and Phillip
"Up There"   Satan
"Wendy's Song"   Wendy Testaburger

Bibliography

Arp, Robert, ed. *South Park and Philosophy: You Know, I Learned Something Today (The Blackwell Philosophy & Pop Culture Series)*. Malden, MA: Blackwell Publishing, 2006.

Arp, Robert, and Decker, Kevin S, eds. *The Ultimate South Park and Philosophy: Respect My Philosophah! (The Blackwell Philosophy and Pop Culture Series)*. Malden, MA: Wiley-Blackwell, 2013.

Chapman, Graham, Michael Palin, John Cleese, Terry Gilliam, Eric Idle, Terry Jones, and Bob McCabe. *The Pythons: Autobiography by the Pythons*. New York: Thomas Dunne Books, St. Martin's Press, 2003.

Hanley, Richard. *South Park and Philosophy: Bigger, Longer, and More Penetrating (Popular Culture and Philosophy)*. Carus Publishing Company, Peru, Illinois, 2007.

Johnson-Woods, Toni. *Blame Canada! South Park and Contemporary Culture*, London: The Continuum Publishing Group, 2007.

Judge, Mike. *MTV's Beavis & Butt-Head's Ensucklopedia*. New York: MTV Books 1994.

Nagy, Bernard and Tom Locke ed. *Colorado's South Park, High Country Paradise*. Colorado: High Country Artworks, LLC, 2010.

Parker, Trey and Matt Stone. *South Park Guide to Life*. Philadelphia: Running Press Book Publishers, 2009.

Parker, Trey, Matt Stone, and Robert Lopez. *The Book of Mormon Script Book: The Complete Book and Lyrics of the Broadway Musical*. New York: Newmarket Press, 2011.

Simpson, Brandon. *The Libertarian Lessons of South Park: An Analysis of Libertarianism in South Park, How Ron Paul, Gary Johnson & South Park Created a New Generation of Libertarians & South Park Conservatives*. Small Town Press, 2013.

Stall, Sam. *The South Park Episode Guide Seasons 1–5: The Official Companion to the Outrageous Plots, Shocking Language, Skewed Celebrities, and Awesome Animation*. Philadelphia: Running Press Book Publishers, 2009.

Stall, Sam and James Siciliano. *The South Park Episode Guide Seasons 6–10*. Philadelphia: Running Press Book Publishers, 2010.

Stratyner, Leslie and James R. Keller, eds. *The Deep End of South Park: Critical Essays on Television's Shocking Cartoon Series*. Jefferson, North Carolina: McFarland, 2009.

Weinstock, Jeffrey Andrew. *Taking South Park Seriously*. Albany: State University of New York Press, 2008.

Index

THE FAQ SERIES

Prices, contents, and availability
subject to change without notice.

HAL•LEONARD®
PERFORMING ARTS
PUBLISHING GROUP

FAQ.halleonardbooks.com